Justice Daniel Dissenting

Other books by John P. Frank

Mr. Justice Black
Cases on Constitutional Law
Cases on the Constitution
My Son's Story
Marble Palace: The Supreme Court in American Life
Lincoln as a Lawyer
The Justices of the Supreme Court

Justice Daniel Dissenting

A Biography of Peter V. Daniel, 1784-1860

BY JOHN P. FRANK

HARVARD UNIVERSITY PRESS

CAMBRIDGE, MASSACHUSETTS

1964

To Mr. Justice Hugo L. Black

*with affectionate good wishes
upon his completion of a quarter century
on the Supreme Court of the United States.*

PREFACE

PETER V. DANIEL was appointed a Federal district judge in
Virginia by Andrew Jackson in 1837 and a United States
Supreme Court Justice by Martin Van Buren in 1841. He
served on the Supreme Court until his death in 1860.

Daniel speaks to the American present with the voice of
an American past which we simply do not hear any more.
Professor Daniel J. Boorstin has caught in a title our problem
of rediscovery when he writes of *The Lost World of Thomas
Jefferson*. As he says in his preface, "Just as America will
never again be the same kind of wilderness that it was in
Jefferson's day, it is surely not in our power to live any more
within the Jeffersonian world of ideas. The spirit of Jeffersonian philosophy can be only imperfectly recaptured, at
best." The intellectual world of Virginia at the turn of the
nineteenth century has for so long been so removed that it
is hard for a contemporary American to realize that it once
existed; and yet the roots then laid down still flower in our
own day.

Our generation has forgotten Daniel because the United
States as a country has moved away from what he stood for.
He would not recognize our world, and we can scarcely comprehend his. He was not a great judge, nor a great prose
writer, nor a great thinker whose works dominate the intellectual life of the early nineteenth century. He was a good
judge and a good thinker and a fair prose writer.

Daniel was something else. He was determined. He was
the last Jeffersonian to hold public office in the United States.

He was so true a Jeffersonian that his adherence to the early ideals of Jefferson and of the Jefferson party outlasted even the adherence of Jefferson himself. He was an intransigent, indefatigable, stubborn outpost of eighteenth century thought in nineteenth century United States. He was the last exponent of the Virginia and Kentucky Resolutions of 1798, and very possibly the first prominent exponent of secession.

What he stood for never had a chance. His social philosophy was formed while the United States was an agricultural country, before capitalism as we understand it came to America. He was one of the last opponents of capitalism, not in favor of any ism of our own day, but in behalf of agrarianism. He clung longer than most of his contemporaries to what was once a dominant American ideal. He is a kind of bench mark in American history, for by measuring what we have become as against what he was, we discover how far our country has traveled.

He may not have had good judgment, but he had courage, and he never faltered. When, in the great fight over the United States Bank, the bank men in Richmond had him at the edge of ruin, he characteristically commented to his friend President Van Buren: "Damn the contemptible slaves of the Bank, I put them all at defiance."

Daniel was born in Stafford County, Virginia, on a farm or plantation called the Crow's Nest. He studied law in the office of Edmund Randolph in Richmond and married Randolph's daughter. He practiced there and from 1812 to 1835 was a member of the Council of State of Virginia. For most of that time, under a peculiar system of the day, he was also the lieutenant governor. He was one of the principal friends of Andrew Jackson and of Martin Van Buren in Virginia and, as a newspaper publicist, took a very active part in electing Van Buren to the presidency. Because he was such a strong antibank man, Jackson offered him the post of At-

torney General of the United States when he made Roger
B. Taney Secretary of the Treasury at the height of the
struggle over the United States Bank. Daniel declined; he
could not afford to take the position because of its low pay.

As a member of the United States Supreme Court, Daniel
was one of the most extreme anti-business and pro–state's
rights man ever to sit on that Court. He was a warm friend
and coworker of Chief Justice Taney's, and his own extremism helped place Taney in the center both of the Court
over which he presided and the country in which he lived.

The passing of Daniel from the scene is somehow drama-
tized for me by the physical disappearance of the paths of
his life. His home in Richmond is completely gone, and replaced with other structures. The farm which he kept near
that city has long since been replaced with streets and urban
housing. The state capitol building in which he served still
exists, but the rooms in which he functioned have been so
completely remodeled that contemporary capitol staff do
not know that those suites ever existed.

Daniel's old family homestead, the Crow's Nest, was a little
south of present day Alexandria, on a point of land along the
sides of which two little streams, Aquia and Potomac Creeks,
enter the Potomac River. Today the exact spot of what was
once a fine plantation home is very nearly impossible to locate.
When I searched for it in the late 1940's, there was still alive
an elderly woman in the neighborhood who according to her
own account had once seen buildings on the land, but she
could point out no path by which the site could be approached overland. An old coon hunter who knew the area
finally took a companion and me to it by boat. We found ourselves at the top of a high bluff in the midst of a complete
wilderness, with not the faintest trace of even a single foundation stone. All that remained near where the hunter said the
house had been was a peculiar hollow, perhaps four feet

deep, which he said had once been a well but which was now filled and grown over with grass.

Near the well site was the old family cemetery. Here were simple gravestones in every stage of ruin. Two or three still stood upright in the woods, strange markers among the trees. Most of the stones had long since toppled over, many had been reduced to pieces by the weather, and some had been broken apart by weeds which had grown completely through them in nature's effort to bury the last trace of human passage.

For all its desolation, the scene had dignity, and we examined the markers with quiet care. Justice Daniel had been buried in Richmond, so his could not be here. But there were the stones of immediate members of his family. Those that were down had to be lifted carefully, for snakes hid under them; and moss had to be removed with sticks before inscriptions could be read. Flat on the ground and broken was a stone which recalled the glories of the past. There, it declared, lay a daughter of a signer of the Declaration of Independence.

Soberly, we went away. For this is what is left of the civilization from which Peter V. Daniel came: a path which an old woman thinks she can find; a location which will be lost forever when an elderly coon hunter dies; a hollow in the ground; and some broken stones which may never again be seen.

In truth, the twentieth century has moved a long way from the world of Peter V. Daniel. And yet, though the philosophy known as agrarianism is quite gone, many Americans today inherit its attitude even if its teachings do not directly govern them.

My wife, Lorraine W. Frank, had a substantial role in the writing of this book. Much of the research we did together and many of the working notes are hers. The editing was done by her and by my partner Paul M. Roca, who gave many hours to the consideration of every sentence in the manuscript.

The secondary and widely republished original sources on which this study depended are apparent from the notes. The most important manuscript collection examined was the Grymes Papers at the University of Virginia Library at Charlottesville. I want to thank the Grymes family of Orange, Virginia, descendants of the Randolph-Daniel line, for permission to quote from this collection and for sharing other family mementos as well. I also consulted the Jefferson, Van Buren, Polk, Jackson, Rives, Story, and McLean Papers in the Library of Congress; the Taney, Howard, and Carroll Papers in the Maryland Historical Society at Baltimore; the Department of State appointment papers in the National Archives; and scattered other manuscripts of the Library of Congress, the University of Virginia, the University of North Carolina, and the Huntington Library.

Also of great value were the records of the Virginia State Library at Richmond, including those of the Virginia district and circuit courts and the various records of the Virginia Council of State for the 1830's; the Richmond property, tax, and probate records for the period; and the original journal of the United States Supreme Court, which because of the inadequacies of reporting in Daniel's time is essential for the understanding of many Supreme Court opinions.

The Richmond *Enquirer* has been closely studied, both in the Library of Congress and the New York Public Library, for the years 1808 to 1860. Other newspapers, too numerous to mention, have been studied for particular episodes and are duly cited.

Research was done in various Virginia points, Washington, New York, and Arkansas, and I am indebted to the

American Philosophic Society for a travel allowance. I am grateful to law students at Indiana University and the Yale Law School for assistance in the early stages of this study. Typing of a much revised manuscript has been in the competent charge of Lynn Swisher. I am particularly appreciative of the warm personal encouragement of Professor Carl B. Swisher of The Johns Hopkins University, whose work on Chief Justice Taney is the leading biography in this field.

Finally, my gratitude goes to my long-suffering partners who put up with my maintaining a double life as an author and a practicing lawyer.

John P. Frank

Phoenix, Arizona
October 1963

CONTENTS

I	THE EARLY YEARS	I
II	THE WAR OF 1812 AND COUNCIL DUTIES	21
III	FAMILY AND PRACTICE	49
IV	REVOLT, ACTUAL AND POLITICAL	63
V	A GROWING ROLE IN NATIONAL POLITICS	77
VI	THE CAMPAIGN FOR VAN BUREN	92
VII	DEFEAT AND VICTORY	127
VIII	DISTRICT JUDGE	140
IX	THE SUPREME COURT APPOINTMENT	150
X	DANIEL TAKES HIS SEAT ON THE COURT	168
XI	DANIEL'S ROLE, IN GENERAL AND ON EXCLUSIVENESS	181
XII	REGULATION OF BUSINESS	200
XIII	THE STATE AND THE NATION	213
XIV	PERSONAL RELATIONS	227
XV	SECTIONALISM AND SLAVERY	243
XVI	ROUTINE COURT BUSINESS	259

XVII THE CIRCUIT   275

XVIII THE LAST DISSENT   285

      HERITAGE   290

NOTES   295

CASES CITED   325

INDEX   331

The frontispiece is reproduced from H. L. Carson, *The Supreme Court of the United States*, Philadelphia, 1891.

Justice Daniel Dissenting

Chapter I

THE EARLY YEARS

PETER VIVIAN DANIEL was born on April 24, 1784, in Stafford County, Virginia. That he was born in Stafford County seemed to him in later years almost the most important fact of his life; except for his birth and death dates, it is the only fact recorded on his tombstone.

And yet another fact, if he had thought about it, was clearly more important. For the purpose of establishing him in his future career, one tidewater Virginia county would have been as good a birthplace as another. What meant more, though he was not given to bragging of it, was that he came of good family.[1] In a Virginia society dominated by a little interlocking group, it was important to belong to the inner circle.

Peter came of Daniels and of Vivians, of Travers and Moncures. His mother, Frances, almost forty years old when he was born, was the daughter of a minister, John Moncure. His father, Travers, was a direct descendant of Captain William Daniel who came from England to Virginia in about 1630. The line may go farther than this, perhaps to the Daniels of Lancashire in the fourteenth century; but assuming it to be so, those distant Daniels were an obscure lot and what really mattered was Peter's descent from one of the earliest settlers in Virginia. His daughter Elizabeth, an incurable romantic, was later to search for connections with noble families in England, but there is no reason to suppose that

Daniel himself would have cared even if those dubious connections had been established.

Stafford County, a tobacco and agricultural center, was bordered on the northeast by the Potomac River, and on the southwest by the Rappahannock. The family farm, known as the Crow's Nest, was located about fifty miles south of Washington, and about sixty miles north of Richmond. Daniel gained there a permanent interest in agriculture which remained his hobby for the rest of his life and which permanently conditioned him to cherish above all else the way of life of an agricultural community. By the middle of the nineteenth century the county was to be farmed out, and much of it has now been abandoned. The whole white population in Daniel's time must have been fewer than two thousand and the county seat at Stafford Court House had fewer than a dozen dwellings.[2]

Daniel's precollege education came from private tutors who took small groups of students. While his education was doubtless as good as the county afforded, it was not impressive. If he retained any Greek he never showed it later, and he used very little Latin. In maturity he was concerned almost solely with law and politics; there is no evidence that other enthusiasms had been kindled at an early age. He lacked the manifold intellectual interests of a Jefferson or the comfortable and extensive culture of a Madison. His personal library in later years was filled with law books, though it contained the inevitable Waverly novels by Scott as well as the *Edinburgh Review* and *Southern Review*.[3] Though he later served on the board of the Richmond public library, he does not seem to have read very widely among the works thus put under his direction.

Daniel topped his education at home with the barest taste of training at Princeton, the northern college of highest prestige throughout the South. Here such Virginians as James

Madison, Charles Lee, and William Branch Giles, with whom Daniel would have later tussles in politics, had studied. He arrived on the campus in 1802, admitted to the junior class at the age of 18.

His enrollment came at a black hour for the college, for only two months before his entrance Nassau Hall had burned to the ground, destroying almost all of the three thousand volumes in the college library.[4] While Nassau Hall was being reconstructed, the students boarded in the village. They were soon able to move back into the main building, but the new iron roof was leaky, and showed signs of collapsing on the inhabitants. In these unpleasant quarters the students spent their disciplined days. At 6:00 A.M. came the morning prayers and from then until breakfast at 7:30 the student was expected to study his morning recitations. Classes were held by a faculty of a half dozen, including President Smith who taught the juniors something of the liberal arts, philosophy, theology, and politics. The balance of the day was spent either in actual recitations or in policed study in the rooms. At 9:00 in the evening there was an inspection to be sure that all students were safely in their quarters. The rare diversions included the debating societies; Daniel was a member of the Cliosophic.[5] The excess of control led to great resentment upon the part of the students who retaliated with every imaginable kind of destructive horseplay; pistol shots, firecrackers large enough to be considered explosives, and barrels of stones sent rolling made frequent disturbances. Daniel was not a man to see humor in practical jokes, and it is doubtful that he either participated in or enjoyed them. He left Princeton after a few months, and the whole experience had a negligible effect on his life.

What Daniel did take away from his adolescence was a deep interest in politics, and a fixed set of political principles. The most significant political event of his early life was the adoption of the Virginia and Kentucky Resolutions of 1798, and Madison's Report on the Virginia Resolutions. These documents, instigated by Jefferson and Madison, were the bristling reply of those states to the Alien and Sedition Acts. Whether Daniel, as a boy of 14, actually comprehended the issues of 1798 is doubtful, but the political principles of the Resolutions did remain with him. They asserted three basic premises: first, that the powers of the Federal government were to be most strictly and narrowly construed; second, that it was the duty of every true patriot to resist the slightest extension of Federal power; and third, that the states, when the Federal government did exceed its power, "have the right, and are in duty bound, to interpose for arresting the progress of the evil." What the last proposition meant, which is to say just how the states were to "interpose," was the great source of ambiguity in the Resolutions and became a matter of great importance to Daniel in later life.

Upon the return from Princeton, Daniel stayed at home for two years and then went to Richmond in 1805 to study law in the office of Edmund Randolph. He was admitted to the bar in 1808. He could have found no more influential a preceptor than this head of one of the foremost families of Virginia. Randolph, an aide to General Washington at the very beginning of the Revolution, had soon after become the first attorney general of Virginia. He sat in the Continental Congress, he was governor of Virginia, and he led the Virginia delegation to the Constitutional Convention of 1787. The basic draft from which the Constitutional Convention worked, though largely prepared by Madison, bore his name and was known as the Randolph Plan. At first not wholly satisfied with the Constitution, and unwilling to sign it, Randolph swallowed his doubts and became one of the leading Virginia ratificationists along with Madison, Pendleton, Marshall, and others.

Under Washington, Randolph became the first attorney general of the United States. When Jefferson left the cabinet, Randolph took his post as Secretary of State, a position he held until 1795. Then came the crisis of his life. A confidential memorandum of the French minister casting grave doubts on Randolph's personal integrity was captured by the English and made public. Whether in this episode Randolph was virtuous or corrupt does not much matter for purposes of this story, since his position in Virginia was not appreciably shaken by the incident. However, it left his family, which was to include Daniel, permanently somewhat on the defensive. In 1795 Randolph himself published a vindication which was republished by Daniel's son Peter Vivian, Jr., some eighty years later.[6] A collateral descendant, Senator Daniel of Virginia, was still attempting to erase the stain as late as 1889. But putting aside the sense of outrage, the incident had no real effect on Daniel's life, except that it may have intensified his antifederalism.

The Richmond to which Daniel came in 1805 was a small town, its better homes located near the capitol on Shockoe Hill. Only a few days after Daniel's arrival Thomas Jefferson was inaugurated for his second term as President, and perhaps Edmund Randolph took his young clerk to the Inauguration Day celebration dinner at the Eagle Tavern. If so, Daniel had his first Richmond experience with that inexhaustible entertainment, the toasting party. After a good dinner the table was cleared except for the glasses, and toast after toast was drunk. This was the Richmond equivalent of the British coffee house of a century earlier; the epigram which an English gentleman might have polished at home to toss off casually in play at cards was supplanted here by the pithy wisdom which accompanied each glass. After the official toasts called for by the chairman of the evening came the voluntary offerings, one dealing with the Supreme Court. Jefferson's party had but lately made an unsuccessful effort to impeach Supreme Court Justice Chase. An irrepressible volunteer, determined to find a silver lining even where there was none, offered "Judge Chase: late in trial before the Senate of the United States; may this prove to the judiciary that they are amenable to the people." [7]

Peter had little money, but there were plenty of ways for him to spend what he had. If he wanted to rub elbows with legislators, he might go to the Washington Tavern, some 200 yards from the capitol, which boasted of its capacity to put up thirty of the legislative gentlemen and also kept large stables well supplied with clover, hay, and corn for their horses. Or if he wanted a dinner of oysters and beefsteak, he could get it at Watson's. If he had anything left, he might even buy a law book or two for his private collection. Tucker's Blackstone was for sale for $20 a set, and the English reports were being offered at $3 to $3.50 a volume.[8]

But Daniel did not have to go to the taverns or the streets for his entertainment. Randolph took the young man not only into his office, but into his home. There one met the best of Virginia society, including the Randolph's allies by marriage, the Carters and the Nicholases. Indeed, Randolph kept two homes, one a farm named Spring Farm, located a few miles from downtown Richmond in an area since become a part of the city; and the other, his city residence. The town house, a two-story brick structure immediately across from capitol square, was one of the newest in the city when Daniel came. Following the plantation style of keeping the kitchen separate from the main house, the cooking was done in an adjacent brick building.[9] This splendid edifice was one of the sights of Richmond, and Daniel counted himself fortunate to be often within it. Here he met the son and three daughters of Edmund Randolph, though when he first arrived in 1805 he did not pay much attention to the fifteen-year-old school girl named Lucy, later to become his wife.

By 1808 young Daniel had finished his law studies in Richmond and had returned to Stafford County. There he fought a duel with John Seddon of Fredericksburg, a duel which has been so encrusted with misleading legends that the full truth about it will never be known. The most widely publicized twentieth century account of the duel dates the event at four years after the actual occurrence and then ascribes as its cause something which happened in the erroneously given year.[10] No one knows the exact cause, but given Daniel's personality it seems probable that it was political.

According to one of the accounts, Seddon had previously challenged Daniel, who had declined to fight, whereupon Seddon posted him at Fredericksburg as a coward. As this tale goes, Daniel was at the time engaged to Lucy Randolph and the implication is that she dissuaded him from the combat. Seddon subsequently gave a second challenge, which, after further consultation with his Lucy, Daniel accepted.[11]

The story is pretty, but incredible. Daniel was probably not engaged to Lucy at the time and, more to the point, one would as well expect D'Artagnan to run from a fight as to believe that Peter Daniel would suffer himself to be posted as a coward. For the fifty years that we know him well, from 1810 to 1860, he walked everlastingly upright the better to balance the chip he carried on his shoulder; and it is inconceivable that he should have been so different two years earlier. Moreover, had Daniel suffered posting quietly, his reputation would have been such that there would have been no point in a second challenge; his disgrace would have been so great that no man would have been obligated to notice him. The rule of the code was that a man might refuse a challenge from "one that has been posted; one that has been publicly disgraced without resenting it; one whose occupation is unlawful; a man in his dotage and a lunatic."[12] If he had declined the first challenge, Daniel would have been regarded either as a coward or a fool.

Whatever the cause and background of the duel may have been, the two men met on Saturday, November 15, 1808. Seddon was the challenging party, and his second presumably called upon Daniel's second to arrange the details. The distance chosen was ten paces, and the place was immediately across the Potomac in Maryland. The parties could thus escape the Virginia law against dueling which would be inapplicable to them when they were out of state, and they would never be punished under the Maryland law which could not reach them after they returned to Virginia.

On the appointed day the two combatants, with their seconds and a surgeon, went their separate ways to the field of battle. Both arrived at precisely the proper time. Instructions were read and the arms were inspected. These were presumably smooth-bore pistols under nine inches in length which, if not breechloaders, were usually filled by the seconds with a careful loading of powder and the insertion, at the muzzle, of a ball pushed into place with a rod covered with kidskin. The second then handed the pistol to his principal, giving it to him with the muzzle away from his enemy. The duelist when at his station put the pistol in his right hand pointed to the ground.[13]

At this point, or a little earlier, something occurred which somehow gave rise to a legend most discreditable to Daniel's reputation. Seddon, it was said, wore a white vest, the fringe of which showed slightly across his abdomen. According to one story, "Daniel suggested that he remove the garment, as it was a rather shining mark. Seddon indignantly declined to do so." According to the other story, Daniel is supposed to have remarked in a subdued tone to his own second just before the exchange of shots, "I think I shall strike Mr. Seddon about the button on the white line."[14]

No one will ever know what thoughts were in Daniel's mind when the two men took their positions. Doubtless he was standing slightly sidewise, so as to give the smallest possible target. Doubtless he was nervous, for it was almost certain that one man would die; in ten Virginia duels between 1800 and 1810 nine men died and one was seriously wounded.[15] Perhaps he planned to fire quickly before his hand might tremble; perhaps to avoid the same misfortune he remembered to keep a loose grip on the pistol. However it was done, it was done. At the signal to fire the two men raised their pistols and fired almost simultaneously. Seddon's shot was wild. Daniel's entered his adversary near the center of his body, on the right side, about halfway between the hip and the shoulder.

Daniel's second asked whether Seddon as the challenging party was now satisfied. Seddon was not, whereupon the second offered him another shot. In a moment it became apparent that Seddon was unable to raise his right arm to fire again. His second then put the matter up to their surgeon, and in a few minutes Seddon's second announced that his friend was unable to fire again; that he was now satisfied; and that he had no further call on Daniel. Daniel, accompanied by his second and his surgeon, left the ground. Seddon was carried to the boat in which he had come. He was taken to his home where he died two days later.

Rumors about the vest episode quickly spread. It seems probable that Seddon wore a morning suit, with a swallow-tailed coat and a white waistcoat. If he did, his judgment was bad, as the white against the black would have given a better target than completely dark clothes. It was for this reason that the wise duelist wore a plain costume, avoiding even brightly colored buttons. In any event, Seddon's costume was a worry for Seddon and his second, and Daniel could with propriety, under the code of honor, be only a beneficiary of their poor judgment. The rules precluded any direct conversation at the field and precluded with equal vigor any asides which might have the effect of irritating or upsetting the adversary. If Daniel had made either of the comments attributed to him in the legendary accounts he would have been guilty of great impropriety.

A story rapidly circulated in northern Virginia, Washington, and Richmond asserting some such impropriety. The tale gained such currency that it became necessary for the seconds of the two men to take the unusual step of issuing a press release denying it. Their joint statement gave an account of the duel, noting that "not a word was exchanged by the principals." The statement concluded: "in direct contradiction to some shameful and slanderous misrepresentations which have gone into circulation, it is stated on the authority of both of the seconds, that every circumstance of the unfortunate transaction just stated was perfectly fair and honorable. No indecorous word or action escaped either party; the utmost civility and politeness prevailed on the ground, and the conduct of every individual concerned was unimpeachable, and completely characteristic of the gentlemen." [16]

This statement was prepared on November 17, 1808, the day that Seddon died, and only forty-eight hours after the duel. This means that the rumors must have spread extraordinarily quickly. There is no reason why Seddon's second would have agreed to the statement if it were false. However, the press release, although it received good circulation in the immediate area, was apparently forgotten; as usual, the scandal outlived its refutation.

The Seddon duel undoubtedly colored attitudes toward Daniel, but it had no traceable consequences in his later life. He never referred to the episode again in any recorded way. The affair may, however, cast light on Daniel's personality. Was he, then or later, something of a bully, spoiling for murderous fights on political questions?

The answer is pretty clearly no. Daniel never fought another duel, although he came close to it on occasion and he gave strong moral support to a favorite nephew who had a duel in 1852, when Daniel was on the Supreme Court.[17] As has been noted, he went through his political life as an extremist with a chip on his shoulder. He was always ready for trouble, and his savage pen and tongue put him into many a situation in which trouble might have arisen; but he always stayed within the technical bounds of courtesy in his published statements. When called upon to account for himself he was quick to explain, without yielding an inch, that he had not meant to be personal. There was many an instance in later life when he went hustling down to the office of the Richmond *Enquirer* to inform the editor that if some adversary wanted to make something out of one of Daniel's bristling anonymous letters, he, Daniel, was ready; but this was always accompanied by a courteous exposition of his view of the matter which his adversary could, without loss of honor, accept. There was to be an incident in 1834, to be examined later, in which his adversaries were to charge that he had deliberately attempted to stir someone to an attack; but that charge was probably unwarranted.

Whether the Seddon incident gave Daniel a reputation which made it easier for him to avoid trouble later, no one can know.

Up to the year 1809, when he was 25, Peter's personality and experiences are largely lost to view. After 1809 these blinds begin to fall away and his path becomes easy to follow. In that year he went to the legislature as a representative of Stafford County, where he had an utterly undistinguished career. This brought him back to Richmond where he rediscovered Lucy Randolph. Before Lucy there had been other romances; indeed, as he recalled later in life, "some pointed attention known to have been previously shown by me to another" made Lucy keep him waiting a bit after he finally made his offer to her.[18] But he was scarcely to be blamed for not having seen Lucy's promise earlier than he did. She was a second sister, and ill-health as a child and a young woman had given her a somewhat retiring disposition. Until her older sister was married, she was obscured. But when her sister married, Lucy was, as the saying went, "brought forward," and her natural timidity was forced to yield to her duties as a hostess for her father in one of the greatest houses in Virginia.

With this new prominence and with a pleasant if not a large dowry she soon had any number of suitors, some of them with better prospects than Peter. He proposed; she demurely declined; she exercised the woman's prerogative, and on April 20, 1810, they were married.[19] To the marriage he brought his prospects as a promising politician and as a young lawyer of negligible personal estate. She brought as her dowry her father's country place, Spring Farm, with its furniture and much of the Randolph silver, some of which, still handsome, is in good use in the middle of the twentieth century.[20] Better still, she brought her name; for by this marriage Daniel moved into the Randolph clan, becoming a part of the ruling clique of Virginia, to the great advantage of his own career.

We have no contemporary description of the physical attributes of the young couple. We know that she thought him handsome, and he thought her lovely, one of the most beautiful women of her day. No other evidence bears out these enthusiasms and one may suspect as the truth that he was of good height, slender, and passable in appearance; she was slight, frail, and also passable in appearance. The overwhelming evidence of their correspondence is that they loved each other devotedly so long as life kept them together. After Lucy's death, twenty-five years later, Peter attempted to prepare a memoir for his children telling them the story of his courtship and of their mother's virtues. He was no good at this sort of thing, and his prose creaked with the embarrassment of his self-revelation. Yet for all the heaviness both of his word and of his spirit there was a sense of terrible loss. He referred to "the delightful playfulness of her temper and conversation," to the "decided pleasure in her society" which he had always taken. True to the romantic standards of his time, he thought of her almost as an ethereal being, who might literally become the "guardian angel" of her husband and her children.[21]

The girl Daniel married was Episcopalian, devout almost to the point of eccentricity. She was extremely gentle, an influence all to the good on Peter with his savage uprightness, but she was also something of a scatterbrain. Her few extant letters are striking for their disorganization, a circumstance for which she was sometimes a little apologetic. Her interests, in the spirit of the times, were basically the interests of her family, her home, and her church. She read a little, but nothing heavy. Pope's *Essays* proved far too much for her.

Lucy's primary concerns are reflected in a letter she wrote her husband in the first summer after their marriage.[22] She spoke of her general contentment with her "darling husband," a happiness which would quite run over if only she could induce him to read the Bible with her so that they might pray together. She stressed her willingness to economize: "You will not surely let an anxiety for elegance make you unhappy?" She instructed him on preserving the peaches while she was gone, and told him just how to use each of their three large jars, one brown, one black, and one which they had been using for a butter churn. From the problems of the cellars she jumped to the pins and needles which she had left behind and then to her sewing. Best of all to Peter, certainly better than the instructions about the curtains and the shawl and probably better than the news about the pants and the gaiters that she had made for him, was her conclusion. It is so artless and yet so sincere; to read it is almost to intrude: "Now dearest husband do not you know that I long to see you . . . Bless you, your wife longs to lay her head on your bosom and then she wishes for nothing more. Her husband's affection and good health, is all that your wife wants my husband . . . good-bye dear, dear husband; your wife — your fond wife L.D."

The financial condition to which Lucy referred was a plague which was to torment the remainder of their lives. For all that industry Lucy speaks of, and for all her economy, the family's condition was never to be completely comfortable, and there would be times when they were to feel acute financial pressure.

When Daniel settled in Richmond with his bride he in effect committed himself as a permanent resident to a city in which he was to live for forty years. The city became a part of him, and he of it. He and Lucy are buried there, on the scene of his triumphs and defeats and his endless political fights. In this city of 5000 people on the James, in addition to the capitol building and the governor's house and the little fringe of houses, stores, and taverns, there were also a penitentiary, an armory, and a poorhouse. Of real industry there was none. The river was poorly used, with cataracts and shoals which could be navigated only by an inferior system of locks, and very little power development. Richmond was the capital, the commercial center for an agricultural community, and very little more.

The men of the city were intensely political, with a substantial majority of Federalists and Whigs throughout the years of Daniel's life. His own Jefferson or Republican Party, which did not come to be known in Richmond as the Democratic Party until about Jackson's time, received much of its intellectual leadership from Thomas Ritchie's Richmond En-

quirer, which circulated throughout Virginia. This party usually dominated the state but not the city. Hence in his actual daily contacts and in the development of his law practice, Daniel was in the center of a group which disagreed with him over politics, and this in no placid way. Daniel was keenly and sometimes bitterly aware that the big financial interests of the state, as these later developed, saved their legal patronage for those who agreed with them.[23]

At the same time this was a hospitable, kindly, and generous people, and Daniel made some of his own difficulties by his own stiff preoccupation with politics. Even so, life was sociable enough. As a contemporary observer of 1811 described the people of Richmond, "they entertain with a plentiful table, a sparkling glass, and a flowing bowl, and are only discontent when the satiated guests can no longer enjoy the profusion." [24]

The Virginia Council of State, membership on which was to be Daniel's principal public service for almost a quarter of a century, met regularly in Richmond. This body was one of the most incredible structures in the history of American politics. The Virginia state constitutional structure had its monuments to pure theory. It was devised in a time of overriding concern about the dangers of a strong executive. Virginia developed a system under which the legislature had great power and the governor had practically none. Having given the governor almost nothing to do, the Virginia Constitution proceeded to bless him with a Council of State to help him do it. To keep the governor from obtaining too much power even in his petty province, he was compelled to consult this Council of seven on almost every activity he might undertake and to abide by its decision. Together the governor and his Council were known in Virginia as the executive department.

The Virginia fears of an overbearing executive were not

allayed by mere dilution of executive power. The Council, too, might grow evil, and what good the dilution if power were merely transferred from a passing governor to a permanent body of Council members? Hence the ingenious system of election to the Council of State. A member once elected served for life, or until he resigned or was removed. Every three years the legislature, by joint vote, was compelled to remove two of the seven councilors, a process colloquially known as "the scratch." At the time of the scratch, the legislature balloted until a majority had chosen the two to go. Then, by the same process, it chose their successors. Thus a member could serve for as long as he was not scratched. This system, as will be readily apparent, was not contrived to achieve perfect harmony among the members of the Council; every three years each necessarily became the political rival of the others, as each attempted to induce his friends in the state legislature to go after someone else.

The senior member of the Council, which Daniel very rapidly became, was the lieutenant governor of Virginia. The Council itself was necessarily chosen largely from the tidewater area and particularly from Richmond, since the pay, $1000 a year, would not sustain a person who had to come from any distance for the meetings. Meetings were extremely frequent, sometimes running as often as three times a week during a busy season.

By a most unusual set of circumstances, there were not two Council vacancies but five to be filled in 1812, resulting from four resignations and one death. In addition to his ability and his standing as a young lawyer, Daniel had three excellent qualifications for entering the contest. First, he had been a member of the legislature and had friends there. Second, he was readily available in Richmond. Third, he was a member of the Randolph family and thus a member of the ruling group in Virginia. He was elected and took office on January 9, 1812.[25]

The first two or three items of business are a sample of the incredible quantity of governmental minutia which was to pass across this Council table in the following years. The very first bit of advice given by the Council was the certification of a pension warrant for a veteran of the Revolution. Next, the Council referred to its own previous order that the slave June should, for some crime, be sold for transportation to the West Indies. John Prunty, slave trader, handled the sale to the satisfaction of the State of Virginia, and by action of the Council of State he was allowed five dollars for those services. Third, some ninety veterans were claiming land bounties; all their claims were rejected on the ground that they had already received bounty. Then came the first division in the new board: a dispute over the pardon of a convicted criminal. No decision was reached, and the matter was put over to another meeting.[26]

Between 1812 and 1835, Daniel must have been in Council on something between 1500 to 2000 days with only occasional absence when he might be on circuit attending to his legal duties. The unceasing flood of decisions included minor opportunities for patronage, as when it was necessary to select a coroner, fill a warehouse inspectorship, or give out some other little favor.

Occasionally important matters arose. The massing of such matters culled from twenty-five years of experience would, from the very concentration of their presentation, give a misleading impression. Basically the Council was tending to the housekeeping of the State of Virginia. These chores were without drama; they were merely useful. They were the kind of chores which an agricultural state, with a not very active government, was likely to have in the first part of the nineteenth century.

Daniel managed to stay in at least seeming agreement with his colleagues for a year, and did not file his first dissent, a most lengthy document, until March 16, 1813. By this time the war with England had begun, and the issue was one which arises in time of war in any country which has compulsory military service. A gunpowder manufacturer asked that, to keep up a satisfactory flow of powder to the state, his employees be exempted from militia duty. In view of the severe need for gunpowder the Council gave the workmen a six months' exemption. Daniel and another member noted their dissents.

His document began with his exposition of the reasons for writing it: his "unqualified disapprobation" of the action taken and his respect both for the Commonwealth and for the integrity of his own judgment made him speak. Fully recognizing "the value of harmony in public council, wherever indeed instantaneous action is required since it at once gives dispatch to business and adds weight to determinations when formed," [27] he felt nonetheless that this solidarity had its proper limits.

After his preface, Daniel in an orderly and comprehensive way developed his argument. This militia exemption was twice wrong, first because it was unconstitutional, since only the legislature and not the executive had power to make such a policy; and second, because even if the executive had power to take such a course, this was an unwise occasion for its exercise. It is typical of Daniel that he should give his constitutional objections first and get to the merits second. He began his discussion of the constitutional question with "a short view of the nature of our state government." Under the constitution, the governor has no general lawmaking power even over the militia; far from it. Rather, that power rested with the legislature, "the proper and natural authors of all rules for civil society." His reasoning thus brought him to a great fundamental truth, "every departure from which is at war upon the theory of and practice of republics, that executive officers who hold in their hands the machinery, the very apparatus of power, should never be entrusted to determine the extent of its application." [28] There was no act of the legislature which even remotely suggested that the men here involved must not serve in the militia as did anyone else, and this executive action therefore was not merely unauthorized by the constitution and laws but was in conflict with the statutes which required service.

Turning then to the merits, "it is alleged that the public exigencies, the force of the crisis demands the course now pursued by the executive." Daniel not merely rejected a conclusion as to the necessity, but "would most deeply deplore the arrival of that time, when public officers, especially ministerial or executive officers, would make *their* opinions paramount to the law. When this time shall arrive, legitimate government will be no more." Is there any conceivable occasion when the executive is justified in changing the law? He would not say no, but if there were ever to be such a time, "it must be when the salvation of the state imperiously called for the infraction; or at least where essential public mischief would have followed from the observance of the law." [29] The present situation did not even remotely approach such an emergency. There was no evidence that the state would be unable to get powder elsewhere if this particular mill closed down, nor that it would close down; Daniel was sure that there were in fact other sources of powder. Moreover, the penalty for nonappearance in the militia was the payment of a fine, and the company could pay for these men if it really wanted their services.

He concluded by ripping into the company which sought the exemption. He spoke of the company's "grace and favor to the commonwealth" in selling powder to the state at scandalous war profits. The company, he conceded, was composed of amiable gentlemen, but they had no legitimate claim to special favor over the rest of the public.

Not only in its form but in its substance, too, this opinion is typical of the Daniel of the next fifty years. As always, he had begun with first principles, for with him most concrete questions were decided by reference to first principles. His argument is simple, for his was never a devious or complex mind. The executive has exercised a power; the constitution does not say that it has that power; therefore the executive acted wrongly.

Typical too is the near violence of his attack on the company seeking the exemption, and by implication on those of his brethren who gave it to them; yet he carefully avoided giving direct offense. He was the junior member of the Council, and he probably in fact offended his colleagues, but he tried not to and was probably unaware that he might have done so. And it was characteristic that he should have seen here a shabby attempt by a few merchants to achieve a special favor. He was always alert to that kind of favoritism. Typical too was his capacity to exercise himself over a small point. There was here no basic question about a policy of exemptions. Under the statutes as they then existed, the legislature already exempted a miscellany including professors, tutors, students, millers, ferrymen, and tobacco inspectors. The question of whether powder mill workers should be added was fairly one of reasonable difference of opinion. The legislature was not in session, and a six months' exemption would, in effect, simply hold the question open until they met. Moreover the governor certainly had some general powers over the militia which might arguably have permitted this delay in the muster. The only serious question was the one on which Daniel put his finger, the question of distribution of power. It was very like Daniel to think it worthwhile to fight this particular issue on general constitutional grounds.

Chapter II

THE WAR OF 1812 AND COUNCIL DUTIES

FROM 1812 TO 1815 Daniel's contribution to the prosecution of the war was his most important public work. England and France had been engaged in the death struggle of the Napoleonic wars since 1803. The increasing tension caused by interference with America's trading rights as a neutral and by British impressment of seamen on American vessels, added to the expansionists' ambitions for Canada, took the United States into the war in June 1812. War fever was already high in the spring of that year in Virginia. On April 15, 1812, the Council of State met to discuss and advise the governor on the foreign situation. Solemnly they canvassed the military resources of the state and directed that the militia of the vulnerable tidewater counties in particular should be ready to march. The Council directed Governor Barbour to inspect the state's defenses, to consult with the Federal government on the best means of defense, and to prepare plans for the assembly of troops.[1]

Thus Virginia prepared for war. It remained to select an opponent. For Virginia, like the rest of the country, was still split over the question of which of the European belligerents was America's enemy. On the morning of Saturday, May 30, the people of Richmond met at the capitol building. Governor Barbour was elected chairman of the meeting and a committee was chosen to report on the situation. The resolutions committee, which included Daniel, brought in a sizzling report. It denounced the British interference with American trade, continuing in high indignation: "our own harbors imperiously blockaded by ships of war — and our brave tars torn from their country's colors and their homes, cast into British ships! . . . and to crown the whole, we have seen a serpent, in the shape of a spy, stealing to our firesides and altars, and attempting to sting us in the very heart of our union." [2]

The allusion to a spy was to a British agent, one Henry, whose activities had been recently exposed.[3] The most obvious fact about this verbal fit of passion is that Daniel did not write it. The style is not his, and he did not completely agree with its militant conclusion, a call for "prompt, open and vigorous WAR against Great Britain."

This resolution ignored the offenses of the French which, except for the British impressments, were as severe as those of the English. Virginia had not three but four parties, though it may well be supposed that the fourth was exceedingly small. One faction wanted war with England; another, war with France; a third, peace; and the fourth faction, to which Daniel belonged, wanted to fight both England and France. That the fourth program would prove a tall order did not dissuade its adherents. It was on motion of this faction that the meeting adopted a further resolution noting that the French also were victimizing American commerce and expressing the belief "that, unless the negotiations now pending should speedily eventuate in an honorable adjustment of these aggressions, we trust that our government will, in due season, mete out the same measure to France, which they are about to mete out to Great Britain."

Having duly informed the President and Congress that the people of Virginia were ready to take on the whole of the civilized world, the Richmond meeting adjourned. Soon after, a Richmond Federalist paper sponsored an anti-French memorial to counter the effect of the prowar mass meeting of May 30. This memorial was placed for signature at the Hygeian Fountain for any who cared to subscribe. Here, after a few persons had signed it, Daniel saw the petition and wrote in his own observations:

> The undersigned supposing himself called on to declare in common with the rest of his fellow citizens in his opinion of the above memorial; hereby protests against the same —
> First, because its statement of facts, to him appears to be discolored and incomplete.
> Second, because the temper it evinces, to him appears to be that of party rancor.
> Third, because to him it appears to be disgraceful to attempt an extenuation of, or any apology for the violence of the crimes of his country's foes.
>
> P. V. Daniel [4]

This insertion sat poorly with the friends of the memorial, who marked it out, though not so completely that it could not be read. The anti-English *Enquirer* in an amused report of the episode alluded to Daniel, "to whose Republican firmness this is not the place to pay the Eulogium it deserves (who had voted against the public resolutions because in his opinion an *immediate* war ought to go against France as well as England)," and derided the Federalists.[5]

On June 18 the United States declared war on Great Britain. Richmond went to war with enthusiasm. On June 20 the Society of Friends of the Revolution met at the Washington Tavern. Daniel's brother-in-law, Peyton Randolph, served as chairman. A gigantic Fourth of July celebration was planned, with Daniel on the committee on toasts. Amid reports that West Canada was about to be taken by American forces and with the contagious excitement of the young men of Richmond organizing into militia companies, the great Fourth of July celebration was upon the city.

A gun salute at sunrise inaugurated the festivities. The governor reviewed the troops and gave them an inspirational address. At noon the troops, whose "line was displayed in all its elegance," assembled in the capitol building and there the Society of the Friends of the Revolution shared the glory. After a reading of the Declaration of Independence, the audience heard the message of President Madison requesting a declaration of war, and finally the declaration itself. The soldiers fired their salutes in the square, and then the entire population adjourned to the various banquet tables. It was a magnificently happy Fourth of July, filled with rumors of the enemy on the run and with no omens of the coming sack of Washington. The climax was splendid illumination of the city, with first honors going to Mr. Beck, owner of a confectionery, who covered his store front with wreaths of lamps.[6]

Daniel's committee had done a splendid job of arranging the toasts. The Society of the Friends of the Revolution, as befitted their pre-eminent station, gave the main banquet at the Bell Tavern. A hundred people were in attendance, and seventeen official as well as fourteen voluntary toasts were offered. At least one official toast was offered which, while it may have reflected Daniel's views on that hot July day, did not later do so: "*Our Union*: the rock of our safety — the first storm broke harmless upon it — the *second* shall find it immovable." In the other official toasts, he could join with unlimited enthusiasm, particularly those to Thomas Jefferson, to James Madison, and to "the majority in Congress."

Reality quickly followed the high jinks of war's dawn. By September 1 Richmond knew of the defeat of the American forces at Detroit, and the *Enquirer* was calling for the removal of the Secretary of War.[7] On September 5 a meeting was held for the people of Richmond, with Governor Barbour presiding. A committee of eleven, which included Daniel, was established to receive blankets and contributions of money for the care of soldiers. A visiting minister gave the meeting tone by an energetic short speech which he concluded with a contribution of $20, and $2110 was promptly subscribed. Within a few days, the contributions were up to $5700. Blankets were harder to come by than money: only 41 had been obtained.[8] A few days later disaster hit Richmond when a powder factory blew up and fifteen persons were killed.

Routine council duties went side by side with war activities. The meeting of Wednesday, December 30, 1812, is a fair sample of the humdrum business that remained to be done. An agent of the state whose job it was to collect delinquent taxes in certain counties was allowed an extra $20 because he ran into some unexpected difficulties. Payment of miscellaneous bills was authorized, as for example $37 for the use of three wagons which moved arms for the benefit of the militia; $18 for axes for a detachment of the militia; and so on through a dozen other bills for military supplies, down to charges of as little as $1 or $1.50 for small services.[9]

Later in the winter there was variation enough from this petty routine. In early February 1813 five British ships of war were sighted off Hampton Roads, and the state turned to self-defense with a frenzy. A voluntary cavalry association was organized to defend Richmond; whether Daniel was involved is unknown, but the elderly head of the Society of the Friends of the Revolution became captain of the company. Daniel along with every inhabitant of Richmond was required to have a musket, a bayonet, a cartridge box, and six rounds of cartridges available in his home. The legislature speedily appropriated an extra $50,000 for munitions and authorized the governor and the Council to raise numerous new companies of infantry, artillery, and cavalry.

In mid-March the Council met in a spirit of grave danger,

believing that the continued presence of a hostile fleet in the waters of the state presaged an attempt on Richmond both for purposes of plunder and to destroy the arms industry there. It directed the Richmond militia to prepare for field operations, the preparation to consist in part of parading three times a week with full fighting equipment and in part in extensive field maneuvers.[10]

During this crisis, the Virginia legislature passed a law the operation of which led to a sharp split between Daniel and the remainder of Governor Barbour's administration. By the winter months of 1812–13 the militia system of defense was failing. A citizen soldiery is generally thought to be the great bulwark of a free people, but whatever virtues such a system may have for momentary crises, or short term insurrections, it was hopelessly inadequate for a long war. The militia system was a conscription system. Since the menace was along the coast, vast numbers of western militia men had to be brought east. As the demand grew, heads of families were taken, and agriculture and industry were disrupted. The theory of the state militia was that trained regulars or long-term Federal soldiers would bear the brunt of the battle, the militia doing that share which their inexperience would permit. But in 1813 the Federal government totally failed to produce its share of the troops necessary for such a partnership. In Virginia the militia system had become the *whole* system for the defense of the state.

As a result, during the legislative session of 1812–13 the legislature decided to supplement its own militia system by authorization of a regiment of volunteer, long-term Virginia regulars. The act was passed with a visible cocking of the snoot at the Federal government; the point was that if the Federal government could not furnish an army, Virginia would organize its own. This statute stirred Washington both to indignation and to action. The two thousand Virginia militia in the Norfolk area were integrated into a Federal plan for defense of that area, with some Federal assumption of financial responsibility. At the same time the Federal government expressed strong displeasure with the organization of state regulars, hinting that a state army was unconstitutional. To this the friends of the Virginia legislation had a ready reply; the Constitution prohibits the states from raising troops in time of peace, but it certainly does not restrain them in time of war.

The Federal resistance to state regulars, coupled with the improvement of the Norfolk defenses and the lessening of the enemy pressure in March 1813, led to a genuine constitutional crisis in the Council. Barbour had no wish to oppose the Federal government, which was headed by James Madison, a Virginian, with its War Department in the hands of James Monroe, also a Virginian. At a bitterly tense meeting of March 24, 1813, Governor Barbour offered and the Council accepted a proposal "that it would be inexpedient at this time to proceed to the execution of the act" to set up the state regular forces. From this conclusion, two members of the Council, one of them Daniel, dissented separately. Daniel synopsized his dissent in a few words: "They speak of the inexpediency of their carrying into execution the law *at this time*. It should be recollected that the law is *general* and *positive*, that it contains no proviso for *executive discretion*. The advice is not given with reference to any such condition or proviso, nor because the executive have not the practicable means of carrying the law into execution; but for the purpose of *preventing the operation* of the law," and the executive has no power whatsoever thus to suspend a law of Virginia.[11]

The burst of dissents and the public reaction left Barbour in a most uncomfortable position. The plain fact was that, whether for good reasons or for bad, the executive had acted in absolute defiance of its duty in suspending the act; as Daniel had said, the executive had no option whatsoever as to which laws it would enforce and which it would ignore. Hence in the few days after the Council meeting of the twenty-fourth, Barbour decided that his position, though seemingly victorious, was untenable, and he retreated to a proposal that a special session of the legislature be called to repeal the law. This proposal he offered at the meeting of March 31, with the understanding that the operation of the statute would be suspended until the special session could meet sometime in May.

This was a substantial retreat from Barbour's position of a week before, for then the suspension had been indefinite and now it would be only until the legislature could come together to reconsider the matter. But the tactical significance of the move was larger than this. It took Barbour off the defensive, leaving to Daniel the worries about his political position. There was no possible constitutional obstacle to calling a special session of the legislature, so that Daniel's course was either to go along with the call of the special session, and perhaps claim for himself a victory in having forced it to be called, or resist the call altogether. But if he took the latter course, he could no longer employ constitutional objections to protect the plan for a regular Virginia force. Instead he must come out squarely to oppose President Madison and Secretary of War Monroe, the two most powerful officers of the Federal government and the two most powerful Virginians.

As always, Daniel chose to take a clear stand, to make it known and to take the consequences. He dissented from the call of the legislature on the flat ground that the Virginia statute was a good statute, and should not be repealed, and that therefore there was nothing to put up for legislative consideration. He raised no personal issue with Barbour, conceding completely to him an honest zeal for the public service; but he felt that he would be guilty of cowardice if he did not let the public know his stand on a matter of such great concern to the general welfare.

Daniel believed that the regular Virginia force was a sound plan for the defense of the state and that it should not be tossed aside because of some "frail and temporary expedient the general government might casually afford." The fact that the War Department was presently integrating Virginia militia into the Federal system of defense seemed to him an occasion for neither surprise nor gratitude since this was obviously the minimal duty of the Federal government. Indeed, it had no alternative: "The whole maritime frontier was bare to hostile incursion — the foe was at hand: the general government had not, it is believed, fifty, certainly not one hundred men at or near Norfolk. Virginia promptly supplied them completely equipped and provided." Daniel did not criticize the Federal government; it had done all that was within its power to do. But the very impotence of that government was an incentive to Virginia to act, and not to acquiesce.[12] As for Washington's counterproposal to create a Federal regiment manned by Virginians, it was still a dream: "The probable period of their descent to a station on our coast, or even on our planet," no man knew. As for the political objections, by its loyalty to the Union Virginia had placed itself beyond all merited jealousy; instead of hostility the state was entitled to the applause of every friend of the Constitution.

For the remainder of 1813, Daniel was more occupied with his law practice than with either the national defense or his Council duties. During the summer he doubtless withdrew as usual from the unhealthy climate of the city, and during the early fall his time was preoccupied with the death of his father-in-law, Edmund Randolph, and questions in connection with the settlement of the Randolph estate. Near the end of the year Daniel was again engaged in a constitutional controversy arising out of the war. The episode then occurring, while in a sense appalling, nevertheless illuminates his constitutional conceptions with exceptional clarity.

The incident arose when James Stogdall, a militiaman, wore out his pants. Stogdall and a few other militiamen who were stationed near Norfolk, as their commanding officer reported, were so destitute of clothes that their lives were endangered by the winter weather. The Council was asked to appropriate thirty dollars as an advance to buy trousers for three of these men and to get socks or shoes or a necessary blanket for one or another of them.

It was without doubt the duty of a militiaman to clothe himself, but these men lacked the money. The thirty dollars was therefore appropriated, with instructions to the commanding officer to give it to the men as an advance and to hold back enough out of their subsequently earned pay to cover the amount appropriated.[13] This compromise would seem on its face to be an ideal solution, and Daniel alone dissented. His objection was simple: the statute required the militiamen to clothe themselves and did not allow for advances; the executive had no power to amend the statute by making an advance where the law did not allow one.

Surely this was a use of constitutional doctrine of which not even the most rigid constructionist could be proud. Here were three men at a danger point awaiting a not improbable enemy. Without clothes they could not survive. The legislature was out of session and obviously could not be called back to appropriate a pair of pants for James Stogdall. True, the law did not authorize an advance; but neither did the law prohibit it. This was not at all like the case of the organization of the Virginia regiment, where the executive chose to violate the expressed will of the legislature. It was, in short, absurd.

The Stogdall incident should not leave the impression that Daniel was a petty obstructionist. He dissented frequently from Barbour, but he supported a strong policy. In February 1814 Barbour, fearing invasion, proposed the calling of additional militia for defense of Richmond. At a poorly attended meeting the Council, by a vote of three to one, rejected the proposal on the ground that attack was unlikely. Daniel, dissenting, was tart with his colleagues, for to him the necessity of the added defense was self-evident. As he saw it, Richmond was almost defenseless before an enemy with every disposition to plunder. Worked up to a frenzy of concern, Daniel excoriated the majority:

> When your city shall be in ruins, and the blood of many of its people shall be mixed with its ashes, those who may survive to want and every distressing recollection will find small alleviation of their misery in your assurance that had the enemy only waited for you, you would have retaliated on him the mischief he had done. As little will they be consoled to know that by your tenderness for the public money, you have lost both your darling treasure and the country's still dearer children.[14]

In retrospect, Daniel was right. Richmond escaped burning only because the enemy chose to pass it by and burned Washington instead. The British thereupon left the Chesapeake area, not from compulsion but from choice, and withdrew to the West Indies. For the remainder of the war, Richmond was out of the main line of excitement.

Meanwhile, internal political changes of considerable importance to Daniel were occurring in Virginia. In 1814 Governor Barbour was elected to the Senate. His place as governor was taken by Edmund Randolph's brother-in-law Wilson Cary Nicholas. The entry of Nicholas, Daniel's relative by marriage, into the governorship, along with certain other political developments, put the control of the Virginia administration firmly into the hands of the "Richmond Junto," of which Daniel was a member. As a result, Daniel moved from dissent to participation in policy making. When the treaty of peace was finally signed on Christmas Eve, 1814, Daniel's position within the government was better established than at any time since he had taken office.

Essentially, the new coalition was an interfamily cabal. Though Richmond was a small town, the city was in a position of leadership out of all proportion to its numerical significance by virtue of the concentration of state business there and because of under-representation of western Virginia. Its population was in the zone of 12,000 of whom only 3460 were white males. With due allowance for children, the voting population of the city must have been something under 2000, a condition which made significant alliances easy to form. Intermarriage among the leading families of the state, and especially in the tidewater, where they were common, made for strong alliances, led from Richmond.

Before the American constitutional convention of 1787 the political faction headed by Edmund Randolph and the Nicholas family was known as the Old Party.[15] At this time there was a group centering around Spencer Roane — who in Daniel's time was to be chief judge of the Supreme Court of Appeals of Virginia — which opposed the ratification of the Constitution. Roane himself described the ratification as "distressing and awful."[16] Since Randolph, after some vacillation, finally supported the Constitution, his faction and Roane's were not friendly during the 1790's. Meanwhile Roane was developing as a principal Virginia lieutenant of Jefferson.

When Randolph was forced out of Washington's cabinet, he began to move toward the Jeffersonians, and, along with Roane, supported the Resolutions of 1798. As its share of the spoils, the Old Party placed Robert Smith, one of its number, as Secretary of the Navy under Jefferson and Secretary of State under Madison.

During this period the Roane faction was developing its own leadership. In 1804 Roane's cousin, Thomas Ritchie, founded the Richmond *Enquirer* as a mouthpiece for Republicans in Federalist Richmond.[17] This paper became the most vital political force in the state, and Jefferson, Madison, Monroe, and Roane regularly contributed to it. It also became the major vehicle of expression for Daniel. In that same year, the bank of Virginia was established, headed by Roane's brother-in-law, Doctor John Brockenbrough. Others of Roane's family were in Congress or in the state legislature. This group of friends and relatives became known first as the Essex Junto and later as the Richmond Party or the Central Junto.

Sometime around 1812 the Junto and the Old Party united and Daniel as an affiliate of the Old Party was swept along into what became known as the Richmond Junto. In 1811 three new judges went to the Supreme Court, all affiliated with the Roane group. In 1814 the Junto supported Wilson Cary Nicholas for the governorship, a position he held until he resigned in 1817 to become president of the Richmond branch of the United States Bank. Very rapidly all major banking positions in Virginia were under Junto control, and by 1822 four of the eight members of the Council of State were members. The overwhelming Junto dominance of Virginia affairs lasted until about 1830 when it was momentarily displaced by the friends of Calhoun and the enemies of Jackson. Thereafter the Junto returned to power, and while its solidarity began to crumble in the depression of the late 1830's under President Van Buren, it did not exhaust its effectiveness until late in the 1840's. Its amazing dominance in the legislature, and hence its control over appointments which were largely made by the legislature resulted from the caucus system. The Republican majority in the legislature, which was sometimes not large, voted as a bloc, as a result of decisions made by a majority of its own members assembled in private meeting. Hence the Junto, by influencing only a little more than a quarter of the legislators could control the state; and a few Richmond families — Daniel among them — controlled the Junto.

The most important Council problem of the immediate postwar years arose from the banking crisis of 1816. The episode is of the greatest importance in appraising Daniel. If ever, from his entry into public life to his death in 1860, there is one discovered instance in which Daniel failed to live up to his own principles, his response to the banking situation in 1816 is that instance. The evidence is unclear; but on that occasion perhaps he sacrificed his own deep convictions to the demands of the Junto.

In the first part of the nineteenth century, banks were still a new, and to many a dubious, institution on the North American continent. The Bank of the United States, chartered by Congress in 1791, was allowed to expire in 1811 and was rechartered in 1816 over the opposition of many Virginia Republicans who thought it unconstitutional. Meanwhile, all over America the states were granting charters to banks, many of which rapidly became insolvent. These failures plus widespread hostility to the Bank of the United States led to the development of an antibanking philosophy.[18]

The antibank movement, resistant equally to both national and state banking, had strong support among Virginia agrarians. The intellectual leader of this group was John Taylor of Caroline, with whom Daniel regularly agreed.[19] Daniel's later views on banking, as expressed in his mature years, were vigorously antibank and were similar to Taylor's. Taylor, in a book published in 1814, stood as a tower of the antibank movement. Banking, as he saw it, was "a paper feudal system," which turned the people into serfs of the corporations. National and state banks were equally objectionable; "Will climate, or the names of stockholders have the effect of making bank paper sometimes a curse, at others a blessing?" he asked. Bank charters in Virginia, he asserted, were flatly unconstitutional. Banking was avarice, and "avarice breeds the treacheries of privilege against liberty." He poked biting fun at the pretentions of the old and the new banks: "Established banks exclaim that others would be pernicious, just as one established or chartered religion exclaims against chartering another . . . but though the established bank contends that others would be pernicious, an application for a new bank as loudly insists that the old one is a hateful monopoly, which a new one will destroy." [20]

Having proceeded to an elaborate demonstration of the ill consequences of banking itself, Taylor turned to the vices of paper money. Paper money he regarded as quite unnecessary: "Virginia, by an utter exclusion of paper, would have been supplied with specie."

These issues came squarely before Daniel in 1816. During the war, Virginia banks had been relieved of the necessity of redeeming their paper in specie. By an act of the legislature, specie payment was to begin again on November 16, 1816. This prospect terrified the banks, and in July of that year the president of the Bank of Virginia and the president of the Farmers Bank in Virginia both petitioned the Council to call a special session of the legislature to repeal the law requiring the resumption of specie payment that winter.

The whole question of banking policy was thus before the Council. The Taylorites, seeing no good and much bad in banks, and believing that specie payment was far superior to the limitless circulation of bank notes, would necessarily oppose the special session. Presumably from those very motivations, on July 2, 1816, Daniel joined the Council and Governor Nicholas in a unanimous refusal of a session for this purpose.[21]

But the matter was not closed. The banks besieged the

Governor and the Council during July and August in a vigorous effort to win a reversal of their position. Meanwhile Daniel left town, taking his family away from Richmond for the
summer months. Sometime between the July 2 meeting and
late August the banks persuaded Governor Nicholas (who
was himself to resign the next year to become the head of
the Richmond branch of the Bank of the United States) to
reverse himself and to agree to a special session. This left to
Nicholas the job of persuading the rest of the Council, and
he set out to do so.

What Nicholas' arguments may have been, no one knows.
From the letters returning to him from wandering Council
members it appears likely that he offered different arguments
to each. What, for example, did he tell Daniel? Did he simply
refer to economic considerations such as the chaos which
might result from too speedy a resumption? Did he speak of
the comparative disadvantages to Virginia banks as against
banks in other parts of the country, should Virginia go
through with the plan for immediate resumption? Or did
he point to the practical considerations of politics and Junto
welfare? The last is the one course he surely did not take;
for no contemporary could have known Daniel so little as
to approach him with a proposition, however political its
purposes might be, which did not have at least a coating of
principle.

Daniel sent in his proxy to vote for the calling of a special
session. His own health and that of his family were such that
he was unwilling to come immediately back to Richmond.
There is no reason to consider this a pose; he never came back
to Richmond in summer if he could avoid it. In a letter to
the governor he said:

> The subject of your letter of the thirtieth ultimo, I have
> thought much of particularly of late; and after the position
> assumed by the banking institutions north of Virginia, taken
> in connection with other considerations which have presented

themselves, that subject to my mind certainly wears an aspect differing much from that which it formerly presented . . . If when the question of convening the legislature shall be submitted, my brethren of the Council shall be willing to receive my vote (and I am very desirous of having it recorded), it may then be considered as declared in favor of convening the legislature.[22]

What were those "other considerations which have presented themselves"? If Daniel were a man of less firm integrity, if he had not been a man for whom principle was the razor which cut into every problem, one would be less concerned. But the man who changes his mind always risks the charge that he did so for some wrong reason, and here Daniel not merely changed his mind but also voted in seeming conflict with what was at all other times a fixed principle. If in so much of his life of which we have a record Daniel ever did a major favor for a bank or corporation, this is that time.

He was not the only one to suffer in reaching his decision. Another Council member, John Campbell, was also asked by Nicholas to switch positions, and he too plumped for the special session. Campbell wrote, "The great danger to our banks, I conceive, is to be apprehended from the United States Bank and the suspension of the law but a short time would relieve them from this danger . . . It is from the U. S. Bank alone I wish to see ours protected." [23]

In other words, Campbell could rationalize his shift in terms of a judgment that immediate resumption would favor the United States Bank as against the state banks, and faced with a choice of evils, he put the welfare of the state banks ahead of the United States Bank. On September 30 the Council met and called a special session of the legislature for November 11. Two Council members, Smith and Carson, stood pat, dissenting in detail on the ground that the law was a good one and should not be changed to favor the banks.[24]

Daniel's political career moved ahead smoothly after the bank vote. In 1815 and again in 1818, he successfully survived the "scratch," and went on to another three years of service on the Council.

Not always in the future was Daniel to have so easy a time. Local issues were on the horizon which were to involve him, and the number of his enemies was bound to increase. At the same time, he had gained seniority which added to his prestige. When in October 1818 the presiding officer of the Council of State resigned, Daniel was chosen as his successor by vote of the Council itself, and he thus became lieutenant governor of Virginia. For thirteen years he was to hold this position, the highest office ever given him by the people of his own state. By twentieth century standards, this is a trifling accomplishment; indeed, we might think a man wanting in basic qualities who would hold the office of lieutenant governor for so long a time. But in Daniel's day, the office was only part-time, and his very permanence in office made him for over a decade the most fixed point in the Virginia executive department. He was that figure whom we so much admire in the British civil service, the career undersecretary, the man who held office under many top men and who by his counsel could maintain a stability of administration. Moreover, he was not without duties. For these years Daniel was governor for every purpose whenever the governor was out of the city of Richmond. For example, from the day of his re-election on October 31, 1818, until November 25, through all meetings, the governor was gone and Daniel was the governor.[25]

In 1819 it developed that the state treasurer, John Preston (an officer elected by the legislature), had stolen a substantial amount of state money. The Council, which had nothing to do with the matter, was nonetheless criticized. Daniel was determined never again to warrant such criticism. When in

1823 he headed a Council committee to examine the state finances, he did a thorough job. By personal inspection the banks of deposit were investigated to insure that the state's funds were on hand, and all seeming discrepancies in the books of the state, which covered about $400,000, were scrupulously considered. After Daniel gave the state treasurer and the state auditors an exhausting and not altogether pleasant time, variances of $20 and of $1000 were explained to the satisfaction of the committee. The final inexplicable variance between the books and the actual cash on hand was exactly one nickel. Daniel, with his customary humorlessness, concluded his report with the statement that "This small variance a greater degree of attention might perhaps have removed." [26]

This was typical Daniel care. He was meticulous in every duty. For example, at the time he was conducting the treasury investigation, he also inspected the penitentiary to see whether certain prisoners who had been moved out during a period of repair could be returned. He personally inspected the premises, going over the jail cell by cell, examining the walls, the roof, the possible points of escape, and the methods of handling the prisoners. On the basis of the mental and physical health of the prisoners, he recommended their being moved to the penitentiary.[27]

There were during these same years more intellectually stimulating problems for a Virginian than finding a missing nickel in the state bank vaults. The Chief Justice of the United States lived in Richmond, and the decisions which he handed down a few miles away in Washington were of deep concern to Virginians.

Peculiar indeed was the status of John Marshall in his native Virginia. As the last great Federalist still holding office after twenty years of Republicanism, his views earned him more sympathy in Federalist Richmond than in the rest of the state. To Jefferson and Roane, chief judge of Virginia, Marshall was the most powerful single enemy of Republican principles, and their attitude toward him verged on personal hatred. The invective of Ritchie and Roane against some of Marshall's opinions was unlimited. And yet bitter as the controversies grew, Marshall's personal charm made him a hard man to hate. His simple Republican manners, his want of pretense, his modest attire, and his friendly cordiality as he walked about the streets of Richmond were scarcely compatible with the symbols of aristocracy attached to his opinions, and even the most violent of Republicans must occasionally have been a little embarrassed at the extremes of their own press assertions that Marshall was paving the way for a new monarchy.[28]

On the merits, Daniel was utterly opposed to Marshall's views. How far this extended to personal hostility, no one knows. Since Daniel was a man who usually took his politics personally he probably had a hostile personal attitude toward Marshall at least during the critical years of 1819–1821. Perhaps on other, happier occasions he was one of those Richmond lawyers who gaily joined in the bar dinners which Marshall gave for the attorneys of the city.[29]

There were interludes less calm. For a moment in 1817 Junto members had been in the Bank of the United States, and for a time the tongue of the Junto was quiet on the constitutional issues which the bank raised. But by 1819 the bank management had been changed, and Republican vigor was at the same time unshackled. The antibank spirit and states' rights theories combined in 1819 to create bitter Virginia resistance to what posterity has probably come to regard as Marshall's greatest opinion, *McCullough v. Maryland*.[30] In that case, the Supreme Court upheld the constitutionality of the Bank of the United States in terms so broad as to be a flagrant menace to every Republican states' rights conviction.

The *Enquirer* hailed the opinion with astonishment and apprehension and to a man the Republicans denounced it. Jefferson, now long in retirement but still a senior Republican statesman, on this occasion made his famous statement that "the Judiciary of the United States is the subtle corps of sappers and miners constantly working underground to undermine the foundations of our confederated fabric. They are construing our constitution from a coordination of a general and special government to a general and supreme one alone." [31] It was to answer Marshall in *McCullough v. Maryland* that John Taylor wrote his most famous book, *Construction Construed and Constitution Vindicated*, published in 1820.

Daniel completely shared the common Republican alarm. At the Fourth of July celebration in 1820 he offered as his toast: "The government of the United States, the creature of the state sovereignties; formed for their security and convenience only — may these sovereignties never want the wisdom or vigor to restrict it to the purposes of its creation." [32] The thought was wordy for a toast; of the thirty offered on this national anniversary occasion, his was the longest. But it made his point.

Daniel was drawn directly into the states' rights controversy with Marshall. The matter arose simply enough as a result of a Virginia statute of January 1820 which prohibited lotteries of particular kinds. For some years, Virginians had been enjoying the lotteries managed by two Baltimore entrepreneurs named Cohen, and the statute put them out of business. However, lotteries in the District of Columbia were still authorized by acts of Congress, and the Cohen brothers, in the course of managing a District of Columbia lottery, sold tickets in Virginia. They were convicted in the Virginia courts of violating the Virginia statute, their defense being that the statute was invalid because it conflicted with the act of Congress which permitted the lottery in the District of Columbia. When their conviction had been affirmed by the highest court to which it could come in Virginia, the Cohens petitioned the United States Supreme Court to review the judgment. As the case came to the Supreme Court late in 1820, there were two central issues: first, whether the United States Supreme Court could review a criminal conviction by a state court for violation of state law, and second, assuming that the Supreme Court did have such jurisdiction, whether the state law was valid.

The Virginia legislature authorized special counsel in the lottery case. The details of retaining counsel and instructing it as to its duties were left to the Council of State. The Council chose Philip Barbour (later to be Daniel's immediate predecessor on the Supreme Court) and Alexander Smythe.[33] Early in December, the Council met to give them its detailed instructions and spread the credo of strict construction upon the Council journal. The Council expressed its alarm at the continual encroachments upon states' rights by the national government which they attributed to a love of power and to a weakness on the part of the states in defending themselves. If these convictions of the Cohens were to be set aside, "every trace and vestige of state independence will be obliterated."

In the face of this attack upon its very sovereignty, Virginia was utterly defiant; "the state of Virginia does not recognize the power in any tribunal under heaven to arraign and adjudge away her sovereignty." The Council thereupon directed its lawyers to enter formal and solemn protest against the Supreme Court's jurisdiction and then to withdraw from the case. No representative of Virginia was so to demean himself as even to offer in this Federal body a defense of the policy of the Virginia statute.[34]

Since this is Daniel's story rather than Marshall's, we may almost leave the matter there. Marshall decided the jurisdictional question against Virginia, holding that the Supreme Court of the United States could review the validity of a state's statute involved in a criminal conviction.[35] As planned, Virginia then withdrew from the case.

Spencer Roane himself was at the forefront of the attack on the ruling. In a series of only faintly anonymous letters, signed Algernon Sidney and Hampden, he attacked the opinion of Marshall, and particularly the Republican Justices who had gone along with it. In commenting to Associate Justice Story on the attacks, Marshall said, "There are other minor gentry who seek to curry favor and get into office by adding their mite of abuse, but I think for coarseness and malignity of invention Algernon Sidney surpasses all party writers who have ever made pretentions to any decency of character." [36] Whether Daniel was one of those "minor gentry," no one can tell, since the anonymity of the other writers in the *Enquirer* (and there were several) was better protected than was that of Roane. If he did not write, he showed a more than normal restraint. It should be noted, however, that when he finally came to the Court himself he challenged the authority of many of Marshall's opinions, but he never took the position that *Cohens v. Virginia* was wrongly decided.

Daniel was soon to have enough of his own fights to think about. In December 1819 Thomas Randolph began his series of three one-year terms as governor of Virginia. Randolph, a nephew of Thomas Jefferson, was a hotheaded, vigorous, fellow who delighted in controversy. Personally, he and Daniel were unsympathetic to one another, his dashing spirit meshing very poorly with Daniel's dedication to the letter of the law.

For two years Council meetings were occasions of friction between the two. In January 1821 came the triennial scratch. If he could, Randolph would then have attempted to eliminate Daniel, but any such maneuver, even if contemplated, was forestalled when two other members of the Council voluntarily offered themselves as "victims of the constitution." The replacement of the two volunteers increased Junto strength, making the year 1821 particularly difficult for Randolph. In the middle of the year Randolph wrote a despairing letter to his uncle, Thomas Jefferson, describing the situation of the executive department. Jefferson answered him with blunt candor: "I have ever considered the organization of our executive as the crudest part of our constitution, a mere mongrel kind of Directory. Yet I see no hope of amending this or still worse things in it." [37]

Encouraged at least in principle by his distinguished uncle, Randolph attacked the situation directly. Upon his re-election for a third term in December of 1821, he publicly declared war. The executive department, he said, was divided into two branches, one the plural branch (the Council) and the other the single branch (the governor). He had protested "strongly against the unconstitutional encroachment, now so long continued as to threaten to become permanent, of the plural branch of the executive department upon the single branch, which I have the honor to represent at this time." He declared his intention to resist the Council because any other course would "violate my conscientious interpretation of the laws." [38]

He proceeded to specify his grievances. First, he objected to the practice of the Council of giving commissions to sheriffs, a power he believed was his alone. Second, he objected particularly to the interpretation by the lieutenant governor (Daniel) of the meaning of the constitutional language which caused the lieutenant governor to act when the governor himself was "absent from the seat of the government." (In the twentieth century, when we are accustomed to the notion that the President of the United States carries his presidency with him wherever he goes, it is difficult to realize how constrained some nineteenth century state executives were.) Randolph contended that he did not lose his powers as governor by leaving Richmond, particularly so long as he was in the county in which Richmond was located.

Randolph then went after Daniel directly. He blasted at "the usurpation, now openly acknowledged in the gazettes of this place, which converts the constitutional executive of Virginia into an Executive Directory with two presidents, one chosen by the general assembly, and another by itself, who may be fully installed by it in the office of chief magistrate whenever it may think proper to decline acting with the other, until weary of inaction, he withdraws from the capitol." The phrasing is clumsy but the meaning is clear. A Richmond-based Council of State could always outlast an out-of-Richmond governor by refusing to permit a course of action until the Governor went home, at which time the Richmond-based executive branch could do as it pleased.

While this public attack was against the Council as a body, Daniel was the prime target. Yet all of the Council was entitled to join in the reply, and every member but one did so in an excessively lengthy joint newspaper statement.[39] This rebuttal shrewdly stressed that Randolph was the first governor who had been unable to get along with his Council.

In these letters, and others which followed, one trifling item became the most tangible controversy. Randolph contended that the governor alone was the commander-in-chief of the militia and that he alone could direct it. The preceding Fourth of July had been rainy. As the road adjacent to the public square was in poor shape, Randolph had asked that the Norfolk and Richmond militia, which were to appear in the parade, be allowed to march on the public square. There was a gravel pathway here which could have been used and, as Randolph put it, the "cavalry had a right to march in order where Negro hack drivers are permitted to go for fares." This privilege had been refused by Daniel and the Council.[40]

Perhaps only a Virginian of the first part of the nineteenth century could have made this into a serious constitutional question, but there it was. If the governor had power to order the militia, why could he not order them into the public square? The Council replied that it was responsible for the care and upkeep of the public square, a property which had been developed at great cost.[41] A horde of horsemen with the resulting crowds would certainly be destructive of the grounds. As for the constitutional question, they contended that a Fourth of July celebration was a voluntary meeting, and that meetings for pageantry or amusement, even if engaged in by militiamen, did not make the militia anything other than another crowd.

After this stormy beginning, it was hardly to be expected that Governor Randolph's last term would be anything other than frosty. As the next Fourth of July (1822) drew near, both sides were looking for trouble, and they found it. Randolph was clever enough to choose an issue in which popular sentiment was sure to be with him. He ordered the adjutant general to give powder to the militia for use in firing salutes on the occasion. The cost was $60, and the Council refused payment on the ground that this was an unauthorized expenditure.

For a moment, the Council had scored a point. But when the legislature returned to session in December, Randolph in the course of his annual message asked for a special appropriation to pay for the powder and at the same time unleashed a new attack on the Council. With all the prestige which attaches to the farewell words of one retiring from office, he hit hard. Recalling the Preston scandal he said, "I sincerely respect the scrupulous conduct displayed on this occasion, and heartily rejoice that vigil has again come into fashion. But I feel at the same time, in common with other taxpayers, the hardship of having to contribute, from the now scanty fruits of industry, to make up the enormous loss sustained by the commonwealth from the scandalous peculations committed while these watchmen slept on their posts earlier." [42]

He bitingly reviewed the functions of a Virginia governor, a post which had proved not "so exalted, or the office so dignifying, as I had expected from the theory of our constitution." He had worked hard, he had rarely been able to get through a meal without being interrupted by the demands of some citizen of the state for some service. In the Council, he cheerfully reported, he had done his part faithfully. He had read aloud all the communications and documents to the Council and he had put up with their bad manners, their interruptions, and their conversations. He made it very clear that he was glad to be done. Affairs might have been worse than they were — at one point he had threatened a duel with someone (presumably Daniel) but the episode had passed.

As ex-governor, Randolph continued the fight. In the spring of 1823 he was elected to the legislature, thus coming back to the House of Delegates in the winter of 1823–24 when the triennial scratch was due to operate on the Council. He then made a vigorous but unsuccessful effort to unseat Daniel.

Thus, for the moment, Thomas Randolph lost his fight against the Council of State and Daniel. But he helped to begin the process of change which within a few years was to reconstitute the executive department of Virginia. Only a few months after this election there was a mass meeting in Richmond to consider whether to urge a state constitutional convention. The popular objections to the constitution went to points other than the structure of the executive department, but there were sharp comments about the Council. Animated conversation on the subject continued in Richmond for many days, until finally Benjamin W. Leigh, a leading lawyer, came publicly to the defense of the Council. Leigh and Daniel were friends, at least until a later political crisis, and undoubtedly Daniel was one of those who induced Leigh to take a public stand.

Leigh defended the existing executive department of Virginia on the ground that it did reduce the powers of the governor to the "lowest degree practicable," and that this was highly desirable.[43] Leigh's name was sufficient in Richmond — before long he was to be elected United States Senator — so that the opponents of the Council switched ground. At the next mass meeting, in May 1824, they opposed not the Council itself but its construction. They objected to the long term of service, to the size of the Council, and above all to the scratch, which they accurately described as an "odious process." [44] The mass meeting particularly decried the almost ludicrous position of the governor, who could not even cast a vote at the Council meeting and whose powers consisted simply of complying with the Council's advice. Randolph's complaint had indeed caught fire!

At several consecutive mass meetings, the fight for the Council system was carried by Daniel's friends. Principal advocates of the Council were Leigh and Daniel's fellow member of the Randolph clan, Philip Norborne Nicholas. After a time interest dribbled off as attention was turned to the national election of 1824, and at the end of 1824 Daniel was still well ahead of his enemies. He had survived the embezzlements of Preston (for which he certainly had no direct responsibility), had outlived the scratch, and had seen the rage against the Council wane into temporary ineffectiveness. At the end of 1824, the lieutenant governor and not the governor was the top man in the executive department of Virginia.

Chapter III

FAMILY AND PRACTICE

DANIEL WAS a man of endless principle and endless controversy. He was also a human being, a man who loved his wife and children, who made a living and owned modest properties, who had social friends as well as political enemies. One wonders just how warm his friendships may have been. That he was a man of great courtesy is evident, but whether this was a warm courtesy is something else again. One contemporary observer speaks of his "frozen deportment." [1] Did it seem thus to all? He liked people and he liked to be liked; his personal relations with Chief Justice Taney were later to be a source of pleasure to him. But his warmth so often took the shape of fervor that it may have lacked the softer touch of sheer humanity.

Certainly he loved Lucy, and she loved him, and he loved their three children. The first was Elizabeth, who was born in 1814 and who never married. Between her and her father there was a special intimacy never achieved with the others. His son Peter, born in 1818, became a practicing lawyer in Richmond and was far more of a financial success than his father ever had been. The baby was a second daughter, Anne, known as a child as Nannie, whose happy-go-lucky ways were sometimes a trial to her serious father.

Perhaps as a balance to the excessive strain of public life, Daniel had an intense affection for his family. Lucy's preoccupation in life were her home, her children, and her "*Dear, Dear* husband" as she sometimes addressed her letters to him.

Even before Daniel became a judge, they were necessarily apart when Daniel's practice carried him around the state. Those separations were hard for Lucy to bear, the more so because she could not be sure when he could return. Here, without knowing it, she marked the borders of her world:

> I write for fear you should not come home today. I was sadly disappointed at not seeing you last night, I had been thinking all day what could contribute to your comfort, and with some sorrow did I see another evening close without your being with us. I have looked for you ever since Thursday. I got your letter on yesterday; it came in good time to satisfy my unreasonable temper. How often I had repeated to myself, 'he has been absent a fortnight without writing' I cannot say. After reading the letter I did nothing for some moments but bless my husband, and say that he is the best of human beings.
>
> I have had our house swept from top to bottom and three rooms scoured, and a good deal of rubbing done to the parlour grate — but I am determined not to fatigue myself. Every time I go into the house I like it better and better — I would rather it were smaller, but I am pleased, most extremely pleased with my *home*. I should have had more done in the way of cleaning, but the early part of the week was a holy day, and for nearly all the week Lena has been sick — I was afraid she was going to have one of her serious attacks, but by using calomel (etc.) I have got her apparently and professedly quite or nearly well. As *you* were not at home I had no doctor by which I have saved $2.00 toward the house.[2]

She then recounted a bad dream about an accident to little Peter and described the horror of her nightmare. But she assured her husband that the two children (this was before the birth of Anne) had never looked better. She had taken them twice to Spring Farm and let them run. Little Peter was looking forward to the time when he could travel with his daddy. She reported her reading — a book on scriptural history — and then she took a little slice at the Richmond

Baptist minister, of whom she did not approve. She concluded, "The warmest feelings of my heart are yours my husband — my *treasure*."

Daniel's own religion was never ardent enough to suit Lucy. He did not reject religion, but his associations with it were largely formal. Lucy's almost passionate desire that she and her husband should throw themselves down on their knees to pray together was probably rarely if ever satisfied. The family belonged at first to the Monumental Episcopal Church, switching after 1845, along with most of polite Richmond, to the new St. Paul's.[3] The children were confirmed in the Episcopal faith. But no recorded word of Daniel's reflects any real concern with religious matters. His only preserved writing on the subject is a copy of a translation of a sermon by the eighteenth century French Bishop Jean Baptiste Massillon.[4] And though he doubtless went regularly to church when he was in Richmond, he seems only occasionally to have done so when he was away. Lucy's faith was personal and sustaining. Hers was an uneven temperament, light and happy at times, depressed at others, but she always turned to religion in her hours of vicissitude. Daniel's personal self-righteousness gave him less need for such a reliance, and one may suspect that he looked on the divine a little speculatively.

Lucy's influence on Daniel was for balance and restraint. Her affection, her chitchat, her domestic concerns, all moved and interested him, and her sweetness of manner made crises seem less critical. She did not share her husband's bitter partisanship. When Daniel Webster came to visit Richmond in 1840, Daniel was incensed almost to the point of fury at the manner in which the Whigs fawned on the great man. Lucy, in her sweet way, confessed guiltily that she took a wholly different view of it: "I never saw a more gay scene, and although I disapproved the cause of their rejoicing, and that they should use such improper means to obtain their end, yet I saw so many smiling faces I was obliged to smile too; and I smile whenever I recollect their good tempered cheerful faces." [5]

On the little things, Lucy managed her husband like any good wife. The question of this or that expenditure for a bonnet or a bit of cloth usually came out as she wished it. Her elder daughter, Elizabeth, was later to learn this skill. But in a sober moment, Lucy once gave her basic credo. The question was whether she should take a little trip. She decided not to: "I would gladly go to Stafford myself immediately if your father would let me, but although his words are 'Go', yet his manner says 'Stay', and I have not yet learned to thwart his wishes." [6]

Peter was Lucy's "darling, charming boy." He thought of her as irresistibly lovely. With his eternal rectitude, Peter must have been at times insufferably hard to live with and, financially their life was not easy. But if Lucy ever showed serious exasperation, there is no evidence of it. Every expressed thought was in the tone of "blessings attend my husband, dear husband." [7]

Daniel and Lucy were deeply fond of their children. Lucy idolized them and Peter counseled them, worried about them, and spent time with them. His correspondence with Peter and with Anne is lost, but enough remains of his correspondence with Elizabeth to show a relationship which (at least until near the end of his life) was in the best sense friendly. She was the first to be old enough to go on his judicial circuit with him, and it was a great treat for them both. Young Peter stayed home making great plans for the time when he also could go. [8]

The children's education was of special interest to Daniel. Peter, Jr., had to be educated not only in book learning but also in the manners of a gentleman, for while the last thing that the father wanted was that his son should become a fop or a dandy, he did want the boy to have both the values and the manners of a Randolph and a Daniel.[9] With Peter, Sr., dignity meant a great deal. But though he influenced the children, he at least tried not to dominate them entirely. When at the age of 18 young Peter seriously determined to become an engineer, his father, though not liking his choice of professions, nonetheless encouraged him to give engineering a try.[10] As the father suspected might be the case, the choice was not final and young Peter became a lawyer. In the last ten years of his life, after he had closed his Richmond home, Peter, Sr., made frequent visits from Washington to the home of Peter, Jr., in Richmond, and it was from his son's home that he was buried. In 1846 he transferred to young Peter the bulk of the Stafford County Crow's Nest property which had been handed down from his father before him.

Anne, his youngest, he loved and occasionally teased. He thought of her a little as a lightheaded miss and as she grew older he would save for her the diverting social tidbits picked up in his travels.[11] When she married Charles Moncure of North Carolina and moved to that state, Daniel continued his affectionate interest in her and her welfare. He noted her children's birth with great interest, had the usual grandfatherly curiosity as to which side of the family they resembled,[12] and expressed frequent concern for the care of her health. But she was always the youngest — when she was almost thirty and had children of her own, he was instructing her not to show her distaste for one of her neighbors.[13] He thought of his Nannie as a "lazy huzzie," and he was delighted to indulge her in any way he could.[14]

But Elizabeth, his first born, was always his favorite. After Lucy, she was for many years the most important person in his life. Elizabeth was a little of an invalid, at least in the sense fashionable for maiden ladies. After Lucy's death, she kept her father's house for several years, and his correspondence with her shows deep concern for her welfare and a sensitive perception of her interests. By the very selection of the topics he chose to tell her about, Daniel revealed a respect for his daughter's interests and understanding. From her second year, when she gave herself the nickname of "Dautie Bet," Elizabeth had a central spot in Daniel's heart.

Elizabeth as a young woman was about what could be expected of a faithful daughter of Lucy Daniel. She had suitors, and it is not clear why she remained unmarried. She had an interest in things religious and things sentimental, and collected poems of a saccharine sort. But she had a sense of humor too, and enjoyed a joke or a jingle when she came upon it. One treasure was a poem entitled "The Puritan," which perhaps she read to her father. It began

> The old Puritan was a solemn man,
> Sombre and sad were his features.
> He talked through his nose and wore plain clothes
> And seemed the forlornest of creatures.[15]

Elizabeth was well educated by the standards of her time, or indeed of any time. Her personal books included the works of the contemporary novelists including Scott, but it also included a translation of the works of Xenophon, two volumes of Cicero, and an old edition of the works of Racine, in French. Particularly cherished was the Book of Common Prayer, which, Elizabeth noted on the flyleaf, she shared with her mother in her mother's last illness. She made a little study of Beethoven for her own curiosity, and while it reveals some of her mother's inclination to scatteration, she had enough of her father's clarity to note in the margin, "I might have arranged this better." [16]

Daniel gave constant counsel about Elizabeth's health in the period after her mother's death. He worried about her going to bed late, and he encouraged her to go horseback or carriage riding every day. He urged his "dearest Bet" to keep the house socially lively and herself comfortable when he was away, despite their limited income.[17]

Daniel's properties, on which the children were brought up, were three. First there was the Crow's Nest in Stafford County, in which area the family occasionally visited in the summers. This property was of no great interest to Daniel in the last years of his life. The second was Spring Farm, the farm adjacent to Richmond which was Lucy's dowry and which Daniel managed through a foreman. The third was the house in town.

Spring Farm was an important part of Daniel's life, not merely for such income as he drew from it, but as a hobby. He had a lasting interest in agriculture, and later, while on the Court, enjoyed bringing in samples of his best products for the common mess maintained by the Justices.[18] Spring Farm was a part of what had been the Mt. Comfort plantation which has now completely disappeared.[19] It is in that part of Richmond now known as Chestnut Hill or Highland Park. In Daniel's time, the farm was still a good horse and buggy ride from town. The property contained an owner's house, an overseer's house, and small buildings as well as the usual farm structures. Daniel was not a man given to handiwork, and had the most simple repairs at the farm done for him by a local carpenter.[20]

The house in town, which was the real headquarters of the Daniel family, was at the corner of Seventh and Grace streets in what is now downtown Richmond. Here a block of row houses was built in 1834, and Daniel's was a substantial four-story structure with a very small porch.[21] In the same row of houses lived Thomas Ritchie, the editor of the Richmond *Enquirer* and Daniel's fellow Junto leader, and the two must often have put their heads together coming from or to their many meetings.

Daniel's establishments, insofar as they were not self-supporting, were maintained by his income as a practicing lawyer. His Council duties gave him $1000 a year and some subordinate state services added a little; but his basic income came from his practice, and it was not much. By the standards of his social contemporaries, Daniel was poor and in many ways this circumstance dominated his life. Even a new bonnet for Lucy had to be planned and saved for. They lived pleasantly, with a fair amount of entertaining, travel, and regular vacations, but it was still a frugal life.

Daniel's practice was of a general sort. What big, lucrative business there was in Virginia, he did not get. He was proud of the fact that at the bar he was diligent, careful, and successful. Yet just before going on the Federal bench he summed up his experience this way: "I never had the patronage of a bank or a merchant scarcely in my life. Their *easy*, *regular*, *gainful* business has been thrown into the hands of men of opposite political opinions. 'Twas only when they found themselves beset with difficulties, or when they feared my efforts against them, and wished to buy them off, that I have shared their custom. And I have generally therefore made them pay pretty well, as I felt I owed them nothing on the score of favor." [22]

The last touch was probably vainglory. It is true that the most substantial business of Richmond was largely controlled by the Federalists, and there is no evidence that they were often so desperate for help that they turned to their most conspicuous enemy. At the beginning of his practice, his work included the typical young lawyer's errand boy activities. One of his first cases was an effort to get a land grant approved by the legislature on behalf of a woman who claimed that it had been promised to her by responsible Virginia officials some twenty-five years before. A few years later he attempted to get a court martial decision reviewed for a militiaman. These two cases put him respectively in touch with Thomas Jefferson [23] and James Madison,[24] and are the only recorded evidence of any direct contact between him and those two Virginians.

The bulk of his practice involved simple property sales and debts between individuals. He was often in the Court of Equity, reporting in 1824 that he had to look over some ninety-seven cases before the next Equity Term.[25] He was often a trustee in real estate transactions, some of them involving fair amounts of money.[26] The Richmond property records show him in numerous land transactions.[27] The few remaining records of how he conducted his business show exactly what would be anticipated from the personality which unfolds in his political life: he was meticulous, thorough, and assured.

In the Virginia Supreme Court of Appeals Daniel had thirty-five cases all told — not a large number compared with the titans of his bar. He lost the first seven, but in his last years of practice won appreciably more than he lost. These cases came from an area within fifty miles of Richmond and involved, usually, wills and real property. Six cases concerned slaves. Twelve hundred dollars was the largest sum of money in any of his cases [28] and a 560-acre farm the largest piece of real property.[29]

From this practice he drew his income, usually in the form of small payments, as a fee of $5 for defending a suit in one of the county courts.[30] At the height of his practice in the 1830's his total income was between $3000 and $4000 a year including the $1000 and miscellaneous income from the state.[31] His living expenses came to something around $3000 a year [32] and when, after he went on the district bench, his income fell below this figure, he was in anguish.

This was not a large income even by the modest standards of the first part of the nineteenth century. There are no figures on average legal incomes for this period, in Richmond or elsewhere; but top lawyers in the major commercial cities were making from $10,000 to $40,000 a year, with a few outstanding individuals earning much more; and routine incomes in many cities must have been about $5000 or roughly almost double Daniel's.[33] In part, it was true that wealth was hard to come by for an intense Republican, and that a political career required much expensive hospitality. During the early 1820's even Thomas Jefferson was facing bankruptcy atop the lovely hill at Monticello, and plans were afoot to rescue him with a state-sponsored lottery which Daniel supported.

With this mediocre income Daniel maintained his house and farm, kept usually four or five slaves principally for work on the farm, had two to four horses for his own and farm use, and kept a carriage for himself and for the use of his womenfolk. He wore a gold watch, and his household furnishings included a piano.[34] Some understanding of his status and that of his more well-to-do friends is gained by comparing him with Philip N. Nicholas or John Brockenbrough. Daniel had four slaves; each of those gentlemen had nine. Daniel had one watch; Nicholas had two. The Brockenbrough and Nicholas carriages were incomparably superior in quality and in trappings to Daniel's. But in one respect, Daniel led the pack. His silver tableware was much more elaborate than Nicholas' — the old Randolph plate, which Lucy had inherited, was the glory of the house. The mahogany dining table, too, came from Edmund Randolph, and it glistened with the silver platters, the covered silver bowl, the silver soup ladle, and two silver gravy spoons which bore the Randolph coat of arms. Much of the miscellaneous silver and the china, including the excellent Canton set, also came from the Randolph household.

The care and handling of slaves was of great concern to Virginians. Many gave the matter systematic thought, just as either personnel management or animal husbandry gets elaborate thought today. For example, James Barbour, the governor of Virginia with whom Daniel served during the War of 1812 and who later became senator, owned some one hundred slaves. He thought their proper diet should be all the bread they wanted, a little meat each day, preferably bacon, and milk when available or cider if milk was short. To this he would add "a small quantity of whiskey — six or seven gallons to a laboring hand during the year." [35]

A modest slaveowner like Daniel had none of these mass care problems. He had his own set of common sense notions on the management of slaves. He vacillated between the use of white servants, hired by the year, and Negroes. On the one hand he liked white help, and on the other hand he found the annual turnover an annoyance.[36] (In this, as well as in some other respects, Daniel would have found the twentieth century really insufferable.) On the whole, both the management and the selection of servants for the house was left to Lucy or, later, to Elizabeth. On one occasion he gave Elizabeth the authority to buy any necessary servants, a cook, a house servant, or a driver with a carriage, if they were not too expensive; he expressed the hope that a driver could be obtained who would take good care of the horses and the carriage, though he was pessimistic over the prospect.[37]

At the same time, he gave his womenfolk some guidance on slave handling. Fearing that a household slave, Phil, might attempt to escape, he directed that Phil be kept as busy at his employment as possible. This, Daniel thought, would keep him from forming bad habits or making poor associations. He also congratulated Elizabeth on having brought the servant Betsey around to a good humor. Daniel's reason was most practical: "I believe that although violent in her temper, she has kind feelings, and it is desirable (while too much familiarity is to be avoided) to cultivate feelings of kindness with those with whom we are compelled to have daily and hourly contact." [38]

On rare occasions Daniel was a firm disciplinarian. When his "rascal James" consistently behaved badly, Daniel instructed his son Peter either to whip James himself or, if the task were too unpalatable, to have the job done by a constable. The only alternative was to sell the slave, which he very much disliked doing.[39] In Daniel's will he expressed the hope that James would not be separated from the Daniel children (who had known him from infancy), and he specifically commended James to their kindness. If James were not to stay in the family, Daniel directed that he be hired out to some kind and humane person.

This concern for the welfare of others, so typical of Daniel's feeling toward those about him who did not cross his political path, resulted in his taking one of his dining room servants to the seashore so that her health might improve.[40] If household slaves were sick, Lucy did all she could to take care of them. The essence of his attitude was expressed in a note to Elizabeth about an operation on one of the slaves: "Peter almost made me weak at his account of poor Beaufort's sufferings under the surgical operation performed upon his shoulder. Poor fellow, I could hardly have witnessed it; though I know it was in truth a kindness to him and indeed necessary to save his life. Tell Doctor Rawlings that I hope he will see that his prescriptions are faithfully applied, for I know that Negroes especially are very inattentive to such matters as require attention and trouble." [41]

The Daniels were of the oldest of Virginia families, and were entitled to move freely in the best of Richmond society. With an occasional sneer at the "parvenu aristocracy," they did.[42] Daniel enjoyed entertaining and going out, at least when his occasional rheumatism and Lucy's variable health permitted. He therefore had a position of some prominence in what was perhaps the greatest social event of the early nineteenth century, the visit of Lafayette to the United States. Lafayette, who as a young man had been with Washington at Valley Forge and at Yorktown, came again, fifty years later, to the scenes of his sufferings and of his triumphs. Wherever he went the dreams of glory of every American went too, for he symbolized the foundation of the Republic. In New England, in New York, in the middle and in the southern states, each community struggled to outdo all others in the magnificence and in the eloquence of his reception. Every American followed the newspaper chronicles of the "Journey of the Nation's Guest," and proud Virginia, scene of the ultimate victory at Yorktown, prepared to do its share.

On Saturday, October 15, 1824, the dignitaries of Virginia converged on Williamsburg.[43] Lafayette came by boat from Alexandria, stopping at Mount Vernon for two hours. Upon his arrival in Williamsburg the governor presented the Council to him. At Mount Vernon, the home of the man whom he regarded as the greatest he had ever known, Lafayette had knelt to kiss the coffins of George and Martha Washington. At Williamsburg there were further reminders of the past, the house where George Washington had been married in 1759, and the still visible remnants of the British trenches, sunk from the tread of cattle and from rain, but not entirely effaced.

There followed a period of entertainment at Williamsburg, the nicest touch of which was the use at one of the dinners of some wax candles which had been taken from the stores of Lord Cornwallis when the English force had surrendered forty-three years before. Then Lafayette went to Richmond, where the round of dinners, balls, and entertainments left the city with no need to apologize for its hospitality. The best amusement was a race for a $1000 prize at the Jockey Club, at which the winning filly was immediately renamed "Virginia de LaFayette." [44] Without a doubt the high point was a superb address by Chief Justice Marshall, himself a veteran of the Revolution, who welcomed Lafayette in the capitol square. With gracious simplicity and strong authority, he spoke of the affection which the fighting men of America had felt for their former commander.

The social climax was a great ball at the Eagle Tavern, magnificently festooned with greens and flowers for the occasion. There were fifteen hundred guests on the floor, and hundreds more in the gallery.[45] Peter and Lucy were there of course, Lucy dressed in a lovely gown of brocaded taffeta. Lafayette took a turn around the floor with her, and one may suspect that even in the economical Daniel family that fleeting contact with the great man was enough to warrant putting the dress away forever as a memory of the occasion. To this day Daniel descendants carefully preserve a section of the cloth of the dress worn by Lucy Randolph Daniel when she danced with Lafayette.[46]

There were also the formal dinners with the after-dinner toasts. At one such, the toast offered by Daniel was long in sentiment but short in neatness: "The assertors of human liberty in every age and nation; may they, like LaFayette, live to hear the success of their exertions resound in the benedictions of free and happy millions." [47]

As was usually the case, Marshall had the best word. He offered: "Rational Liberty — the cause of mankind. Its friends cannot despair when they behold its champions." [48]

Chapter IV

REVOLT, ACTUAL AND POLITICAL

IN THE DECADE 1825 to 1835 Daniel emerged as one of the primary Jackson–Van Buren men in Virginia and was gaining national stature. By 1835 his position in Virginia politics was based on something more substantial than persistent attention to small duties and longevity in office.

But notwithstanding his more substantial position, there were still the little duties. He had the usual chores of a man prominent in community life. He sat on the Richmond public library board; he presided regularly at the Fourth of July dinners (and improved somewhat in the quality of his toasts). He continued to do the basic work of the Council both before and after a change in the structure of that body, and he had always his own political fences to tend, his job to hold, and, during the Constitutional Convention of 1829–30, the Council itself to preserve.

One of these continuing unspectacular jobs was the work of the Council in the administration of justice. The Council gave pardons, and the governor himself had to approve extradition warrants for persons wanted by other states. Virginia being a slave state, the Council was almost the only defense for Negroes accused of crime. In this role as a criminal judge Daniel appears at his best: his was a forceful voice for fair play and for modification of harsh penalties.

Daniel's approach in criminal law was one of strict adherence to established procedures coupled with moderation of penalty. He was extraordinarily sensitive to the thought of physical pain in those about him, including his slaves, and he could not look on the death sentence with the casual indifference of many of his contemporaries. As might be expected, he stuck to established procedures even when they were inconsequential or awkward. Thus, in extradition cases the slightest failure to live up to the literal requirements of the statute by way of affidavits, notarizations, and so on caused him to refuse to extradite.[1] He adhered firmly to the principle that "The punishment of the guilty is not of more importance than is a strict conformity with the powers under which the criminal jurisprudence of the country is to be dispensed. In the high concerns of life and liberty the forms of the law become of the essence of the law."[2]

Application of these principles to slaves was of considerable benefit to them. For example in 1829 the slave Henry was convicted by the Goochland County Court for committing an assault on a white man. For this offense he was condemned by the court to sale in the West Indies (more formally, to transportation beyond the limits of the United States), a penalty which, next to the death penalty, was the most severe which the court could give. Condemnation to transportation meant the breaking of every familial tie and something less than a long life in the cane fields. As no slave ever returned from the Indies to describe his experiences, the terrors of this penalty in the minds of the slaves may have been even greater than the actuality.

In behalf of the Council Daniel set aside Henry's conviction. Under the statute the offense of which Henry had been convicted was a felony, and convictions in felony cases had to be unanimous. In this case one of the trial justices of the peace had dissented from the opinion of his associates. "So far, therefore, from the opinion of the court being any warrant for transporting the slave beyond the limits of the United

States, that opinion is regarded by the Executive as an acquittal by the plain directions of the statute." [3] Daniel, in his indignation at the illegality committed, added a direct reproof to the court.

Virginia needed psychological as well as physical control over the slaves. Particularly in the tidewater counties, where the Negro population far outnumbered the white, the possibility of a slave insurrection was always in the back of a planter's mind. Who could tell whether a sidewise glance was insolence or merely curiosity? Who could tell whether an evening meeting of a number of slaves in one of the cabins was really for a religious ceremony or to plot trouble? Who could tell whether if slaves were permitted to learn to read, they would really use their knowledge only to study the Bible and thus perhaps become more docile, or whether they might begin to communicate by writing and to plot among themselves?

Rumors of impending insurrection frequently ran over the state. In 1829, Daniel was sufficiently upset by such rumors in the neighborhood of a Federal arsenal that he proposed to the Council that the Secretary of War be requested to improve the defenses of the arsenal in case any attempt should be made on it by the slave population. [4]

The evil day came two years later. In Southampton County in southeastern Virginia on the plantation of Joseph Travis lived a Negro slave about thirty-one years of age named Nat Turner. Of somewhat more than average intellectual powers, Turner regarded himself, and was regarded by some of the Negroes, as a prophet. He was born in the United States, but his mother had been born in Africa, and she had cultivated in him a deep religious mysticism. In the summer of 1831 he began to hear "voices" directing him to murder whites. Signs in the sky, particularly an eclipse of the sun, led him to believe that the time had come. At three o'clock in the afternoon of Sunday, August 21, Turner and six other Negroes met in the woods where they roasted a pig and drank considerable brandy. At this wooded rendezvous, they made their first actual plan. No one outside this small central group ever participated in their planning, a point which became of considerable importance later. On that night, the twenty-first, the men entered the Travis house and killed all five of the occupants as they slept. The dead included a baby in a cradle, whose brains were dashed out against the fireplace.[5]

After this savage beginning the marauders cut a swath of some twenty-seven miles through the Virginia countryside in the next day and night, frightfully butchering some fifty white persons, the great bulk of them women and children.

The carnage was essentially aimless rage stimulated by alcohol. At each plantation to which they went the central group added slaves to their number, some willingly and some by force. Their number thus rose and fell, at some points the gang amounting to as many as sixty people, at some points falling to twenty. No barbarism was omitted. The victims were clubbed or hacked to death, and their blood was sometimes used to ornament the slaves. Never in the history of abortive peasant revolts was there one more aimless than this. If Turner had a master plan of any sort, no one has ever discovered it; and the bulk of the slaves participating were acting in blind fury with no understanding of any possible objective. At each bloody stop new liquor and new arms were obtained and were quickly distributed.

The night of the twenty-first and the following day were the high point of the revolt. By the twenty-third the news had reached Richmond, where the governor and Daniel were the only Council members present. Governor Floyd was Daniel's major political enemy, but this was no time to stand on personal considerations. Daniel at once agreed that the governor should take all necessary measures to suppress the insurrection by ordering out troops and taking any other step which the necessities of the case might require.[6] It is a tribute to the extraordinary calm shown by the state administration in this crisis that Daniel also approved a minor postage bill before the meeting adjourned. The revolt was suppressed by August 25.

Throughout this difficult period Daniel maintained admirable poise. In consultation with Floyd he appraised all of the excited requests for help which poured in from all over the state (for insurrections were expected in every corner). He slashed in half some requests for ammunition, concluding, for example, that it was sheer waste to send more than eight or ten kegs of powder to one county.[7]

Before the main trials in Southampton County began Negroes in adjacent counties were tried for attempts at insurrection (the reality of which was dubious) and were sentenced to death. When this first group of cases came before the Council in mid-September, Daniel set the death sentences aside and reprieved the slaves for transportation. He did not argue that these slaves were not guilty, although he did raise a little doubt about it, but he contended that since they were prosecuted under a statute which made it a crime to "conspire to rebel" they could be convicted only upon an actual conspiracy. This meant that they had to participate in the making of some plan. At most these particular defendants were guilty of some form of insolence for which the penalty was less than death. He concluded, "I cannot make them otherwise criminal than the law has done it nor annex to their misconduct a punishment not assigned to it by the law itself." [8]

Fifty-three slaves came to trial in Southampton County in September. The court tried to make these trials fair. The issues were not easy. Though the leadership was steady, the membership of Turner's band changed constantly. Moreover, some of the defendants could rightly claim that they had been forced to participate. About a dozen of those tried were discharged; most of the rest got the death sentence. Daniel reviewed these death sentences with scrupulous care.

He had no finer hour. The spirit of the state, and particularly of the affected area, was one of revenge to the point of blood lust. A month after these cases began to come to Daniel, Turner himself was captured. He was promptly tried and sentenced to be hanged, a sentence to which no one could fairly take exception, since in his case the law squarely fitted his offense. However (although this was no part of the sentence), after his execution his body was cut down and the skin was removed and at least some of it made into ornaments or souvenirs, the flesh was cut off and reduced to grease, and the skeleton was given to someone as a trophy.[9]

One should recall this general state of mind when appraising Daniel's actions. In case after case he reduced the death sentence. In the cases of the slaves Frank, Jim, and Issac, all three condemned to death, Daniel found that the testimony was almost entirely that of one witness, another slave, and this slave Daniel simply did not believe. At most, he concluded, these slaves were guilty of isolated actions which did not amount to conspiracy and therefore did not fall under the death-sentence statute. As a result, their sentences were reduced to transportation.[10]

The Turner episode shows a striking quality of judicial balance in Daniel's makeup. So much of his public service was partisan, and some of it so passionately partisan, that it is hard to realize that there was also in him a strand of contemplative judgment. When, with sixty dead and the state in a frenzy of fear, a man stops to examine guilt or innocence with care, he is, in the best sense of the term, a judge. That there would be excesses in the repression of the Turner rebellion was inevitable; it is to Daniel's immense credit that he did not allow his judgment to be corrupted by the excitement of the moment.

A year later, in 1832, two cases again tested his sense of justice. The first was a remarkable case of rape.[11] The accused slave, Joshua, had allegedly entered the room of a white woman, Mrs. Selbe, in the darkness of the night. Joshua's own black skin (if Joshua in fact it was) doubtless made identification none the easier. He — or someone — had intercourse with Mrs. Selbe. Joshua's brother and sister swore to an alibi for him. The defense attempted to shift the blame to another slave, Tarleton, who was shown to have been in the neighborhood of the crime at about the time of its occurrence and, when Mrs. Selbe had left the house earlier that same evening, had asked him where he was going and who was to be in the house during his absence. However, Mrs. Selbe testified very firmly that she recognized Joshua's voice, and there was some supporting evidence, on the strength of which Joshua was sentenced to death.

What troubled Daniel in this case was not the question of the guilt or innocence of Joshua. He was satisfied that it was Joshua and not Tarleton. What did trouble him was the question of whether Mrs. Selbe might not have encouraged Joshua. If so, he could not be guilty of rape. There was in the record no evidence to support this suspicion, but there was a letter to the Council by a white person which at least hinted at the possibility. Another judge faced with a clear case of sexual relations and a probable rape between a slave and a white woman might have been less careful in his inquiry, but the mere hint of inducement was enough to give Daniel pause. "Whilst I would punish a rape committed even upon a lewd woman," he said, "I certainly should be disposed to mitigate the punishment in relation to an accused, when it was clearly shown, either that his accuser was wholly unworthy of credit, and stood uncorroborated in her statement by circumstances,

or where it was manifest that preceding familiarities authorized on the part of the accused the reasonable expectation of
their recurrence." He thereupon suggested delay of the execution to permit the possible uncovering of some evidence
(other than mere rumor) either that Mrs. Selbe was of bad
character or that there had previously been any intercourse
between them. He added, with obvious sincerity, "truth and
justice being the only objects in view." [12]

The second case is one in which, unfortunately, Daniel was
considerably more than a hundred years ahead of his time.
To this day the Supreme Court of the United States has not
been progressive enough to adopt as a principle for free citizens the rules which in 1832 he laid down concerning the
use of the third degree against slaves.

The episode arose from the trial of the slaves John and
Allick, who were charged with breaking into a storehouse in
the town of Petersburg and taking a chest with contents of
a value of $700. The crime was substantial, and the local
police set about to solve it with an excess of zeal. Allick was
seized and tied down in a cramped position which became so
painful that he confessed and implicated John. Apart from
this confession there was no other credible evidence against
either of the two slaves. Bank notes were found in a place to
which John and Allick had access, but so did many others.
The police contended that the thieves had got wet in the
course of the theft, and when arrested, John's clothes were
wet; but the robbery had occurred more than twenty-four
hours before the arrest, in which time his clothes would have
dried out if their dampness had been caused as charged. The
only other evidence against Allick was the presence of three
or four dollars in change in his pocket, which was scarcely
significant evidence that he had stolen $700 the day before.
On the strength of the confession, the two were convicted.

Daniel was profoundly shocked that in Virginia the third

degree could be used against anyone, much less a slave. In his twenty years on the Council there had been only one previous instance of such a means of extracting evidence. He remembered the earlier occasion well, for then the Council had not merely remanded for a new trial — it had ordered the acquittal of the defendant. Daniel now followed the same course:

> The use of *torture* (unknown at all times to the institutions of the common law, and now condemned and abolished wherever the remotest approaches to just and enlightened principles have obtained) is sufficiently abhorrent in situations wherein he who resorts to it may in turn become its victim. But when applied to subjects from whom retribution can never come, and who have not the advantage of a judgment by their peers, it is more than doubly odious and if either its modes, or degrees of application, are left to the judgment, or the tenderness of those who resort to it, the gradations will be short and rapid, from the *tying down in an uneasy posture*, spoken of in this record, to the brand, the screw, or the wheel.[13]

But, said the prosecuting attorney, Allick confessed twice. His second confession was made without threats or promises. This argument Daniel discarded as the ridiculous subterfuge that it was: "When the latter's statement was made, the prisoner had made his previous confessions under the infliction of bodily pain; he knew as he said, that the first confession was reduced to writing; he was moreover still in durance; and the addition of a few circumstances would scarcely vary the consequences either to himself, or to his alleged associates; or if they did, they would in some degree extenuate the offense imputed to himself." [14]

Daniel then wrote a sentence which expressed his most profound convictions: "My purpose is to reprobate, and so far as I have power, to arrest the practice regarded by me as unjust, and cruel, and utterly destructive of safety in any community in which it may obtain."

Like any other public servant, Daniel constantly had not only the duty of filling his job but the task of keeping it. He survived the scratch of 1824, it will be recalled, only after a major tussle. In 1827 he had an easy time of it, facing not even token opposition.[15] It was, however, a bad year for the Junto, with two of the faithful going off the Council. Daniel's own influence was thus weakened; almost never in the minority during the earlier part of the decade, his dissents were somewhat more frequent after this election.

This term, 1827–1830, saw a menace to Daniel's continuance in office far more substantial than the scratch. The drive for a convention to revise the entire constitution, which Governor Randolph had sparked a few years before, flamed up again in 1828.

Reorganization of the executive department was a fairly minor part of the serious questions which called for reconsideration. The major issues were representation in the state legislature, extension of the suffrage, and slavery. On all these issues that portion of the state which was later to become West Virginia was opposed to the eastern or tidewater section. There was also sharp difference over internal improvements, which the West wanted far more than the East.

These disputes led to a constitutional convention in 1830. This meeting became one of the most important state conventions in American history, and it must have been one the greatest disappointments of Daniel's political life that he was not a delegate. The district in which the city of Richmond was located was entitled to four delegates, only two of whom were to be from the city. Chief Justice John Marshall of Richmond was clearly the overwhelming first choice of the entire district, receiving seventy-five percent more votes than his closest Richmond rival.[16] The second Richmond seat went to Philip Norborne Nicholas, Daniel's close friend and relative, and his senior in standing, years, and prestige with the Junto.

Because the districts were not required to choose residents, Daniel had the alternative of seeking election elsewhere. A notice signed "several free holders of the district" was sent out in his behalf to the residents of the seven counties of the district encompassing Stafford County. On this great occasion, it said, "We have the right, and it is our solemn duty not only to ourselves but to posterity, to select men of the greatest ability and experience in whatever part of the state they may live." Such circumstances "demand the services of Peter V. Daniel," who was a native of Stafford County, still owned property there, and had the closest family ties with the district. Moreover, he had represented Stafford County in the state legislature. "Few men of his age have devoted more attention to the science of government than Mr. Daniel," it very accurately said.[17] The attempt failed. The district chose to elect from its own present population; and though Daniel was never formally withdrawn as a candidate, he must have dissuaded his friends from voting for him, because when the actual time to ballot came, no votes were cast for him.

The great convention was held in Richmond. In addition to Marshall, James Madison and James Monroe were delegates, and so was the governor of the state, the two United States senators, and nine members of Congress. On the greater issues of the day, the convention was essentially conservative. By margins of only four votes, it defeated basic proposals for equal representation of the different regions, and for significant increase in the suffrage. On these fundamental questions the most distinguished delegates sided with the conservative faction.[18] A year later the House of Delegates was to defeat a proposal tending toward the abolition of slavery in Virginia, and this by a majority which might never have existed if a democratic system of legislative representation had been adopted the year before.[19]

The convention for a time was strongly tempted to abolish the Council of State altogether. Finally by way of compromise it reduced the number of members from seven to four, the four to choose a lieutenant governor from among their own number. The governor was to preside at Council meetings and cast the deciding vote in case of a tie. The scratch was eliminated, and Council members would serve for four years. The largest change in the new system was that the governor would be compelled to *ask* the advice of the Council, but he was not compelled to *follow* it. The Council's position would be duly recorded so that the governor could be held responsible by the legislature when acting against the Council's advice.

That the Council of State was saved at all was a demonstration that its record had on the whole been good. So long as the debate could be kept on the theoretical level, it was easy to denounce the Council system; and to a limited extent the complaints could be made tangible. The excessive Richmond orientation of the Council was particularly emphasized. Yet when Benjamin Watkins Leigh, who stood with Nicholas in behalf of the Council, pressed the opposition for a concrete example of specific abuses from the Council system, almost nothing was forthcoming. Leigh himself reduced the opposition to a joke by asserting that there had been no more serious problem of abuse than the grant during Governor Randolph's administration of a few barrels of damaged powder for a Fourth of July celebration. (The record adds: "Here a well known voice was heard to remark, that the grant had made far more noise than ever the powder did, for that would not burn.") Doddridge, a western opponent of the Council, went all the way back to a scandal of 1808 to find an abuse to talk about.[20] The Preston treasury scandal of a few years before had, happily for the friends of the Council, been overlooked.

The pro-Council and anti-Council forces were closely balanced, and the stands of individual members changed as other issues were decided. For example, Senator John Tyler supported abolition of the Council when it appeared probable that the governor would be elected by the legislature, but changed his position when it appeared that the governor would be elected directly by the people.[21] The majority either way at any given moment was thin. John Randolph, who backed the Council, denounced the "lean, staggering, rickety majority, tumbling from side to side." [22] On critical votes Marshall and Madison also supported the system.

As a result of the efforts of his friends Nicholas and Leigh Daniel's job was saved, but most of its function was gone. Yet in part he had saved himself. He was by far the senior councilor and his record of service for eighteen years had resulted in nothing with which the enemies of the Council system could attack the institution. Indeed Leigh had mentioned Daniel's personal record as a justification for the Council system, saying: "The ablest men of Virginia have been in the Council; and I shall take occasion to say, that the present Lieutenant Governor [Daniel] is, in point of capacity, abundantly fit for the management of the affairs of this state, or of any other state in the Union; and, in point of firmness, integrity and virtue, there is not a man in the Commonwealth that would be disparaged by a comparison with him." [23]

The convention was in session in the winter of 1829–30. Its sessions thus overlapped those of the state legislature, which convened for its annual meeting in December 1829. This legislature had the job of conducting the last scratch and electing a governor for the last year under the old constitution. The scratch took place on January 5, 1830, and did Daniel's reputation no harm. He was the first man out of danger on both series of ballots.[24] Four days later the legislature met to elect a governor.

This gubernatorial election was triply important. The man elected now would have an excellent chance of being the first governor under the new constitution. Moreover, the national leaders, Jackson, Calhoun, and Clay, would be affected by the Virginia election. Of special concern to Daniel was the fact that the end of the Council was in sight. If ever he was to advance from the Council to the governorship, this might well be his last chance.

As a result of these considerations, Daniel stood for the governorship as the representative of Richmond and of the Jackson–Van Buren forces. He was overwhelmingly defeated by the Calhoun candidate, John Floyd. The vote was 140 for Floyd, 66 for Daniel.[25]

The result was the worst possible conflict within the executive department. For practical purposes, Governor Floyd was of one party, and Lieutenant Governor Daniel, of another. This condition persisted even under the new system, for in 1831 Floyd was elected the first governor under the new constitution, and Daniel again became lieutenant governor. The election of Floyd in 1831 was without opposition, and Daniel won easily.[26] Daniel's supporters stressed his loyalty to Jackson and made much of his experience and his reputation for the highest integrity. At the same time there was a firm if minority opposition to Daniel. The press referred discreetly to the "bitter feeling" which marked the balloting. The first executive department under the new constitution was thus divided and rent by bitter feeling, with divergent policies oriented in relation to the divided policies of Washington factions. The resultant fireworks involved Daniel in sharper clashes than any he had experienced up to this time. To understand those clashes it is necessary to examine his developing role in national politics.

Chapter V

A GROWING ROLE IN NATIONAL POLITICS

THE HISTORY of Daniel's national political activity falls fairly neatly into phases by decades. From 1810 through the election of 1820, which is to say from the beginning of his political career until well into his lieutenant governorship, he took a vigorous interest in national affairs without being a significant state leader. Between 1820 and 1830 his role changed. He continued to be an important state official, and at the same time he had within the state a position of some influence and leadership on national affairs. By the end of the twenties he was a major Jackson–Van Buren lieutenant in Virginia; but his interest in state affairs was still predominant. From about 1830 to 1840 this role was essentially reversed; in this period he was unquestionably a major state leader in behalf of the national interests of his party. In repeated instances his activities in state affairs were controlled by his judgments as to what would further the national interests of the Democratic presidents.

The Republican (soon to be called the Democratic) party in Virginia began each national campaign from 1820 to 1840 with the selection of a ticket of electors. These were chosen by the members of the party in the state legislature. The next step was the organization of a Central Corresponding Committee, consisting of Richmond figures, to lead the campaign. Local committees were then established in each county. The Central Committee raised the necessary funds, saw to the printing of ballots (for this was long before the day of the secret ballot and the voter took his own ballot to the polls), and filled the state with broadsides and pamphlets. Daniel became a member of the Central Committee for the first time in 1820, at the time of the unanimous re-election of President James Monroe. The senior member was Spencer Roane, near the end of his career as chief judge of the Virginia Supreme Court of Appeals. Others were Andrew Stevenson — later to become Speaker of the House of Representatives under Jackson — Philip N. Nicholas, and Thomas Ritchie. These men were also the heart of the Junto. Most of the writing was done by Ritchie because the *Enquirer* led Republican thought in the state; but Daniel was a kind of auxiliary editorial writer, his editorials taking the form of countless letters to the editor.

It was during this period that there occurred the most momentous political event of Daniel's life. All subsequent advancement, including the Supreme Court appointment, stemmed from it. This was the informal national alliance between Martin Van Buren in New York and the Richmond leaders in Virginia, or between the Albany Regency and the Richmond Junto.

Martin Van Buren was one of the greatest political managers in the history of the United States. Approximately the same age as Daniel, he entered state affairs in New York in 1813, about the time that Daniel went onto the Council of State. He rose quickly, with service as state senator, state attorney general, and, after 1821, United States senator from New York. He developed the state organization known as the Albany Regency which until it foundered on the slavery issue was the dominant political force in New York State.

While the Virginia Junto was dissatisfied with President Monroe on principle, Van Buren was having difficulties of a more practical nature. Monroe appointed an anti–Van Buren

man as postmaster at Albany. Van Buren made a public statement of his disappointment and mortification, and pledged
that the Democrats would proceed with irrepressible energy
to correct the unhappy situation.[1]

Shortly after his election to the Senate, and while there
was still much uproar over his statement, Van Buren made
a get-acquainted trip to Richmond. The focus of his trip was
a visit to Spencer Roane already on his death bed but still
a dominant force in the Junto. Roane was propped up in bed
so that he and Van Buren might have a conference of several
hours beginning with the Albany post office problem but soon
ranging over the whole course of national affairs. In Roane's
sickroom were busts of Jefferson, Madison, and Monroe, the
place of prominence being given to the statue of Jefferson.
As a test of Roane's attitude toward his fellow Virginian in
the White House Van Buren suggested that perhaps courtesy
required that the bust of the President be given the foremost
position in the room. Roane replied emphatically, "No! No!
No man ranks before Tom Jefferson in my house! They stand,
Sir, in the order of my confidence and of my affection!" [2]

Whom else Van Buren saw in the course of his Richmond
trip is unknown; perhaps among the other leaders he met
Daniel. In any case, from this time on there was a regular
correspondence between Van Buren and some of the Junto
leaders. Ritchie, his coeditor of the *Enquirer* C. W. Gooch,
and Philip Nicholas began at once, and within a few years
Daniel was a member of this circle of correspondents.[3]

As a first step in their joint efforts, the Regency and the
Junto agreed to support William H. Crawford of Georgia
for the presidency in 1824. In 1822, when the choice was
made, Crawford was the candidate with the greatest prestige.
New England's man was John Quincy Adams, Secretary of
State under Monroe who, though he tried, could not sufficiently disguise his nationalist views to satisfy the states' rights

faction. Henry Clay, another candidate, was a native Virginian who had moved to Kentucky and who had yet to achieve his later prominence. The fourth contestant was the old hero Andrew Jackson of Tennessee, whose popular appeal went back to his victory at New Orleans in the War of 1812. After 1824 Jackson had the wholehearted support of the Regency and the Junto, but prior to this election the combination of a preference for Crawford and a distaste for Jackson's reputation for a quick temper made the perhaps overcivilized forces of Richmond and Albany view Jackson with something approaching alarm.[4]

One other candidate in the field was John C. Calhoun of South Carolina. But Calhoun was still in the earlier phase of his own political development, and stood for a protective tariff and for internal improvements. Incredible as it may seem to our own generation which thinks of Calhoun as a states' rights extremist, in 1824 he could be seriously described by a Virginian as "an ultra politician of the Federal school."[5] Perhaps also because Calhoun was the only southerner who could be a serious menace to Crawford, the Junto fought him with great vigor. In terms of Daniel's own future, the dominant single fact about the election of 1824 is this: the Junto supported Crawford and opposed both Calhoun and Jackson. Its opposition to Jackson was temperate, its opposition to Calhoun vigorous. When Crawford went down in defeat and also in physical disability which for practical purposes took him out of politics, the Junto had burned no bridges which precluded its going to Jackson. It could never easily go to Calhoun.

The Virginia proclamation for Crawford represents in short compass views which Daniel held all his life. Adams, said the statement, would not do. He favored a "splendid national government, with great and overshadowing powers." In other words, he was for internal improvements and for national glory. On the other hand, Crawford, a simple man, objected to all such magnificence. He believed that the state bore the primary responsibilities of American government and that for a national government to watch over the public's interests and to minister to its wants was "subversive of the great ends which were designed by the patriotic founders of our institutions." Virginia wanted a "plain and frugal government which shall be 'neither felt nor seen.'" It sought a total freedom from the national government which would "permit the industry of our citizens, unshackled in every department and walk of life, to reap the fruits of its own free exertions."[6]

The cause waned, and the broadsides of the Junto began to take on the quality of bedside bulletins. In October, as a last effort, the Junto advised the voters of Virginia that Crawford's health was "rapidly advancing to entire restoration," an observation more hopeful than accurate.[7]

In the election of 1824 Jackson was clearly the leader both in the popular and electoral vote, but lacked a majority. In accordance with the constitutional system his name and those of Adams and Crawford, the two runners-up, were referred to the House of Representatives. Clay was now out of the election but was still in a position to control the result, for he influenced enough congressmen to throw the election against Jackson and for Adams.[8] Doubtless by no coincidence at all, Clay became Secretary of State in the new administration.

The election was a disaster to the Junto and the Regency. Van Buren reports that he left Albany after the election "as completely broken down a politician as my bitterest enemies could desire."[9] Sentiment in Virginia was equally distressed. But as is so often the case with postelection depression, the loss was temporary and the despair was needless. The turn of events permitted and indeed almost required the New York–Virginia alliance to give Jackson wholehearted support. At the same time the defeat, and particularly the manner of it, greatly intensified Jackson's determination to get into the White House. The reaction to the "corrupt bargain" between Adams and Clay was almost violent in Virginia. Gone was even a remote possibility that Clay could ever be anything but an enemy.

In terms of Daniel's own career, the significance of the election of 1824 is not so much in what he did as in what he got. He participated a little, he doubtless wrote a little, and he learned a little, though his must have been a minor part. But he gained a place in an organization which was to become the dominant political force in the country.

Almost immediately after the election Van Buren, with his usual shrewd foresight, declared for Jackson in 1828.[10] Calhoun, too, though he served as vice president under Adams, had no practical choice except to join the Jackson parade.[11] Both Van Buren and Calhoun were young enough to hope that they might follow Jackson into the White House, and wise enough to see that they could not precede him.

As the months of 1827 went by, Daniel lined up firmly against Adams. He presided at the main Fourth of July dinner in Richmond, and his toast was a blast at the conduct of the Adams administration's foreign policy — he called for "statesmen, not jugglers" in foreign affairs.[12] By the end of the year the whole state had fairly clearly taken sides.[13] In October an anti-Jackson convention met in Richmond; among the participants were those who eventually formed the Whig party in Virginia.[14] At the same time the Daniel clan in Stafford County was publicly proclaiming itself for Jackson.[15] In response to the Richmond anti-Jackson meeting the *Enquirer* proclaimed Jackson as its first choice for the presidency.[16] These developments not only split Richmond, but chipped at the solidarity of the Junto itself, for some of its members followed Clay into the developing anti-Jackson group. As the *Enquirer* wryly observed, hereafter there would be less talk about "the Richmond Party" — "If there be one, there are 'two Richmonds in the field.' " [17]

The "two Richmonds" met in formal conflict in 1828. As the old Federalist party coalesced around Adams, that faction became ever more respectable. At the state convention of Adams men the chief judge of the Supreme Court of Appeals presided and Bushrod Washington, a nephew of the first president and a justice of the United States Supreme Court, appeared as one of the delegates. Daniel's old enemy Governor Thomas M. Randolph was another.[18] John Marshall, though not a delegate, announced that he would vote for the first time in twenty years in order to do his bit to prevent the destruction of the government by the election of Jackson.[19]

While a strong group thus lined up for Adams, Daniel and the rest of the Richmond Party beat the drums for Jackson. On public occasions Daniel made what he could of his dissatisfaction with the administration's foreign policy. He presided at two sentimental dinners, one for each of the Virginia senators, John Tyler and Littleton Tazewell, both Jackson men.[20] But the work of the campaign was considerably more than speeches. Once again Daniel was on the Central Committee for the ticket of Jackson and Calhoun, again with his Junto colleagues Nicholas and Ritchie. Theirs were the first three signatures on one of the main papers issued by the group.[21] The committee had the full job of organization, of fund raising, of ballot distribution, and of publicity. In Richmond proper it hustled a local Jackson committee into action. With minimum contributions of one dollar apiece, and with the aid of subsidiary committees, funds were raised for desperately needed extra circulars.

Unlimited energy and funds were essential for this incredibly dirty campaign. It began with reasoned arguments, perhaps showing something of Daniel's personal influence in the attacks made by the Jackson men on Adams' foreign policy. But the Adams men all over the country attacked Jackson in every possible way. They painted a picture of him as a near maniac, an adulterer, and a man wholly unable to control his temper. They minimized his part in the Battle of New Orleans, claimed that his marriage with Rachel Jackson had not been legal, and turned the aggressive episodes of Jackson's past into murderous propensities.[22]

The Daniel group made the best use of these attacks by denouncing the attackers. They had more to gain by inciting the Jackson supporters to new efforts than from attempting to answer the various charges. Particularly in Virginia, where public attacks on a lady's virtue were viewed with disgust, the overheated allegations about Jackson's marriage helped Jackson more than it hurt. The Jackson force could easily make the best of the situation by describing the old hero as wounded to the heart by these vicious attacks on his beloved wife.[23]

Daniel's own attitude toward Jackson can be described by the self-contradictory phrase "enthusiastic reserve." Jackson's views were almost Daniel's, but not quite. He never knew Jackson intimately. There had not been any free and full correspondence with Jackson comparable to that with Van Buren. Moreover Daniel thought of Jackson as a true hero of the republic, and men seldom have a sense of intimacy with their heroes. Jackson in turn was perfectly well aware that he had in Daniel a loyal supporter in Virginia, and he repeatedly offered him appointments. But usually each dealt with the other through Van Buren.

Daniel particularly admired Jackson for a quality they had in common, that of firmness. Daniel liked to say of Jackson — using a phrase he attributed to Jefferson — that "He has as much of the *Roman* in him as any man living." [24]

Daniel wanted a government which would abolish the

tariff, make no internal improvements, and pay off the public debt. In this last desire he was aiming at more than simple economy. He wanted to get away from "splendid government," to return to the simplicity which had marked Jefferson's administration. He was confident that Jackson would move in these basic directions. When in 1830 Jackson vetoed a bill for certain internal improvements, even though the vote was not on the strict constitutional grounds which Daniel himself would have desired, he felt that the President had reached the heights of heroism. He realized that Jackson himself was a westerner and was particularly subject to the lure of expenditure of public funds for the development of the West.[25] If Jackson's administration had done nothing but produce that one veto, Daniel would have been more than repaid for his efforts in the election of 1828.

Daniel was eventually to discover somewhat more divergence between himself and Jackson on the subject of the tariff than he had at first supposed, but he was more than willing to make allowance on this score in view of the other achievements of the Jackson administration. He thought of Jackson as a "single minded firm man . . . who nobly throws himself into the breach and hesitates not to risk all for the safety of the constitution." To Daniel, Jackson was an inflexible man, and a moral hero. His strongest hope was "May God preserve to his country so valuable a citizen." [26]

This admiration for Jackson coupled with his own basic views caused Daniel to work hard in the campaign of 1828. His campaign efforts consisted in part of his work for the Central Committee and in part of personal contact. His own special contribution was as a pamphleteer, or more correctly, as a writer of letters to the editor.

Letters to the editor in the first part of the nineteenth century had a significance which the twentieth century reserves for an occasional letter to the New York *Times*. Part of the difference lay in the nature of the newspapers themselves. The Richmond *Enquirer*, one of the most influential papers of the time, was a four-page sheet which printed a certain amount of local news actually collected in Richmond and freshly reported, plus excerpts from other papers around the country which were similarly reporting their local news. This unappetizing collection of snippets was made no more digestible by the interspersion of long columns of reports of legislative proceedings. The quality of the newspaper therefore rested primarily in its editorials, and in the letters which were in effect editorials contributed by readers. Such letters were taken seriously and were closely read. It was not beneath the dignity of a President of the United States to use this form of communication. By this means Adams and his own Vice President, Calhoun, had attacked each other under thinly disguised anonymity.[27] It was in the form of such letters that Spencer Roane had criticized John Marshall's decision in *Cohens v. Virginia*, and it was thus that Marshall had made his reply.[28]

Disastrously for biographical purposes, it was the fixed custom to publish such letters over pseudonyms. Occasionally this anonymity was pierced, as in the instances just mentioned, but usually the cloak was effective. Hence the papers were full of letters from "Crito" or "Man of the People" or "Voice of 98," depending on the taste of the author, and no one usually knows who these individuals were.[29] As a result, although it is clear that Daniel was a regular contributor not only to the *Enquirer* but also to other Virginia newspapers, it is by no means always clear which letters are his. On the basis of internal evidence of style and point of view one may on occasion guess that a particular letter was by Daniel, but there were enough persons in Richmond of similar points of view, and his style was sufficiently commonplace, to make impossible assured identification of more than a handful.

A sufficient number of his letters have been identified to permit some generalizations.[30] Daniel was not a man of temperate political views. In his private discourse his attitude toward the Whigs was one of violent antipathy. Passions were high during the Jackson administration, and none were higher than Daniel's. He thought of the Whigs as illiberal, selfish, malignant, and profligate, as trucklers to the banking interests and as devoid of any quality except greed.[31] The Whig paper in Richmond he alluded to as "that common sewer of defamation," [32] and he thought of his political enemies as menacing not only the existence of the state but the very survival of his family. Excerpts from a letter to Van Buren at the time of the national election of 1832 will suggest the heated state of his mind: the immediate forthcoming election is a "great struggle between democracy and the constitution on the one hand, and corruption and profligacy unexampled on the other." "The conflict we are now waging [is] against that worst of all influences; that which puts intelligence, probity, patriotism, falsehood, venality, vice in every form, all upon an equality, that is, values them merely as they can become means to be wielded to its purposes — *the influence of money*." [33]

The letter to Van Buren just quoted was not mere election time heat; this was his normal way of thinking about the opposition. At a time of comparative quiet he spoke of the "treachery and defection" of some Jackson adversaries, whose conduct he hoped would lead to "consequences the most signal and condign . . . defeat, disgrace and lasting public odium." [34] At times his stock of specific epithets ran dry and he was forced to such lump categorization as "that combination of all the vilest ingredients called the Whig Party." [35] These attitudes were not merely general, directed against Whigs as such, but were also personal. His strength of feeling could lead to social ruptures in Richmond, and even after he was on the Supreme Court, his intense feeling did not abate. On one state occasion he met Webster and reported "My hand was actually contaminated by contact with his." [36]

Daniel's letter-writing tone is usually extremely emphatic, falling just short of bad taste. But Daniel's opponents were equally irritable, and the annoyance that his outspoken vigor caused gave them every incentive to revenge themselves on him. When in 1835 his adversaries made their major attack on his Council position, it was as much as anything else an attack on his writing activities. One critic charged that Daniel "has used his station, and the patronage of the State, through the columns of a public journal of this city, to support the administration, and destroy the principles which Virginia has ever held sacred. I will not aid in continuing that station and patronage." [37]

A more heated critic was more specific about the tone of Daniel's writings: "He has been one of the most violent partisan writers in the state — those gentlemen with whom I am acting have received a full share of his embittered party denunciations, while the administration, including Martin Van Buren, has been favored with his most fulsome praise and adulation . . . Should he be re-elected — which God forbid! — no sooner shall he be safely seated in office than he will dip his pen in gall — again the columns of his favorite journal will be opened to him, in defense of Andrew Jackson and Martin Van Buren, and in hostility to Virginia principles, and Virginia statesmen." [38]

Daniel's own code of the proprieties of public correspondence permitted him to be vigorous but never directly personal. Some line of distinction was necessary particularly in a society in which dueling was not yet completely abolished. As late as 1846 Thomas H. Pleasants challenged Thomas Ritchie, Jr., son of the editor of the *Enquirer*, to a duel because Pleasants believed that something which young Ritchie had permitted to go into the *Enquirer* reflected on Pleasants' character. In the resultant duel Pleasants was killed.

Daniel's pen brought him to the verge of a similar conflict with a distinguished opponent in 1832. The occasion was the Senate's rejection of Van Buren for the post of minister to England. By 1832 the momentary alliance between Van Buren and Calhoun in support of Jackson had ended, Van Buren continuing in Jackson's favor, and Calhoun becoming one of Jackson's most conspicuous opponents. The rejection of the Van Buren nomination, planned by the Whigs and by Calhoun to give the maximum humiliation to both Jackson and Van Buren, occurred after Van Buren had already reached England to take up his duties, thus making him an international spectacle of defeat. The defeat was a gross act of folly on the part of Van Buren's enemies, because it merely intensified Jackson's loyalty to Van Buren and it gave Van Buren's friends a chance to portray him before the country as a wronged man. Indeed, this petty act of partisanship greatly helped Van Buren to the presidency.

Daniel, in a series of letters in the *Enquirer* signed "Crito," vigorously attacked both the Whig leaders and the Calhoun faction for their treatment of Van Buren. He singled out for special attention the junior senator from South Carolina, Stephen D. Miller, a man of no great national reputation who had been in the Senate only a short time when the Van Buren episode occurred. The Crito letters occupied many columns in the *Enquirer*. The allusions to Senator Miller were brief but pungent.[39] Only momentary mental aberration on the part of the voters of South Carolina, thought Daniel, could have raised Miller to any position higher than that of "an obscure brawler in some petty election precinct."

Senator Miller was understandably offended by the Crito letters insofar as they referred to him. Following the etiquette of the time he wrote to Ritchie, as editor of the *En-*

quirer, asking for the identity of the author. Only by this means could Miller seek direct satisfaction in the form of a duel. This same etiquette required Ritchie to forward the request to Daniel, for if Daniel declined to reveal his identity, Ritchie was at perfect liberty to pass on the refusal to the senator.

Daniel would not yield an inch. He permitted Ritchie to identify him to Senator Miller, with the understanding between them that the letter he sent to Ritchie would be sent on to the senator.[40] Daniel took much care in the composition of this letter; it is a marvel of new insult coated over with seeming courtesy. Of course, said Daniel, he was willing to let Miller know who was the author of the piece; he would certainly not take any action for which he was not ready to accept full responsibility. Daniel did want to make clear that nothing personal was intended in what he had said about Miller, which is evidenced by the fact that until a recent debate he had never heard of Miller and had not even known that the gentleman from South Carolina was in the Senate. "Of him, therefore, as a private man I have known nothing, have said nothing; and could have intended to say nothing." But Senator Miller had made an address to the people of the country, on a public matter, and Daniel had as much right to express his opinion on that appeal to the country, "with full as much moderation as [Miller] had shown towards either the President or the late Minister to London," as anyone else.

When this letter was forwarded to Senator Miller, he wrote Daniel directly asking that he "withdraw so much of this publication as relates to myself or so qualify the same as to divest it of its offensive personal character." [41] The language chosen by Miller verged on a formal challenge to a duel. Daniel responded in complete calm, neither inviting a duel nor retreating. To salve Miller's feelings, he said, "My remarks were aimed exclusively at the principles professed in that speech, the manner in which they were urged, and the tendencies of the one and the other — all as I then thought and yet think, legitimate subjects of criticism." [42] Miller could construe this as a reaffirmation that nothing personal was intended by Daniel's comments.

And so the two firebrands stood. Perhaps the physical distance between Richmond and Washington contributed to the happy result, but for whatever reason, no more was heard of the matter.

It may be safely assumed that Daniel was occupying himself in the campaign of 1828 by writing for the cause in much the same spirit. A little before the election attention turned, as it usually does, from who *should* be elected to who *would* be elected. Wagers were offered in the paper on this county and that, on the size of the majority for the favorite candidate, and on the national outcome.[43] But the Junto was rightly confident that it had done its work. Richmond City, as might have been expected, went for Adams, but the majority was not enough to balance against the Jackson strength in the county of which it was a part, and the margin was for Jackson.[44] The voters throughout the state and country had rallied to Old Hickory. For the first time in Daniel's life the government was one which he had helped in a substantial way to get into office. Most of his political efforts during the succeeding twelve years were aimed at keeping that government in power.

Chapter VI

THE CAMPAIGN FOR VAN BUREN

As is usually the case of the lieutenant in politics, Daniel was often the inheritor of other men's quarrels. Thus it was that when Andrew Jackson went into the White House in 1829, the course of Daniel's life began to be affected by the Washington wars. In addition to Jackson, two men and a lady (if indeed she was a lady, for this was one of the points at issue) were soon to have great influence on the immediate course of Daniel's life. The gentlemen were John C. Calhoun and Martin Van Buren. The lady was Peggy O'Neill Eaton.

Martin Van Buren and John C. Calhoun had many points of difference, but they had in common one ambition. Each wanted to be president of the United States, and each knew, after the election of 1824, that the opportunity could come only after Andrew Jackson had been president. For a moment they made common cause in behalf of Jackson, and between 1824 and 1828 both could be regarded as Jackson lieutenants. Calhoun served the cause faithfully from the chair of the vice president, Van Buren served it as faithfully as a senator from New York. Here on the Senate floor the two men were in daily contact, and moved toward their then common end.

The two were very different. Martin Van Buren was the first great political manager in the history of the United States.[1] This, coupled with his defeat for re-election to the presidency, has tended to diminish his reputation for statesmanship to the level of a mere manipulator. This is wrong. He was a manipulator and a good one. So was Franklin D. Roosevelt. But Van Buren also was, within the fair latitude which is permitted to statesmen who actually hold office over a long period of time, a man of principle. Van Buren's great distinction was a sense of humor, a sense of proportion. He saw the line between the silly and the serious, between those issues which were great and those which were small. He appreciated the foibles of his fellow humans, and because he appreciated them, he could if necessary take advantage of them. In all these things Van Buren was the very antithesis of Daniel, and there is reason to suspect that Daniel's eternal humorless righteousness must on occasion have been a downright bore to Van Buren.[2] What establishes Van Buren as a *great* politician instead of as a *mere* politician is that he was able to bring both the righteous and the unrighteous, the Daniels and the Tammany hacks, to serve his cause.

Somber, tense, ambitious, desperate, are words commonly applied to Calhoun.[3] He was known by at least some of his contemporaries as a "thinking machine," a man savage in his intensity and profound in his thought. When Andrew Jackson was inaugurated on March 4, 1829, Calhoun had already behind him a great career in public life, a career far more distinguished than had been Van Buren's. He had been a leader of the congressional War Hawk faction which brought about the War of 1812, and once in the war he had been an effective national leader. In the immediate postwar period he had been caught up in a temporary nationalism and had supported both the chartering of the second Bank of the United States and the first candidly protective tariff, that of 1816. He served in the cabinet of President Monroe, and was himself a serious candidate for president in 1824. It was then that he, perforce, accepted the vice presidency and made temporary alliance with Van Buren behind Jackson.

Thus on inauguration day in 1829 Calhoun had the advantage in prestige and experience over Van Buren. A man making a wager in 1829 as to which of these two, Van Buren or Calhoun, would be the next president might well have chosen Calhoun.

But the seeds of Calhoun's destruction were already sown. He suffered from one of the great weaknesses which can overtake a national political figure: he had been on the national scene too long, and his control of his state organization was by no means good. Van Buren, on the other hand, was distinctly in charge of the party in New York. In the years 1828 to 1830 the real leaders in South Carolina were the senators, McDuffie and Hayne. The great issue in South Carolina was the tariff, for a protective tariff did this cotton-exporting state no good and cost it much. When, just before the election of Jackson, a new and high protective tariff was passed, it was regarded in South Carolina as the tariff of abominations. A substantial minority of the state was ready to take almost any action to somehow undo it.[4]

The intensity of this rebellion put Calhoun in the worst possible situation. No man irrevocably opposed to the tariff could possibly be the Democratic nominee for the presidency. For all the years from 1816 to 1828 Calhoun had managed to avoid hopeless involvement over that issue — indeed, for a time in 1824 he had the Pennsylvania — or Democratic high tariff — votes for the presidential nomination. In the next selection of a candidate for the presidency Van Buren would at least control New York, and Calhoun could see with an awful clarity that if he lost both industrial New England and Pennsylvania, he would never be president. On the other hand, his whole political life depended upon his strength in South Carolina. If he could not control his home state, he would become a political ghost flying through the air with no place to land.

The summer and fall of 1828 were one of the worst periods of Calhoun's career. Any possible turn meant disaster. Finally, with McDuffie stirring South Carolina opinion to the fever point, Calhoun had no real political alternative but to join the opposition to the tariff. Doubtless principle led him in the same direction. Yet his election to the vice presidency with Jackson would be jeopardized by too open an avowal of his association with his state's stand. And so he managed to stay on the fence a little longer. During the summer and fall of 1828 he prepared the famous Exposition and Protest, a report adopted by the legislature of South Carolina which declared that the protective tariff was unconstitutional and that the state itself could nullify it. Yet Calhoun's actual authorship of this document was kept a close secret in South Carolina so as not to imperil his election to the national office.[5] When the Electoral College met Jackson was elected president and Calhoun was again elected vice president, even Pennsylvania, innocent of his authorship of the Exposition, voting for him.

The odd affair of Mrs. Eaton gave Van Buren a long edge in the jockeying for position between Van Buren and Calhoun. The incident would have been preposterous if it were not so serious. Peggy O'Neill was the daughter of a Washington tavernkeeper, and Jackson had known her for years. She grew up to be a lovely young lady and married a naval officer named Timberlake, who in due course committed suicide, or at least died under circumstances which some said were suicide. She then married Senator John Eaton of Tennessee, with whom, it was rumored, she had had a more than casual acquaintance before her first husband's death. In fact, rumor made that earlier acquaintance the cause of Timberlake's demise.[6]

Except for being Jackson's protégé and Peggy's second choice, Eaton had no particular claim to distinction and is almost an innocent bystander in the events that followed.

But he was personally very close to Jackson, who made him Secretary of War. Mrs. Eaton thus became one of the first ladies of the land, to whom certain social obligations were properly owing.

When Rachel Jackson died, Mrs. Calhoun became the first lady for social purposes. She, a Charleston aristocrat, would have nothing to do with Mrs. Eaton. At the first general social affair of the new administration, Mrs. Calhoun did not "see" Mrs. Eaton. Mrs. Eaton duly paid her courtesy call on Mrs. Calhoun, and the call was never returned. Van Buren, on the other hand, as a widower was able to be most courteous to the Eatons. Jackson strongly disapproved of the Calhoun attitude, and strongly approved of Van Buren's.

The rest of this boudoir tempest is irrelevant here. Suffice it to say that as a result of this and other strains, by the end of the year 1829 Jackson was at severe odds with his Vice President. By the middle of 1830 there was a hopeless rift between the two. Within a year of Jackson's inauguration it was apparent that Secretary of State Van Buren had no serious competition for the post of runner-up to the Chief Executive. This status, it should be added, was earned by more than victory in such wars as that over Peggy's virtue. Van Buren's advice to his chief was good, his loyalty was firm, and he had earned his rank.

The rift between Van Buren and Calhoun was felt to the very depths of the Democratic party. In Washington, itself, Thomas Ritchie had first been offered the opportunity to publish the official administration newspaper. When he declined, the opportunity went to Duff Green, a Calhoun man. When the administration broke into fighting factions Green went with Calhoun. In Richmond Governor Floyd, who had beaten Daniel for the governorship in 1830, was a Calhoun man. Daniel, on the other hand, stood firm with Van Buren and Jackson. The clash between the two heads of the national administration was thus exactly duplicated between the two heads of the state administration in Richmond, one big difference being that the chief Democratic paper in Richmond stayed with Jackson and Van Buren while the chief Democratic paper in Washington did not.

The choice for Daniel between following Jackson and Van Buren on the one hand or Calhoun on the other was not entirely easy. On the single dividing issue of the tariff Daniel agreed with Calhoun and disagreed with Jackson and Van Buren. There were other anti-Jackson factors. Daniel's friend Ritchie, for one, opposed the inauguration of the spoils system, as Jackson's distribution of patronage was called, and came close to splitting with Jackson on this issue even before Calhoun made his break. It was Van Buren who lured Ritchie back into the fold. Daniel probably agreed with Ritchie, though less emphatically, on the spoils system.

Other issues created a strong pro-Jackson pull. As Daniel put it to his friend Brent in 1831, "I disapprove of General Jackson's opinions relative to the tariff; but what do we not gain in his stifling . . . the scheme for national internal improvement, and in his determination to crush that monster of corruption and perdition, the Bank of the United States." [7] Moreover by this time Daniel had enjoyed several years of cooperation with Van Buren. All the arts of affability which made Van Buren so successful had captured Daniel. Calhoun was a less attractive personality, and if Daniel knew him at all in this period he probably seemed excessively ambitious,[8] a quality which Daniel himself never exhibited.

By 1831 Virginia was sharply divided into three factions, the Whigs for Clay, the Democrats for Calhoun, and the Democrats for Jackson. Most Democrats who were for Jackson were also for Van Buren as his eventual successor. The *Enquirer* kept up some pretense of holding an open mind on that question, but when in April 1831 Van Buren amicably resigned as Secretary of State to help Jackson clean out the cabinet after the Eaton imbroglio, the *Enquirer* hailed his record with unlimited enthusiasm.[9] The Whig group was formally and publicly headed by John Marshall.[10] Titular leaders in the Calhoun-Jackson battle were Governor Floyd and Lieutenant Governor Daniel.

John Floyd, a leader of western Virginia who had served in Congress, had long been a Calhoun man. He had supported Jackson in 1828 and was sadly disappointed at his failure to receive a cabinet office in the new administration. Hostile to Jackson, Floyd was equally unequivocal in his attitude toward Daniel, whom he described, along with several others of the Junto, as a wretch who had deserted his "principles and the liberties of the people for the smiles of that tyrant, Jackson." [11]

These circumstances scarcely made for harmony on the Council of State. Moreover, after 1831 the Council, under the new constitution, had merely an advisory role. In his diary Floyd described this situation in a telling fashion: "I am obliged by the Constitution first to require the advice of the Council, then do as I please." [12] Hence all Daniel could do as a Council member was to give nagging advice or to record opinions which he might hope would later be of some trouble to Floyd. But Daniel was also the lieutenant governor, and Floyd, who lived far from Richmond, had a strong desire to spend as much time as he could at his own home. Once Floyd was out of town Daniel was free to seize the reins.

The most colorful controversy between the two was over a trifle. Floyd was away from Richmond during the latter part of June and all of July 1831. In the interim all of Floyd's duties fell to Daniel. For example, it was Daniel who had to make the arrangements for a proper show of mourning when former President Monroe died on the Fourth of July.[13] But Daniel also settled down to more serious matters. He made all the appointments that were required during this period, over the strenuous objection of one of the Council members who thought that such questions ought to be held in abeyance until Floyd's return.[14]

Daniel's chance to start an argument with Floyd came on June 30, 1831, when along with the regular official mail he received an issue of the *United States Telegraph*, Duff Green's antiadministration Washington newspaper. Green was a one-time Jackson man who in 1831 was editing the Calhoun paper in the capitol. The copy, while undoubtedly intended for Floyd, was not directed to the governor, but to the Executive Department of Virginia. Daniel immediately sat down and sent off a quick note to Green:

> As the head of that Department at this time, I have to say to you that I am aware of no legal or regular warrant for the transmission of your paper to the Executive Department of this State. The Council of State never having advised in relation to the subject, I think proper request that no further numbers of your paper be forwarded to the Executive, as under existing circumstances you can have no claim upon the State for any of them.[15]

In taking this position, Daniel was, of course, technically right. Under the Virginia constitution the governor was not capable even of shifting a newspaper subscription without first checking with his Council, although, having asked its opinion, he could do as he pleased. The governor had discontinued the Baltimore *Republican*, a good Jackson paper, and switched to the *Telegraph* without consultation.

Green at once snapped back a reply, and published the correspondence. The papers, he said, had been sent to the governor and not to the lieutenant governor of Virginia. Any issues that had come into Daniel's possession, he suggested, ought to be returned to the post office to be held for the governor upon his return. If Floyd had not asked the Council for its opinion, presumably he did not want it. "It will be time for you, as one of his advisors, to refuse your consent when it is asked." [16]

Daniel kept hammering at Floyd. First as "Justice" and then as "Veritas," [17] he proceeded to answer the counterattacks on himself by the Richmond *Whig*. Daniel had long been at odds with the *Whig's* editor; the two cut each other when they passed on the street. Column after column was filled with blow and counterblow. Floyd's attitude was that the attack on him was personal and self-seeking. He confided to his diary that Daniel's "folly and imbecility has prompted him to this hostility to make himself agreeable to the President or Federal Executive that he may attain from him an office which he much wants." He served notice that he could no longer maintain a friendly relationship with Daniel, and, as his diary shows, he thereafter avoided Council meetings with Daniel whenever he could escape that duty.[18]

Floyd's attacks on Daniel were confined to his diary, but Duff Green's paper was more direct. It charged that Daniel was currying favor with Jackson, explaining that Daniel was a Van Buren man who had thus come into the Jackson movement after 1824. The *Telegraph* conceded that it wanted to keep Daniel, if it could, from receiving any high office; that it had thought that the original publication of the correspondence by it might have such an effect: "The object of our letter was to throw a stone in his path." [19]

Daniel meanwhile was acting in direct cooperation with Jackson. The President and Daniel were together one Fourth of July holiday at a Virginia vacation spot.[20] The relation between the two was sufficiently close at this time that Jackson gave Daniel the duty of making a semi-authorized statement in Jackson's behalf about the Eaton affair.[21]

Some such statement seemed necessary because of the Calhoun propaganda appearing in the Richmond *Whig* concerning Mrs. Eaton. These party writers asserted that Jackson was aggressively compelling his subordinates and their wives to associate with the lady. This, in Jackson's own mind, was not true. He was upholding Peggy, but he was not compelling anything. In an unsigned but obviously authorized letter appearing in the *Enquirer* on July 8, 1831, without signature, Daniel described the manner in which this question came up in his conversation with the President. Jackson, speaking with great earnestness and sincerity, said: "The right of every member of society to the most perfect freedom in the choice of his associates was so notorious — so familiar to every mind — that no man could, except upon the clearest grounds, be supposed guilty of the flagrant absurdity of calling it into question." Daniel himself echoed the sentiment; it was a profligate falsehood that Jackson had ever conditioned a cabinet office upon a personal association.

With the winter came the time of reckoning. Under the new constitution Daniel was up in 1832 for his first election to a three-year term. The lines were sharp, and the Whigs and the adherents of Governor Floyd united to get him if they could. The strategy was adroit: instead of nominating a Whig, the opposition rallied behind another strong Jackson man, so that the Jackson strength in the legislature would be divided. Daniel's opponents did not attack him personally but rather stood on the venerable principle of rotation in office and on the position that the controversies between Daniel and the governor — without regard to which was right — required the elimination of one of them. As one opponent put it, he would equally freely vote against the governor, but it happened that Daniel's term came to an end first. Daniel's opponents pushed the matter to an early vote while some of his supporters were out of town. An advance counting of noses had shown that the choice would be extremely close, so that one or two absences might make the critical difference. But Daniel's friends talked long enough to allow an ailing senator to return to his seat. This senator missed the first ballot, which ended in a tie, but he was present in time for a second ballot, on which Daniel was elected by one vote.[22]

Just as Daniel's enemies avoided a direct attack on Daniel, so his friends were careful to avoid any attack on or even mention of Floyd. No sleeping lions of partisanship were aroused this day. Daniel's friends praised his intrepid independence and his determination to do what he considered right. As one supporter put it, "There was not a Virginian who would deny that Peter V. Daniel was a man of powerful intellect. He was faithful in the performance of his duties and urbane in his manners. He was a man of stern independence and would not allow his hands to do what his judgment and his conscience did not approve." [23] True, he had made enemies, but so would anyone in such an office who conducted himself as Daniel did with the "impartiality and disregard of consequences which he had displayed in the discharge of his public functions."

It was clear at this election, as on every similar occasion in his life, that Daniel's absolutely firm adherence to principle earned him the greatest admiration among his supporters. This granite quality, however, is something less than endearing, and one somehow senses a want of real affection for Daniel even among his friends. If anyone ever loved him, it was Lucy and the children. But he did have respect. As the *Enquirer* editorialized on the election, "Mr. Daniel has more experience in the executive business than any man in Virginia — and an industry and energy, which have never flagged in the public service. As a politician, no man is more firm, and uncompromising." [24] That appraisal could be his epitaph.

Meanwhile a new issue gripped the country. Early in 1831 Van Buren had resigned along with the rest of the cabinet. Daniel had then thought the resignation a mistake which might weaken Van Buren's standing.[25] But, as was likely to be the case, Van Buren's judgment was best. Jackson appointed him minister to England, so as to keep him in a prominent position and broaden his experience while at the same time removing him from the immediate scene of possibly damaging controversies. But as a result of Calhoun's efforts the appointment was not confirmed by the Senate.

Van Buren, upon his recall from London, made it a long voyage home, timing his journey so that he would not arrive until after the party nominations later in the year. Meanwhile the pro–Van Buren writers dipped their pens in vinegar and went to work on the opposition. The principal Virginia author in this campaign was Daniel, in a series of letters by "Crito."

If there had ever been any doubt in Jackson's mind about the desirability of Van Buren for the vice presidency in 1832, his rejection by the Senate removed it. Within a few days of the defeat Andrew Stevenson, the leading Jackson Democrat in Congress from Virginia, wrote Ritchie that Van Buren had to be put upon the ticket for Vice President, and that Ritchie should give up his "former scruples as to Mr. Van Buren" and support him.[26] But this proved impossible. It took all the skill the Junto could muster to keep the Virginia delegates at what was to be the first national Democratic convention from going against Van Buren. The anti–Van Buren faction lit upon the almost foolproof strategy of uniting Virginia principles with a Virginia personality and urged Virginia's own Federal district judge Philip P. Barbour for the vice presidential position. Barbour's strength, in addition to local pride, was that he was antitariff as well as a good states' rights man in all other respects. The Junto thereupon set itself to the strategy of defeating Barbour by indirection and advocated the course of making no nomination for the vice presidency. To settle this issue a major party caucus of the state's Democrats was held in Richmond in mid-March 1832.

A Virginia party nominating caucus was established by law for the purpose of drawing up an electoral ticket for each party. The members of the caucus were the members of the party in the state legislature plus "special delegates" who were chosen by local Democratic organizations in counties which did not have Democratic representation in the legislature. For reasons of convenience the special delegates were likely to be residents of Richmond. At the 1832 caucus Daniel represented one district in this capacity.

The caucus unanimously nominated Jackson and then faced the vice presidential issue. The friends of Barbour stressed the character and principles of their candidate.[27] His opponents discountenanced such theoretical talk, arguing that if Virginia were to instruct its electors to support Barbour, the probable practical effect would be to throw the election into Congress and thus to elect neither Van Buren nor Barbour but the Whig candidate.

Taking the floor, Daniel began somewhat disingenuously.[28] He had come to this meeting to act for the good of the Democratic party, and if that good required him to make sacrifices he was prepared to make them, no matter how much his personal affection, even for Barbour, was frustrated. He could not in good conscience take a step which might throw into Congress the election of the vice president. Daniel stressed that he was personally and politically friendly to Barbour, but the plain fact was that by no calculation was Barbour likely to get more than fifty-three electoral votes, and only the Whigs could benefit from the resultant impasse.

Safely through the preliminaries, he then moved into high gear. If Virginia could not have Barbour, said Daniel, he for one would be willing to accept Van Buren. In a few words he effectively mingled the causes of Jackson and Van Buren.

He conceded that a man might attack Van Buren and also attack Jackson, but he denied that any man sitting in the convention could be for the one and not for the other.

Daniel switched back to a softer tone. He was not here as Van Buren's advocate, but he could scarcely sit by and see a good man done injustice. Van Buren had acted unwisely on the tariff question, but in this he had not been a free agent, for he had been compelled to follow the instructions of his own state legislature. By extensive quotations from Van Buren himself — indeed, his audience probably thought they were too extensive — Daniel showed Van Buren to be a believer in most Virginia principles. After an attack on Calhoun as the real enemy of Virginia, Daniel concluded: "I think all considerations should induce us to avoid a nomination at the present moment, and to leave the question open and untrammelled. I repeat that I am no Van Buren man — no Barbour man — and, God knows, I am no Clay man, and no Sergeant man! — I wish the subject to be left to the people. They are capable to judge, and will indicate their will, by which a proper decision will be obtained." [29]

When the vote came, it was a landslide against naming anyone for the vice presidential nomination. The caucus thus nominated Jackson and a blank, and established a state central committee which, as usual, included Daniel.

It is impossible to know how influential Daniel's voice was in these debates. Perhaps 50,000 words of convention debate have been recorded and much the same arguments were made one way or another by all the speakers. The issue may well have been one which had been settled before a word was spoken, in that each delegate may very possibly have already made up his mind. Daniel's speech was an effective presentation. It drew blood from his opponents, who rushed to answer, and it was probably the most vigorous pro–Van Buren and anti-Calhoun statement made. Therein lay its essential wisdom, for by opposing Van Buren to Calhoun, Daniel left Barbour dangling as though he were a Calhoun man. This was in a sense unfair, for Barbour was nothing of the sort; but he was being used as a stalking-horse by the Calhoun faction.[30] Floyd, who had been one of the architects of the Barbour scheme, was in at least momentary defeat.

Uninstructed electors were almost as good as electors instructed directly for Van Buren, both because the Junto would have considerable influence with the uninstructed electors, and because Democratic electors would have no practical choice except Van Buren. The next job at this point was to select a pro–Van Buren delegation to the national convention of the Democratic party. Daniel and his friends now turned their attention to this new project.

The national Democratic convention at Baltimore, the party's first, was organized on a basis somewhat different from that which is now familiar. Each state sent as many delegates as it wished, but the total of their votes was in proportion to the state's representation in Congress. Under these circumstances, the nearby states could be expected to send more delegates than those at a greater distance. The ninety-six representatives from Virginia were more than a quarter of the total of all delegates.

The Richmond delegates were selected with great care.[31] One evening in mid-May the Democracy of the city had a mass meeting at the state capitol. Dr. John Brockenbrough, state banker and member of the Junto, was chairman. On motion of Peter V. Daniel it was decided that a committee of five should be appointed to prepare a report and resolutions. Dr. Brockenbrough thereupon appointed the committee, with Daniel as chairman and Philip Nicholas as one of the members. The committee stepped out of the room, went through the form of brief deliberation, and then came back to file a report which Daniel had obviously brought with him. The report declared that the people of Richmond endorsed Andrew Jackson for the presidency and pledged themselves to work heartily in his behalf. They strongly approved of the course of the state caucus in leaving the electors free as to the vice presidency and recommended that a group of five be appointed to represent Richmond at the Baltimore convention. The report was adopted and five delegates were then appointed: the same five men who had submitted the report and resolutions. Daniel was again chosen to chair the group.

The first Democratic national convention met at Baltimore on May 21–23, 1832. A presiding officer and four vice chairmen were chosen. To Daniel, as chairman of the Virginia delegation, went the honor of being the first vice chairman of the convention. The first day was devoted to speeches and to organization. The convention adopted without discussion a rule requiring a two-thirds vote of the body to make a nomination, thus saddling the Democratic party with a practice which was to last for one hundred years and was subsequently to give the South added strength in the national conventions. The rule was to be the subject of discussion at the convention prior to the election of 1836, and at that time Daniel was one of those who upheld it. As one of the principal participants in the organization of the 1832 meeting he must have had some hand in the origin of the rule.

After the close of the session on the twenty-first the huge Virginia delegation met in the quarters of Congressman Archer at a local hotel.[32] Daniel presided. The group began its discussion of whether Van Buren or Barbour should get the Virginia vote. No new argument was offered. The case for Barbour was that he represented the views of Virginia more perfectly than did Van Buren. On the other hand, Van Buren was a moderate on the tariff and took the right stand on every other issue which was of interest to Virginia. To back Barbour might be to encourage his candidacy nationally and thus to give the Whigs a chance to slip a vice president into office even though Jackson were elected.

As the discussion continued it became apparent that the Virginia Van Buren faction could have pushed through a Van Buren endorsement on the first ballot. But some of them perceived that the Barbour group would take their defeat in better spirit if the state were to give Barbour a favorite-son vote on the first ballot, thus giving his friends a chance to show how much strength they could muster, and then to switch to Van Buren on the second ballot. This was the strategy finally adopted, although some of the Van Buren group were not content. It proved to be a wise course, for after the vote had been taken scarcely a Barbour man felt that the transfer was unfair to his candidate.[33]

On the first vice presidential ballot, Van Buren had 208 votes, Barbour had 49, and Johnson of Kentucky had 26. Half of the Barbour votes came from Virginia, half from four other southern states. Congressman Archer then moved a short recess, and the Virginia delegation quickly caucused. It immediately endorsed a resolution which Archer then offered to the convention itself, "Resolved, that the delegation from Virginia to the convention concur in and approve the nomination of a Vice-President which has been made by that body, and will recommend the cordial support of it to their constituents."[34] Kentucky moved to make it unanimous, and Van Buren was thus the nominee of the party for the vice presidency.

This left great work to be done in Virginia. Two issues came to loom large in the campaign. The first was the tariff and the ensuing debate over nullification and the other was the question of the continuance of the Bank of the United States.

Vice President Calhoun's role in the assertion by South Carolina of the right of nullification had been kept secret while he still had some chance of national preferment, but by the middle of 1831 the bridges between Jackson and Calhoun were so completely burned that there was no longer any reason not to bring the war into the open. In December 1831, therefore, Calhoun took open leadership of the nullification forces, explaining in detail just how to put liberty ahead of union. The Constitution, he declared, had been formed by the people of the states. The people retained the power to come into convention within one state and there to nullify a Federal statute on the ground of its unconstitutionality, thus making that statute unenforceable within the borders of that state. It was this treatment that South Carolina proposed for the tariff.[35]

Thus the pot boiled from 1831 to 1832. Threats of resistance mingled with fine-spun constitutional arguments, the whole always permeated by suggestions of compromise.

A tariff revision in 1832 was intended by the Jackson administration to be that compromise. It would lower the rates, cut the ground out from under Calhoun, and perhaps pick up the votes for Jackson in South Carolina in 1832. As soon as Van Buren returned from England Jackson put him to work to try to negotiate such a settlement.[36] But the compromisers did not anticipate the strategies of Henry Clay, who had his own aspirations for the presidency to consider. A proponent of the tariff on the merits, Clay had no intention of permitting Jackson to make political capital of reductions. As a result the tariff of 1832 was if anything worse than the bill it was intended to improve. Far from being pushed further into the Jackson camp, South Carolina was placed in the unenviable position of acting or of giving up its nullification convictions. The situation created the most acute difficulties for the strict constructionist friends of the administration in Virginia. So far as the merits of the tariff dispute were concerned, the sympathies of Daniel and his fellow Virginians were entirely with South Carolina. Yet they altogether rejected nullification.

There were other strict constructionists in Virginia, of whom Floyd was an example, who could see no real difference between nullification and the sacred Virginia and Kentucky Resolutions of 1798 and 1799, to which every Virginian pledged his allegiance.[37] The line between those resolutions and the Calhoun proposal was thin — indeed, South Carolina had taken the word "nullification" directly from one of the resolutions. Yet the Jackson group saw a distinct difference. The great resolutions were, it is true, exceedingly hazy as to just what the states were supposed to do about the Alien and Sedition Acts if they objected to them, but it was possible to view them as an invitation to the other states to join in directing their representatives in Congress to cure the evil. So construed, the Virginia and Kentucky Resolutions were the supreme form of political agitation *short* of actual revolution. Nullification, on the other hand, was revolution at least so far as one law was concerned.

Between July, when the tariff act passed, and October, when Barbour withdrew from the vice presidential race, there was always a possibility that antitariff sentiment in Virginia might bring success to the Barbour faction. But this peril was more than balanced by the strength given the Jackson–Van Buren cause in Virginia by the issue of the recharter of the Bank of the United States. The bank had been chartered in 1816 and its charter was not due to expire until 1836. The bank was by far the most powerful institution in the country, in many respects far more powerful than the government itself. It was dominantly a private institution, with one fifth of its capital and one fifth of its directors coming from the government. It was to a great extent dependent on the government for its cash, since government funds were deposited with the bank, but the actual government influence in its management was negligible.

Jackson himself vacillated somewhat concerning the bank. Basically he was hostile to it, but after the reconstruction of his cabinet following the Eaton episode he began to hear a good deal of probank sentiment. To this, there was one notable exception: the new Attorney General, Roger B. Taney. Taney was a prosperous lawyer who had been attorney general of Maryland at the time of his appointment to Federal office in 1831. From that date on, while Van Buren was the strongest political and personal influence in Jackson's life, Taney was the strongest intellectual influence. Despite an unimpressive physique and a poor voice, Taney was a dominating personality by virtue of sheer intellectual pre-eminence; his was a sophisticated and subtle mind.[38]

There was, as has been noted earlier, a body of opinion in the United States opposed to all banks. This was Daniel's view: "I have no interest in any bank on earth," he wrote the governor of Virginia in 1837; I "have always been the declared enemy of all banks, both state and Federal; and I should deem the utter extinction of banks throughout the world, as the greatest possible good which could be done to mankind." [39] This was not the Taney point of view. He was far beyond that stage of economic primitivism which desired a society free of any banks at all; his opposition to "the monster," as its enemies called the Bank of the United States, rested squarely on convictions about that particular institution. As he put it, "It is the immense power of this gigantic machine, controlling the whole circulating medium of the country — increasing or depressing the price of property at its pleasure all over the United States — embarrassing and ruining, if it chooses, the commerce of our country by a sudden pressure on the merchants — and giving life and

security to it in a more favored city — it is this power, con-
centrated in the hands of a few individuals — exercised in
secret and unseen although constantly felt — irresponsible
and above the control of the people or the government for the
twenty years of its charter, that is sufficient to awaken any
man in this country if the danger is brought distinctly to
his view." [40]

This was the view which Taney pressed upon Jackson just
when the Bank of the United States decided that the time was
ripe to drive for a recharter. In choosing 1832 for this attempt, four years in advance of the actual expiration of its
charter, the bank was undoubtedly influenced by the political
necessities of Henry Clay in the campaign of 1832. Passage
of the bill would put Jackson in this dilemma: if he signed it,
he would lose Virginia and other parts of the South; if he
vetoed it, he would risk Pennsylvania. Nicholas Biddle, president of the bank, believed that Jackson would sign.[41] To prepare for the struggle, throughout 1831 the bank extended
credit all over the United States, and fostered the impression
that the prosperity of the country was dependent upon it.

The bank succeeded in obtaining its recharter from Congress. With Taney's help, Jackson fashioned a powerful veto
message. The veto, which came on July 10, 1832, was rested
on the broadest grounds both of constitutionality and of policy. Jackson said:

> It is to be regretted that the rich and powerful too often
> bend the acts of government to their selfish purposes . . .
> There are no necessary evils in government. Its evils exist only
> in its abuses. If it would confine itself to equal protection, and,
> as Heaven does its rains, shower its favors alike on the high
> and the low, the rich and the poor, it would be an unqualified
> blessing. In the act before me there seems to be an unwise
> and unnecessary departure from these just principles . . .
> Many of our rich men have not been content with equal pro-
> tection and equal benefits, but have besought us to make them

richer by act of Congress . . . We can at least take a stand against all new grants of monopolies and exclusive privileges, against any prostitution of our government to the advancement of the few at the expense of the man, and in favor of compromise and gradual reform in our code of laws and system of political economy.[42]

Even if there had been nothing else, this statement would have been enough to make Daniel Jackson's supporter forever. The doubts expressed by the message as to the constitutionality of a national bank were especially to Daniel's taste. He once said when asked to pass upon the claims of someone for a political office, "He has professed a belief in the *constitutionality* of a *national bank*, and that is an objection which with me would overrule any and every recommendation which could be urged for him or for any other person." [43]

Daniel worked hard in the campaign of 1832. He had the interests of Jackson and Van Buren in mind, and he was also interested in establishing himself as the principal spokesman for Van Buren in Virginia. As a Jacksonian he shared prominence with the state's national representatives, and particularly Congressmen Stevenson and Archer. As a Van Buren man he shared standing with Ritchie and Nicholas. In writing to Van Buren's biographer, Daniel broadly suggested that he should be Van Buren's spokesman in Virginia, stressing his loyalty to Van Buren long before this nomination and his public stand both at the state convention and as the author of the Crito letters.[44] In writing to Van Buren himself on election day, he asked for prompt information on the New York results to be disseminated by him so that the state might not be disheartened by false reports.[45] Nothing came of these requests, and indeed nothing very practical could, but they are indicative both of an aspiration to stature and of a right to ask it. By the close of the election of 1832 Daniel had performed sufficient services for Van Buren so that he could reasonably expect to be a spokesman for the new vice president.

The 1832 campaign in Virginia was more a struggle over the vice presidency than over the presidency itself. Almost two thirds of the central committee's official statement is devoted to Van Buren. Barbour did not withdraw until October, and though he could not hurt Jackson, there was still some possibility that he might damage the chances of the party's choice for the second office. Van Buren's friends were very much aware of the potential threat from Barbour, who came closer to representing Virginia principles than Van Buren. The appraisal the central committee made of Van Buren deserves to be a final judgment of history: "To a judgment clear, vigorous and comprehensive, he adds the advantages of years of experience in the Councils both of his own state and of the nation; of an untiring industry, and imperturbable equanimity, and a simplicity and affability of demeanor, the offspring of republican habits and opinions, and most grateful to all who approach him." [46] In other words, Van Buren might not be a Jeffersonian in all of his convictions, but he was a Jeffersonian in the attitudes which Virginia liked to attribute to her great statesmen.

Whether Barbour was convinced by the proclamation, or by the prospect of defeat, or by a patronage offer from Jackson is unknown; but a few days after the issuance of the statement he withdrew from the race on the ground that Jackson's ticket might lose altogether if he remained.[47] His supporters accepted his retirement with bitterness.[48] They blasted the state central committee as the arrogant tyrants of the Democratic party in Virginia, as the "seven wise men of Richmond," who, having allied their Junto with the Albany machine, dictated to the people of their state. The resolution of the great controversy came a few days later. The Jackson–Van Buren ticket overwhelmingly swept Virginia, and Jackson was comfortably elected by the country.

The election of 1832 was the greatest single triumph of the Richmond Junto in national politics. Junto support was not necessary for the election of Jackson, who would have been nominated and elected even if, for example, Governor Floyd's Calhoun wing of the party had controlled Virginia. But without the Junto, it is very doubtful that Van Buren would have been elected vice president in 1832 and, as a result, president in 1836. True, Van Buren had Jackson behind him, but there were other aspirants than Barbour for the vice presidency, and the results might have been unpredictably different without the Virginia strength.[49]

Within Virginia itself, from the moment of the meeting of the first caucus through the national convention and to the end of the campaign, the Junto displayed superb skill in managing Van Buren's affairs. Viewed solely as an operation in politics, the Virginia campaign of 1832 for Van Buren is as flawless a machine performance as can be found; with a maximum of skill, with a canny avoidance of the fights that could not be won, and with a superb care to avoid wounded feelings which might boomerang against the cause, the Junto passed all obstacles. The basic leadership within the state lay with a small coterie of which Daniel was a part. His exact role cannot be separated from that of the others, for the marvel of the Junto was its cohesion. Certainly on every occasion on which his own activities can be isolated from the others he showed a tact, a skill, and a judgment beyond anything displayed in his previous political career. His first Crito letter and his speech for Van Buren at the state convention are two of his outstanding accomplishments. The smoothness of the whole operation suggests a little more of the dextrous Ritchie than of the blunt Daniel, but Ritchie's biographer says that Ritchie wobbled a little on the Van Buren–Barbour issue in the course of the campaign. In this case Daniel's inflexibility may have helped to keep the Junto firm.

Whatever Daniel's exact role in the party's machinations,

it was undoubtedly a strong one. And why? There is not a scintilla of evidence that Daniel wanted any national office or that he craved fame for its own sake. What exhausted his time and his energy in 1832 was a matter of principle. As he wrote to Van Buren on the day before the election, the ultimate issue lay "between democracy and the constitution on one hand, and corruption and profligacy unexampled on the other." [50]

It is one of the oldest traditions of American politics that a newly elected or re-elected President enjoys a "honeymoon period" which may last as much as a year. During that time the administration sets about to fulfill its campaign promises, and the opposition, having been recently defeated on the old issues, sits quietly by until new issues turn up. In the interim the spoils are customarily divided, and the faithful receive the rewards for the virtues of their party.

But the election of 1832 had been too hard fought for customary amenities. The honeymoon lasted barely long enough for the people to read the election returns, and then the most intense series of political crises of the first half of the nineteenth century exploded. Andrew Jackson's second term was probably the most exciting four-year period in the life of the Old Warrior. It was certainly the most tumultuous time in the life of Peter V. Daniel. The day after the election he was one of the leaders of his party; he was being spoken of just a little, at least, for the United States Senate; [51] and he had a fair prospect of becoming governor. He was shortly to be offered one of the highest posts in Andrew Jackson's administration. Yet almost overnight he and his friends were to lose everything, including the state office he had held for twenty-two years. As one of the shock troops in Jackson's forces Daniel was to feel the full weight of the great anti-Jackson upheaval.

South Carolina's response to the election of Andrew Jackson was nullification. During the earlier months of 1832, while the rest of the country had been occupied with the election, South Carolina had been preoccupied with affairs of its own. There the nullification and union factions had reached the point of actual physical violence. At the same time in November that the country was electing Jackson, this state was electing delegates to a nullification convention.[52] The South Carolina Nullification Convention declared that the tariff acts of 1828 were null and void and of no effect in South Carolina. The state legislature at once proceeded to put this resolution into effect, the actual effective date to be the following February first. Anticipating trouble, the governor asked the legislature to raise a military force of 12,000 men. The issue then passed to the rest of the country. South Carolina appealed for support — more than anyone else to the strict constructionists of eastern Virginia, whose Virginia and Kentucky Resolutions of 1798 they claimed as the spiritual basis for their action.

On December 3 Governor Floyd sent his annual message to the Virginia legislature.[53] Without endorsing the doctrine of nullification as such, he thoroughly sympathized with South Carolina. On December 10 President Jackson issued his forceful proclamation against nullification and called for legislation to enforce the tariff. This was passed under the name of the Force Bill. In this controversy Daniel stood basically with Jackson. Jackson's proclamation had denounced nullification and secession. The Junto acknowledged the right to secede in extreme cases,[54] but they felt that this was not such an occasion. And they considered South Carolina's statement on nullification a slander on the Virginia and Kentucky Resolutions, which they interpreted as a call not for nullification but for public remonstrance against unconstitutional acts of Congress. This was Daniel's view, and he used his influence in the events of January and February to secure this position.

The whole situation made Virginia exceedingly nervous. The state anticipated becoming the actual theater of a war between South Carolina and the rest of the country, for Federal forces would have to march through its territory.[55] In this situation, Virginia opinion was so divided that when two senatorial vacancies happened to come at the same time, the pro-Jackson, pro-Force Bill Rives was elected for one seat and an anti–Force Bill man, Tyler, was elected for the other. (Daniel was mentioned for these seats but not seriously pushed.) Virginia attempted to maintain this compromise position, the legislature sending Benjamin W. Leigh as a commissioner to South Carolina to look for some solution.[56]

When the excitement was over faces had been saved but Jackson had won. In December the President sent General Winfield Scott to take command at Fort Sumter, in Charleston harbor, and to guard it from the South Carolinians. In February the Force Bill passed. It became abundantly clear that Jackson was prepared to send overwhelming military forces to insure enforcement of the laws and, if he should actually resist the enforcement of the laws, to hang John C. Calhoun. Forced by these circumstances, Clay and Calhoun reached a compromise which reduced the tariff rates by an act of 1833, and the storm blew over.[57]

The principal effect of all this excitement on Daniel was to attach him even more firmly to the Jackson party. Daniel's absolute defiance of the nullifiers was expressed in a toast he offered a few months later on the Fourth of July. He rose before seventy-five of Richmond's leading citizens, including Leigh and Chief Justice Marshall, and toasted "our fellow citizen, General Winfield Scott — acquiring new claims to our esteem in every station to which duty calls him." [58] This was a direct slap in the face to every nullificationist present.

Meanwhile the running battle between Governor Floyd and Daniel continued. Floyd stopped attending Council meetings, submitting his requests for opinions in writing. Daniel retaliated by sniping at the governor on little matters. When the expenses of a court martial were referred to the Council for payment, it denied payment on the ground that the governor had not consulted with the Council before ordering the court martial.[59] Floyd's administration became one long protest by Daniel, usually over the refusal of Floyd to give the Council adequate information. Again and again the Council heard Daniel say: "I cannot do more therefore, in relation to this account, than to request that such information as may lead to a just comprehension of it, be laid before the Council." [60]

But there were matters infinitely more important than hooting at Floyd. Nullification had barely been suppressed when the bank controversy flared up again. Throughout the summer of 1833 Jackson considered steps to complete his victory over the bank by the transfer of Federal government deposits from the Bank of the United States to state banks. Taney was the principal cabinet advocate of this move; the Secretary of the Treasury opposed it. Finally Jackson decided to go ahead. In late September 1833 he removed his recalcitrant Secretary of the Treasury and moved Taney to that post. Jackson's choice for a new Attorney General to replace Taney was Peter V. Daniel.

This was not Daniel's first opportunity for Federal employment. In 1830 he had been responsibly suggested for a Federal district judgeship which went to Philip P. Barbour instead.[61] During the spoils period early in the first Jackson administration, he had declined the position of United States attorney for the Richmond area on the ground that he disapproved of the spoils system and that the incumbent was perfectly competent to carry on the job.[62] In March 1833 he had been appointed to the diplomatic post of commissioner under a treaty to settle substantial claims with the Kingdom of Southern Italy.[63] He had promptly declined this office on grounds which were explained by him directly to President Jackson, and which are unknown.

But to be appointed Attorney General of the United States was something else again. It exposed Daniel to the most severe temptation of his life, for it meant not only status but also an opportunity to participate in a fight in which his whole heart was involved. His was a life ruled by principles, and on no issue had he ever felt more strongly than on the bank.

Yet there were terrible complications. Because he was expected to be able to devote part of his time to private practice in Washington, the Attorney General was the lowest paid member of the cabinet. His salary was only $4000. In Richmond Daniel was living on an income in the neighborhood of $4000 by careful management. His savings were negligible. If a Washington practice were to come quickly, he could make the adjustment; but the probability was strong that the transfer would put him into a desperate financial condition.

Public opinion on the Jackson administration was already violently split over the bank, and reactions to Daniel's appointment were controlled by reactions to other questions. Perhaps the nastiest comment appeared in the Pittsburg *Advertiser*: "As soon as we can ascertain who this Peter V. Daniel is, we will endeavor to lay the same before our readers." [64] The Whig papers in Virginia set about to inform the country of Daniel's want of qualifications. The Richmond *Whig* contended that he was one of the worst lawyers in the state with no claim to fame except his authorship of some of the papers of the Democratic state central committee and his support of Van Buren in the recent election.[65] The Columbia *Telescope* charged that his was the "most grossly partial appointment to office that General Jackson has yet made." Daniel was worse than even the third-rate lawyers of Virginia and the appointment was a party reward for his many dull essays in the Richmond *Enquirer*. The *Telescope* continued, "He has grown grey filling a sinecure office in Richmond, on a salary of $1,000, with Tommy Ritchie as his oracle." [66] The Norfolk *Herald* attacked him as a worthless lawyer who was no more than a hack writer for Andrew Jackson.[67] The Washington Whig papers reprinted these local attacks, adding biting comments of their own, but predicted that Daniel would accept the position.

Meanwhile the friends of the administration supported the appointment. The *Enquirer*, disgusted but not surprised at the attacks, leaped to Daniel's defense, calling him "A gentleman of strong mind, of great firmness of character, of the most untiring industry, and the most unblemished integrity." Then, with a fine stroke of strategy, it turned back to the discussion at the state constitutional convention of 1829–30. Benjamin Leigh, one of the leading Democrats in Virginia, was in 1833 against the removal of the Federal deposits and was about to be elected to the Senate as an antiremoval man. The *Enquirer* reminded its readers that in the 1829 convention Leigh had praised Daniel by name as one of the outstanding men of Virginia.[68]

Is there significance in the fact that the *Enquirer*, for all its encomiums, did not say that Daniel was a good lawyer? No such omission was made by the out-of-state administration press. Van Buren's organ in Albany called Daniel's attackers the voice of "the Bank and the Opposition." [69] The Albany paper, perhaps mindful of the fact that Van Buren had been one of Daniel's sponsors for the cabinet position, described him as supremely qualified as to legal ability as well as to political principles. The Harrisburg *Reporter* was pleased to find that Daniel was "a distinguished member of the Virginia Bar, and is a Democrat of the Jefferson school." [70]

For the ten days it took him to make a decision Daniel was in torment. On October 27 he went to Washington to can-

vass the situation there. He saw Van Buren and, in all probability, Taney. On the twenty-ninth Ritchie printed an ex-
planation of Daniel's trip in the *Enquirer*, in the course of a
friendly editorial about him. He had gone, said the *Enquirer*,
to get information concerning the "duties, perquisites, and
leisure for private practice." [71] The opposition press landed
with glee on the wording of this *Enquirer* editorial. Daniel
was lampooned as a fool and a money grabber. The Washington *Intelligencer* used the phrase to attack Daniel as typical of all the naïve Jackson officeholders interested in positions
solely for the financial returns.[72] Yet there was no reason at
all why Daniel should have known what the distribution of
the Attorney General's time would be between public and
private duties, nor what the opportunities for a private practice might be; and however much the Whigs might like to
pretend that high office was held only for the honor which
attached to it, Daniel was in no position to proceed on so
disembodied a basis. He doubtless did go to Washington to
learn more about the financial aspects of the position. When
he returned to Richmond a few days later he was still undecided.

The matter could not long be delayed. On November 4
he had a long visit in Richmond with Congressman Andrew
Stevenson, Speaker of the House of Representatives, and an
outstanding Jackson leader in Virginia. The two men went
over the whole situation in what was doubtless an earnest
conversation; Stevenson keenly realized the necessity of having
a strong man in the office of attorney general. When they
parted Daniel was still undecided, and Stevenson persuaded
him to have one last talk with Ritchie.[73]

By the time Daniel reached his home his resolve had hard-
ened, and he wrote the Secretary of State, his official corre-
spondent on the matter, declining the position. He assured the
Secretary that he was wholeheartedly for the administration
and for its policies; but from the first moment that the posi-

tion was offered, he said, "I have been conscious of difficulties arising from my individual concerns, and from obligations previously contracted, that might prevent" acceptance.[74] He had, he assured the Secretary, attempted most earnestly to remove those difficulties, but he could not do so and he was compelled reluctantly to decline. The next day he reported the accomplished fact to Stevenson and Ritchie, and Stevenson immediately notified Taney that they would have to look elsewhere. Stevenson did not burden Taney with Daniel's reasons, explaining that he could do so when they met if Taney desired. "In the meantime," said Stevenson, "rest assured it is all well." [75]

The administration thereupon chose B. S. Butler of New York, one of Van Buren's closest associates, as the Attorney General. Taney explained to Stevenson that he had wanted a southerner but that more important than geographical considerations was the necessity of having "a trained and thorough lawyer." [76] For this reason, after Daniel declined he had recommended Butler. Clearly Taney felt that Daniel had measured up as a trained and thorough lawyer and that no other talented southerner was equally suitable politically.

Thereupon, on November 8, the *Enquirer* printed a palpable lie. Considerably embarrassed by the trouble it had caused Daniel by describing his trip to Washington to explore the "perquisites of office," it sought to extricate itself and him by asserting that Daniel had refused the appointment in writing two days before he had gone to Washington. This left it necessary to account for Daniel's actions, since his refusal might be construed as a want of confidence in the administration. The *Enquirer* therefore reported that he had acted not upon want of confidence in Jackson, but "upon considerations arising from his own peculiar relations, and such as he has not deemed himself at liberty to disregard." [77] Thus it retreated to total ambiguity.

Twenty years later Van Buren gave a wholly different

interpretation of this event. In a wandering, somewhat auto-biographical manuscript written when he was in his seventies and published after his death Van Buren said that Ritchie and Daniel feared Jackson's rashness. He asserted that he had recommended Daniel for the attorney generalship; that Daniel "came to Washington, was pleased with the invitation to take a seat in the Cabinet, which the General authorized me to give him, was pleased also with the office and would have been glad to accept it under other circumstances, but was, notwithstanding, induced to decline it, after a day's con-sultation with me, by considerations of that character ex-clusively. The general was not a little amused, after our friend left us, to hear me attribute his refusal to an apprehension that he might, in the discharge of his official duties be reduced to the necessity of acting against the principles of '98, or against his, the General's wishes — an alternative that he pre-ferred not to encounter." [78]

On every point that can be checked this reminiscence is inaccurate. Van Buren did not tender the appointment, which Daniel had before he came to Washington, and unless his own letter of refusal and Stevenson's letter to Taney are both false, he did not decline because of want of confidence in Jackson. In the suggestion that Daniel declined immediately after his conference with Van Buren the statement is in-accurate by many days. There is no evidence in any part of Daniel's writings that he had any such doubts about Jackson or any want of confidence in him; and if either Jackson or Van Buren had supposed that these were Daniel's views, surely neither would later have offered him a judicial position. The conclusion is inescapable that Van Buren, writing many years after he and Daniel had ceased to be friends, and in his old age, was subject to a lapse of memory. It is possible that in conversation with Van Buren at the time of his visit to Wash-ington Daniel may have expressed some passing doubt as to an incompatibility between some of Jackson's views and some of his own, but certainly any such circumstance was not the mainspring of his action.

Exclusion from the main bout in Washington did not keep Daniel out of the fight over the removal of funds from the Bank of the United States. This was a national free-for-all, with room for everyone. The issue caused a rift in the Democratic party in Virginia. In December 1833 a mass meeting in Richmond, attended by many Democrats, adopted resolutions written by Benjamin W. Leigh, a leading Virginia Democrat, decrying the removal of the deposits.[79] In January 1834 the legislature met to elect a governor to succeed Floyd. Daniel was the administration candidate. The Whigs — greatly strengthened as a party by defections from the Democrats resulting from the bank controversy — supported Littleton Tazewell.[80] Tazewell won easily. For the first time the party of Andrew Jackson was completely defeated in Virginia. Both houses of the legislature proceeded at once to pass resolutions in various ways condemning Jackson's bank decision. The Senate voted 17 to 15 to instruct the state's representatives in Congress to secure the return of the deposits. Of the fifteen votes against return of the deposits, twelve came from senators who were among the thirteen to vote for Daniel for governor.[81]

Throughout February and March of 1834 Richmond was gripped with wild political passion. Threats of recrimination were rampant as old friends stopped speaking to one another. In the face of disaster the Junto began to crumble. Brockenbrough, Nicholas, and Ritchie joined in a recommendation to Congressman Stevenson that he try to induce Jackson to restore the funds for the balance of the life of the bank.[82] But Daniel would not yield. He wrote Stevenson, "You have no idea of the state of society here at this time; and particularly of the life I lead. I am watched throughout the day; every door I enter, every person with whom I speak, is a subject of jealous scrutiny. I am even now, it is said, being hunted to ruin my business, and with personal violence. But damn the contemptible slaves of the bank, I put them all at defiance." [83]

By mid-summer the debacle was so great that the administration party was unable to raise a quorum even for a good Fourth of July celebration in Richmond. The state's main Democratic gathering on that day was at Fredericksburg. Van Buren sent a toast by mail. He offered: "Unquestioning and uncompromising opposition to the Bank of the United States." There was a toast from Daniel, too: "The Democratic spirit of the Old Dominion . . . again it shall triumph over selfishness, audacity, and corruption." [84]

Chapter VII

DEFEAT AND VICTORY

FOR ALL HIS DEFIANCE, the summer of 1834 was the nadir of Daniel's political career. The new legislature was predominantly Whig, and the Junto was wilting before the enemy. Van Buren's star was nowhere in the ascendancy, and Andrew Jackson himself was under relentless attack. Daniel's own term was to expire in the forthcoming session of the legislature, and with that body constituted as it was, his prospect for re-election was slim. As the last months of his official life trickled away, there was not even the joy of a good fight with the new governor, for Governor Tazewell managed his relations with the Council with a perfect, if frosty, decorum, and no conflicts arose.

In short, Daniel, who a year before had enjoyed the choice of several high Federal positions including a cabinet post, now had no prospect of such a position and probably would not have been confirmed by the Senate if his name had been sent in. He had the status of a Van Buren spokesman in Virginia, but Van Buren's prospects were no better than his own. He had for years been a high official of the executive department of Virginia, and he was shortly to lose even this.

But defeat as total as that which faced Daniel and the Junto had at least the virtue of clarifying directions. There was no way to go but up. The Jackson party prepared to fight. Moreover, there were great rifts in the ranks of their opponents. For the moment, the nationalists of Clay and the nullifiers of Calhoun were together, but there were basic incompatibilities between the two groups. For a time in 1834 it appeared possible that the Whigs might be able to unite behind Leigh for the presidency, but this harmony lasted only until other candidates moved into the field. The Junto's great asset was the experience of thirty years of disciplined unity. There were defections in 1833 and 1834, as for example when Congressman Archer, who had been a Van Buren floor leader at the national convention of 1832, deserted to the Whigs.[1] But the core that was left could still strike together.

At the end of 1834 the legislature had three major offices to fill. The first was the position of public printer, a lucrative bit of patronage which had been Ritchie's reward for services rendered since the earliest days of the Junto. The second was the office of lieutenant governor, Daniel's seat. And the third was the position in the United States Senate which Rives wanted back from Leigh.

Ritchie was the first to fall. In early December, by a vote of 87 to 75, the public printing was transferred to a Whig printer. Whatever may have been Ritchie's private anger, he good humoredly reported in his paper that after the decapitation, the victim was "still firm, proud, erect, and unterrified." [2]

The next victim was Daniel, and he put up a better fight. The Whig party caucused in the legislature on the evening of January 15, 1835, to choose a candidate to succeed Daniel, and had great trouble agreeing among themselves. John S. Pendleton, one of the old Floyd Democrats, was finally chosen. But not all the Leigh Whigs could accept Pendleton, and they unsuccessfully sought to postpone the election.[3]

To minimize Daniel's tidewater affiliations, he was nominated by Representative Sherrard, a northern Virginian, who stressed that although his section received few favors from the executive, it was nonetheless deeply impressed with Daniel's fairness. He described Daniel as a man who was at once kind, courteous, and obliging and yet as a man who never yielded, even to his friends, when he thought some request made of him was wrong. Indeed, Sherrard confessed, Daniel had all too often decided controversies against him; but Daniel's integrity was always respected, even when his actions were criticized. Moreover, Sherrard stressed, Daniel was a true Virginia patriot who had resisted alluring Federal offices including the attorney generalship and the commissionership under the Italian treaty, which, he pointed out, would have paid a salary of $3000 a year. He conceded that he had no hope of persuading any of the Clay Whigs in his audience, for they had always sought to destroy Daniel; but he had strong hopes that he might enlist the Leigh Whigs, who had so recently been Democrats standing shoulder to shoulder with Daniel.[4] Since Daniel was doing everything in his power to defeat Leigh, this must have had a hollow ring.

A protracted discussion followed. The pro-Daniel force argued that a good public servant should not be removed as a simple act of spoilsmanship, particularly since Daniel had never himself been a spoilsman in his moments of triumph. Over and over again Daniel's friends referred to the declined Federal offices, and particularly the district attorneyship which Daniel had refused on the grounds that he disapproved of spoils distribution. Daniel had stood on sound principle then, ran the argument, and the opposition should do so now. No enemy expressed doubt about the reason given for Daniel's refusal of this appointment. But some did minimize his refusal of the attorney generalship (which his friends tried to assert was due to loyalty to Virginia) by raking up the unfortunate *Enquirer* story concerning the "perquisites" of office.

The merits influenced a very few legislators who were not Democrats to vote for Daniel. The Whig representative from the district encompassing Stafford County, perhaps fearing the wrath of the home folks but perhaps standing on principle as well, declared that he could not vote to turn a man out who had done a first-class job, no matter what his politics were. In his opinion there was more evil in party proscriptions than in leaving a good Democrat in office.

Some Whigs quickly repudiated the suggestion that they were voting against Daniel on purely political grounds. One advocated rotation in office as a sound general practice. Another objected to Daniel's correspondence war with the judges of the county court the year before, attributing his vote entirely to the fact that he believed Daniel's second letter was an effort to menace those gentlemen with threats of a duel.

But Daniel's real enemies were ready to meet his friends head on, without any detours into specialized reasons for their opposition. As one opponent put it, he was against Daniel because Daniel was a Jackson–Van Buren man: "Who has been a more active and devoted partizan of the administration, and the appointed succession, than Mr. Daniel?" So far as this critic was concerned, Daniel must be eliminated as a matter of pure patronage.[5]

When the votes were counted Daniel had 75, Pendleton had 52, and 25 were scattered. Since it took a majority to elect, the ballot was thus inconclusive. The distribution did, however, clearly indicate the difference in discipline between the Democrats and the Whigs. The voting continued through three more ballots, most of the scattered and absent votes slowly going to Pendleton, so that at the end of the day the vote was Pendleton, 78; Daniel, 75; and 8 scattered. When the legislators met again on the next day, the seventeenth, they had in their hands a gloomy editorial from the *Enquirer*. Ritchie began his report, "The guillotine is again in motion; and it is sufficiently obvious that the head of Peter V. Daniel, Esq. is to be cut off by the Whigs." The 75 votes, said the *Enquirer*, exhausted the Jackson strength in the legislature, though the story predicted, accurately, that the eight who would not give their votes to Pendleton would eventually compel the Whigs to abandon that candidate and substitute someone else. The *Enquirer* decried this slaughter of "one of the most experienced, able, most active and virtuous officers, of whom this commonwealth could ever boast." [6] The events of the day before, the *Enquirer* conceded, meant "heads off," but, reiterating the slogan which it was using for the forthcoming campaign, it also meant "heads up" and an eventual victory for Jacksonian principles.

Ritchie may have been ready to give up, but Daniel was still fighting. The second day's voting was a battle. The legislators rehashed the debate of the day before. In all this heat, there was one truly objective appraisal of Daniel. The speaker, an experienced legislator, was satisfied that Daniel was a valuable public officer despite the attacks on him. He continued, "It was true that [the speaker] had observed some acts of Mr. Daniel as an active and zealous politician, which he thought detracted somewhat from his usefulness as public functionary. But he weighed the whole, good and bad, of Mr. Daniel's qualities together, and formed his opinion from the aggregate. Were he called on to particularize, he should say that Mr. Daniel's violence of temper was an objection to him. Nay, more, he should say that his political course was also objectionable. But they do not deprive him of a claim upon our candour, nor invalidate the ability which all admit he possesses." [7]

But this was not the day for objectivity. The dominant anti-Daniel feeling was summed up by one member in these words, "Mr. Daniel [was] one of the depositories of the Jackson Party — as the pen in the hand of the President." As another opponent put it, Daniel had both the talent and the experience for the job but the speaker would never vote for the author of the "philippics for the party press." [8]

There were of course legislators who had no strong feel-

ing for either Daniel or Pendleton and who merely wanted
to finish the business at hand. Since it appeared that neither
Daniel nor Pendleton could be elected, some of them began
to urge the withdrawal of the candidates. But a Jackson man
threw down the gauntlet, declaring that the Jackson party
would never relinquish Daniel and that the Whigs would
somehow have to unite to defeat him if they could. In this
militant spirit two more votes were taken, and on each Daniel
kept his 75 votes, while Pendleton got 70, and 17 were scattered. It was apparent after six votes and two days that it was
impossible to act and the legislature therefore postponed the
whole matter until January 30.

The solidity of Daniel's support persuaded the Democratic
leadership to go down fighting. There was not a serious word
to be said against Daniel's execution of his office and his removal would obviously be solely for political purposes. The
Enquirer, heartened, called the tune for the party: the friends
of Daniel "will not abandon or withdraw. They will adhere
to him to the last — and die in the last ditch." Then they
would appeal to the people.

For two weeks Richmond had no business but politics. On
January 29 the legislature was scheduled to choose between
Leigh and Rives for the Senate, and on the thirtieth it was
due to elect a councilor. Strategems were formulated and
negotiations were endless. In Daniel's case every inducement
was used to get needed votes. For example a Whig member
of the House of Delegates named Allan Wilson was told by
friends of Daniel that if he voted against Daniel in this election, the Democrats would, if they were successful in the
spring elections, remove his brother from the Council. He
was assured that if he did vote for Daniel now, his brother,
whose Council term expired in a year, would then be retained.[9] Wilson, whether on principle or because he did not
believe that the Democrats would be in a position to carry

out their threats, stayed with his party and voted against Daniel.

Neither threats nor negotiations nor promises were enough. On the twenty-ninth Leigh was elected to the Senate over Rives by a vote of 85 to 81. On the thirtieth, after another extended debate, the legislature voted again for councilor. On the first ballot Daniel gained strength, coming up to a vote of 79. Pendleton received 66 votes and a new candidate, W. H. McFarland, received 11. The rest of the votes were scattered. The new Whig strategy was now clear. Pendleton was to be given a last chance to develop strength of his own; if he could not do so McFarland, a strong Whig from Norfolk, would come forward in his place. On the second ballot Daniel crept up a vote to 80, only three short of the majority. On the third ballot he gained still another, bringing him to 81. The Whigs now dropped Pendleton and swung to McFarland in force. The fourth vote put McFarland in by a margin of 83 to 81. If delegate Wilson had been a little more sensitive about the prospects of his brother, the vote would have been a tie.[10]

And thus ended for Peter V. Daniel twenty-three years of service on the Council of State of Virginia, for seventeen of which he had been lieutenant governor. The abundant reports of this debate clearly show that he left an honorable record. What is significant in the debate is not the charges that were made against Daniel, but the charges that were not made. As most legislators candidly admitted, he was being removed because he was a strong Jackson–Van Buren man and an enemy of the Bank of the United States. For all the heat, not one man cast a serious aspersion either on Daniel's character or on his record. No one challenged his efficiency or honesty; not even the strongest Floyd supporter went back to the battles with that governor to suggest that Daniel had misinterpreted his duties. It was a great tribute to Daniel that his adversaries could find nothing of substance to attack.

If Daniel shed a tear over his defeat, he had scarcely time to dry his eyes before he returned to the fight to restore Virginia to the Democratic column. Within seventy-two hours he was chairman of a committee to promote a Democratic candidate for Congress from Richmond.[11] For the next year he devoted more time to pure politics than in any other like period of his life. He and Ritchie never worked more closely together. Later in February Daniel presided at a Democratic mass meeting in Richmond at which Ritchie proposed resolutions strongly endorsing Andrew Jackson and applauding his firmness in putting down the Bank of the United States, "an unconstitutional and aristocratical institution." [12]

Through all these activities Daniel was sustained by a grim-lipped energy; his party had been so long victorious that he was mortified by defeat. His temper was edgy, and Lucy must have found him extraordinarily difficult to live with; he snapped at Van Buren when the Vice President did not respond to one of his letters quickly enough.[13] His social and political isolation in his dominantly Whig city was intensified, and even his personal safety was menaced. He believed, with some reason, that on at least one occasion a Whig spy peered through a crack in the Council room door at one of his last meetings, intending to set thugs upon Daniel when he left for home.[14]

Better days were ahead. March and April were a period of vigorous campaigning and Daniel filled the *Enquirer* with letters. Then came an overwhelming Democratic victory in the spring election for the legislature. The Junto was in the saddle again, and at the December legislative session could restore the faithful to their posts.

But meanwhile there was work of the first importance to be done. The national Democratic convention was to be held in May 1835, more than a year in advance of the election.

Andrew Jackson wanted to make sure no new candidate came along to eclipse his favorite, Van Buren.

As the convention drew near, the Virginians set about to select a vice presidential candidate to run with Van Buren. Their choice was the recently defeated Senator Rives, whose nomination would vindicate all those Virginia Democrats who had stuck to Jackson throughout the lean times. The nomination of Van Buren himself was so well assured that Daniel had not planned to attend the convention, but the Rives candidacy was worth supporting. He therefore went to the convention at Baltimore via Washington, where he hoped to negotiate administration support for Rives. The other candidate was R. M. Johnson of Kentucky, unsatisfactory to Virginia because he was not irrevocably opposed to the Bank of the United States, internal improvements, and the tariff. The Virginians wanted the convention to readopt the rule of the 1832 convention requiring a two-thirds vote for a nomination. For it was apparent that the success or failure of Rives might depend upon the two-thirds rule. Virginia could much more easily muster a third of the convention against Johnson than it could one half. The Virginia delegation elected Daniel its chairman and made him the Virginia representative on the rules committee. After a vigorous dispute in which Daniel took the floor in behalf of the two-thirds rule, it was adopted by a thin margin.[15]

The convention met on Wednesday, May 20. On Thursday the Virginia delegation established an official conference committee of three to negotiate on the vice presidency with other delegations. For this purpose it chose its three most experienced politicians, J. S. Watkins, a long-time legislator, Andrew Stevenson, until recently Speaker of the House of Representatives, and Daniel. The conference committee was in effect given carte blanche to reach agreement on a satisfactory vice presidential candidate, subject only to the instruction that it was authorized "to sacrifice men, but not principles." In other words, the committee should attempt to defeat Johnson even if at the cost of Rives.[16]

In later years the Democrats were to learn to manage not merely their conventions but also their off-stage conferences with greater éclat. The first caucus was distinctly anticlimactic. The Virginians had reserved a committee room for the purpose, but rooms were short and privacy was unknown, so that delegates freely moved in and out, creating much confusion. Moreover, the Johnson forces had everything to lose and nothing to gain from such a meeting, so most of them stayed away. After an evening of waiting about for someone with whom to confer, the Virginians were convinced that Johnson was in.[17]

If Virginia could not negotiate, it could defy. Just before the vote for the vice presidential nominee began the Virginia delegation announced to the convention that it would not recommend to its constituents any "nominee who does not maintain and carry out the principles Virginia has ever held dear." [18] Thereupon Johnson was nominated by a vote of 178 for him to 87 for Rives. Johnson thus slipped in with one vote over the two-thirds margin. Virginia held to its position and in November gave its vice presidential vote to Judge William Smith of Alabama. As a result Johnson received less than a majority of the votes of the electoral college and the selection of a vice president was forced into the Senate. There Johnson finally won, becoming the only vice president ever selected by senatorial vote.

By the end of 1835 Daniel's prospects were good. The Democratic legislature elected in the spring convened in December, fully prepared to right the wrongs of its Whig predecessor. The legislature quickly set about to restore Ritchie and Daniel, to drive the two Whig United States senators out of office, and to give all possible aid to Jackson and Van Buren. The Whigs were soon complaining that the legislature was marching with the inexorability of a Roman legion.

Ritchie was returned to his position as public printer and Daniel was elected again to the Council. Daniel's success was at the expense of Council member Wilson, whose term had expired and who had stood for re-election. This led to Whig charges that the Democrats were now engaging in exactly the same kind of political proscription of which they had accused the Whigs the year before. The Democrats replied that Wilson would have been re-elected to the Council had his brother not refused to vote for Daniel the year before. As the *Enquirer* put it bluntly, "But for that event, not a hair of D. A. Wilson's head would have been touched." [19]

The Junto planned to keep Daniel on the Council until they could get him elected governor. As state Judge Richard Parker, Ritchie's brother-in-law, reported events to Van Buren, Daniel "will be our next governor if he remains in the executive department." [20] The qualification was occasioned by the rumor common in Virginia that President Jackson would appoint Philip Barbour to a Supreme Court vacancy and that Daniel would then take Barbour's place on the district court.

But the major task of securing the vote of the state for Van Buren still lay ahead. Having failed in 1832 with one candidate, the Whigs determined this time to run a series of favorite sons, each of whom might capture enough votes to keep Van Buren from getting a majority and thus throw the election into the House of Representatives. In Virginia they were reduced to a complicated double offering of Senator Hugh White of Tennessee, who was essentially a Democrat estranged from Jackson, and William Henry Harrison. The plan was that the Virginia Whig electors were to be unpledged but were to vote for either White or Harrison, whichever seemed best under the circumstances. The Van Buren men were thus campaigning against what they mockingly called a "double-shotted ticket."

As usual, the Democrats organized behind a central committee including Daniel, Nicholas, and Ritchie. Daniel's job involved both organizational activities and writing. He prepared the formal statements of the central committee, and he filled the Democratic press with his letters. This was no casual operation — as the campaign progressed it came close to being a full-time job. Thus within one week at the height of the campaign he published five letters. He was variously "The People," a "Whig of 1798 and 1800," "Justice," and "Plebian." He hit repeatedly at the Whigs' want of a single candidate. Their strategy was derided as a new form of "divide and conquer," since the Whigs instead of dividing their opposition had divided themselves. The dubious procedure of putting up a number of candidates no one of whom could hope to get a majority offered many lines of attack, and the Democrats took advantage of all of them.

The central committee worked diligently, and November brought victory. Martin Van Buren was elected President of the United States, carrying Virginia by a margin of 5000. One month later the legislature met and elected a good Democrat as governor.

But the new governor was not Daniel. He had gone out of the running six months before, and, indeed, had done his final work in the campaign not as Council member Daniel but as Federal District Judge Daniel. Jackson had made the predicted appointment. John Marshall, who had died, was replaced as Chief Justice by Roger B. Taney. There was thus no judge from Virginia on the Supreme Court, and the vacant associate justiceship was given to Philip P. Barbour. In March 1836 Andrew Jackson appointed Peter V. Daniel Federal district judge for the eastern district of Virginia. Despite the best efforts of Daniel Webster, Barbour was confirmed for the Supreme Court and shortly thereafter Daniel was confirmed for the district court.

On April 25 Daniel resigned from the Council, ending twenty-four years — with a one-year hiatus — in state office.[21] His public life was thus divided sharply in half, for he was beginning a twenty-four-year career as a Federal judge. On May 2 he left Richmond on the steamboat *Patrick Henry* to conduct his first admiralty court at Norfolk, and on May 23 the Federal court sat for the first time at Richmond with Daniel as judge.[22] On that day one Hawkins was indicted on a charge of robbing the mail. Daniel had begun his judicial career.

Chapter VIII

DISTRICT JUDGE

DANIEL'S APPOINTMENT to the district court came only after a last-minute fight, remarkably enough a fight within the Junto itself. From 1834 to 1836 the relationship between Daniel and Ritchie, the dominant personality in the group, gradually deteriorated. Daniel had stood resolutely with Jackson and Van Buren during those two difficult years while the worried Ritchie had wobbled. Now ensued events which further divided the two neighbors of Grace Street.

As the prospect of a district court vacancy loomed, state Judge Richard E. Parker, Ritchie's brother-in-law, determined to go after the job. This meant both winning support for himself and pushing Daniel out of the way. One of his devices aimed at Daniel's elimination was a letter to Van Buren which, in the tone of great admiration, stressed the necessity, for the party welfare, of Daniel's becoming governor.[1] Then at the last minute, in March 1836, when the appointment seemed imminent, a number of strong Parker recommendations were sent to Jackson.

The office, which had seemed so assuredly Daniel's, now began to slip away. As soon as indignation had cooled sufficiently to permit action, Daniel's friends put in a frantic day or two in his behalf. A widely circulated petition was skillfully worded to support Daniel and at the same time give no offense; it stressed that "no man could be more acceptable to the whole state than Mr. Daniel." [2] Among the signers was former President James Madison.

There can be no doubt that Daniel had a managing hand in the project of obtaining support, though amenity required that his role be covert. The basic job in his behalf had to be done by someone else, and the task fell to his very close friend Charles S. Morgan. In writing to Jackson Morgan stressed Daniel's loyalty: when Jacksonianism was defeated in Virginia Daniel went down with it, into proscription and retirement. Moreover, Morgan noted, he was the choice of the people. A petition signed by sixteen Democratic state senators and fifty-seven members of the House of Delegates in behalf of Daniel included every Democrat in the legislature actually available in Richmond except two. Mrs. Morgan, in a naïve — or perhaps clever — personal note to President Jackson, even tossed Lucy into the scale. "Mrs. Daniel has ever been, as her husband, your tried friend. In advocating your cause, she has ever pursued a firm and decided course, notwithstanding she is surrounded by your enemies. In her estimation there is none like General Jackson . . . Mrs. Daniel is the daughter of the distinguished Edmund Randolph, and let me assure you, does not form opinions from those around her, but is influenced by her own reason and judgment." [3]

In addition to this petticoat warfare Daniel's friends thought it necessary to convince the President that this time Daniel would actually accept an appointment if offered. A mutual friend sent an authorized note to that effect to the President.[4] Finally, it was necessary to throw a few sticks in the path of Judge Parker. Jackson was told that if Parker were appointed, the governor would appoint a strong anti-Jackson man to his state court vacancy; that Parker already had in the district judgeship an office of approximately the same prestige and pay and could only desire the Federal court job because it meant less work; and finally that it would be bad for the Democrats to put another member of the Ritchie family into office.[5]

For whatever combination of reasons, Jackson chose Daniel. Since the state courts were then in session, Daniel had to transfer to other lawyers all his business on hand, an activity sometimes interspersed with pauses to savor the joys of his promotion.[6] He had a robe made for himself. It stood for a time in the tailor's window, exciting the pleasant comments of his friends and the jibes of his critics.[7] Since Richmond was a Whig town and the Whigs hated him thoroughly, he had comparatively few personal friends with whom to share his pleasure. He doubted the sincerity of the few congratulatory words from Whig sources — which were few.[8]

The transfer to the bench did not mean a transfer out of politics. It did not even totally cut him off from his old Council duties. Just as Chief Justice Taney continued to be a principal adviser of President Jackson, so Daniel occasionally acted in an advisory capacity for Virginia's governor. More than a year after his judicial appointment, he gave the governor an informal but written advisory opinion on a point of interpretation of the state constitution.[9]

In the Federal court structure of the time, a Federal district judge had two different sets of duties because he sat as a member of two different courts, the district and circuit courts. The district court heard the admiralty (shipping) cases and the suits by the United States for forfeitures and penalties. It also had minor criminal jurisdiction. The circuit court had jurisdiction over the general run of law suits in Federal courts, at that time largely suits between persons of different states, and the more important criminal business. In some matters there could be an appeal from the district court to the circuit court.

Daniel was the only judge in the district court. In the circuit court he was one of two judges, the other being the Supreme Court Justice for the area which included Virginia, Philip P. Barbour. If for any reason Barbour did not appear for a circuit court session, Daniel became the sole judge of that court. It was an odd system, for insofar as it permitted appeals from the district court to the circuit court it permitted appeals from Daniel to Daniel, and insofar as it permitted appeals from the circuit court to the Supreme Court, it permitted appeals from, among others, Barbour to Barbour. It was nonetheless a well-established system which was to exist until long after Daniel's death.

Barbour, with whom Daniel now had regular contact, was a man very like Daniel himself. This was the same Barbour who had been the anti–Van Buren nominee for the vice presidency in 1832. He was a brother of the Governor Barbour with whom Daniel had served on the Council during the War of 1812.[10] The Justice was a very strict states' rights Democrat whose principal earlier political position had been as Speaker of the House of Representatives. He was a man of engaging personal qualities, given to close reasoning and classical quotation. His relations with Daniel raised no difficulties.

The office of Federal district judge for the eastern district of Virginia was a post of more honor than labor, and little financial reward. Daniel himself estimated that the office left him with almost ninety percent of his time free.[11] The May and November terms of the district court, which sat in Richmond and in Norfolk, ran no more than a week each. Since eastern Virginia was falling farther and farther behind the rest of the country commercially, there was very little substantial commercial business for the circuit court. The law practice here was leisurely, the number of items of business disposed of in a court day was small, and the attorneys were a little group who appeared regularly. The United States attorney was, inevitably enough, one of the Nicholas clan, and received his very limited compensation strictly on a fee basis.

Daniel's work as a district court judge is not of any intrinsic significance to the twentieth century. A reader would be bored beyond tedium if asked to consider all the items of evidence which go into that judgment, and yet may have a moment's curiosity as to how a Federal district judge was occupied in a basically agricultural center in the first part of the nineteenth century. The total number of all of the cases handled in the district court at the Richmond sessions during Daniel's five years of service was under fifty.[12] These can be divided into four categories. First there were the admiralty cases, of which there were fewer than a half dozen. These involved very small boats used in the coastal and river trade. In one, for example, the value of the whole ship was less than $400.[13] Criminal cases form the second category. These were almost nonexistent in this court. A third category includes cases of forfeiture of goods imported in violation of the tariff rules. The most substantial of these items was a bale of broadcloth valued at more than $600 brought in by a captain who attempted to delude the revenue officers into thinking that the cloth was domestic.[14] The fourth category, encompassing by far the largest number of cases before the court, consists of the suits by the United States not to forfeit goods but to recover penalties or damages either for violation of the tariff act or for failure to perform a duty under some other statute.

Sometimes these last two categories merged in one suit. For example, one Koster was accused of smuggling five half pipes of brandy. A forfeiture action was brought against the brandy and a penalty action was brought against Koster. On the first trial the jury was unable to agree, but in a second action it found for Koster.[15] The case against him and against the brandy was thereupon dismissed, leaving poor United States Attorney Nicholas in a dubious position as to his fee. If he lost such a case, he could be paid only if the district judge would certify that it had been reasonable to bring charges in the first place. This Daniel dutifully did, and Nicholas collected $100.[16]

There was much post-office litigation. The 1830's were a sorry time for the postal service, in which Jackson had found a great many jobs for the faithful when distributing the spoils. There had been a major turnover of personnel, and the appointment of Barry, an incompetent, as postmaster general, contributed nothing to stability. Moreover, in this prerailroad era small contractors rather than government employees distributed and transported most of the mail. The result disgraced both public and private enterprise, and became a national scandal. The inept accounting in Washington invited embezzlement in the local offices, and the individual contractors were far in arrears in their duties and payments. After congressional investigations, of which the Whigs made at least as much capital as the situation warranted, the government cracked down and sued for some of its losses.[17]

Many of these suits, usually for trifling sums, came before Daniel. An example is a case against Messrs. Turner and Flint, who as bondsmen had guaranteed the account of a Richmond postmaster who had died without rendering any accounting at all for several months of his service.[18] These gentlemen attempted most ingeniously to slip through a seeming loophole in the statutes which provided that if any postmaster failed to render his accounts "for one month after the time . . . prescribed by law" he should have to make up the delinquency and in addition pay the amount of the postage for "any equal portion of time previous or subsequent thereto." The defendants took the position that this meant double *one month's* postage which, if the statute had contained no more than the passages just quoted, might have been correct. However, a preceding section showed fairly clearly that the phrase "any equal portion of time" did not refer to the one-month period but rather to a *three-month* period. For the postmasters were required to make their payments at the end of each three-month interval, and the one month was merely an additional period of grace within which to close the three-month accounts.

These details are worth a moment's notice because of the light they cast on the manner in which Daniel did his job. The point of law is minor and not very difficult; nonetheless Daniel dealt with it meticulously. He did not overwrite the subject, nor attempt to make a great case out of a little one; but he did exhaust the topic. By verbal analysis and logic he showed that a postmaster was supposed to settle his accounts at the end of each three-month period, that he had one additional month of grace, and that thereafter was liable for double the three months' postage. Several motions for new trial, which required the analysis and distinction of cited cases, were carefully handled, and Daniel concluded, "the court being satisfied that the defendants have in no instance whatever been wronged or oppressed — and inclining to the opinion that they have escaped a portion of their just liability — is constrained to overrule and doth overrule their motion."

The disputes in this district court involved sums so small that the aggregate of the claims would not have equaled Daniel's salary. At the two 1838 terms in Richmond a total of eleven cases were decided. In one the defendant prevailed. The penalties in eight others totaled $565. One other case involved $670, and one admiralty case concerned a small boat worth $400.

Daniel's circuit court work, though not heavy, was more substantial. In 1838, for example, the circuit court had sixteen cases.[19] Almost without exception, these were cases in which a Virginia purchaser was sued for payment either by a northern merchant or by a bank to which a northern merchant had passed the Virginian's promissory note. The disputes involved amounts of from $500 to $3500, with the average being about $1000. Procedure in these matters was simple and informal. The pleadings were written out by hand and the judges, when required, added their handwritten opinions to the records of the cases. Normally Barbour and Daniel tried the cases together, without dispute. There is nothing about these cases which indicates on the part of Daniel any novelty of view on points of law. It is noteworthy, for example, that although he developed, when on the Supreme Court, the doctrine that corporations should not be allowed to sue or be sued in Federal courts, as a circuit court judge he heard such cases without question. At trial he followed the precedents. On the Supreme Court he was free to try to make new ones.

In sum, a Federal district judge in the eastern district of Virginia in the late 1830's was in a position of honor and utility in the community, the utility lying in the disposition of a small number of small matters which nonetheless had to be settled. The records of the circuit court are not sufficiently available to be sure that in the entire five-year period of his judgeship Daniel had no momentous cases, but the strong probability is that he did not. What emerges, though faintly, is a picture of a judge both careful and fair who was developing experience and confidence as a trial judge and who was gaining an insight into commercial affairs and into the ways of the Federal court.

At the same time, these were most unhappy years for Daniel. His judicial salary of $1800 a year was wholly inadequate for his support. His normal income prior to this appointment must have been approximately double that figure. Moreover revenue from the farm undoubtedly fell materially with the depression of 1837. He had accepted the position with the confident hope that its pay would be increased, and he was intently concerned with the prospect of such legislation during much of his district court service.

Peter and Lucy practiced strict economy, but they had scarcely been living lavishly even before he took the new position, and economy very rapidly approached hardship. Within the first year of his judicial service Daniel gave up his carriage and even his riding horse.[20] True, Richmond was a small town and he could get about by foot, but in addition to making his situation embarrassingly evident, the new transportation arrangement made it awkward to get to the farm. With three children to educate, and with a white house servant costing $150 a year in pay, the Daniels began to run into debt at a rate of about $700 a year.[21]

In these circumstances, Daniel began to think seriously of returning to his law practice. His practice had never been rich, but the approaching end of the careers of three of the lawyers of the city gave him new prospects,[22] and his irritation at withdrawing from social life for reasons of economy was some incentive to give up the judicial position.

In this period the salaries of the various Federal district judges were not uniform but varied from district to district. They were set by special legislation and were determined by the amount of work thought to be involved. Senator Rives proposed an increase for Daniel's district, and the House Judiciary Committee reported a bill in 1838 to raise the salaries in seven districts to amounts ranging from $1500 for New Hampshire to $3000 for the eastern district of Pennsylvania. The salary in Daniel's district was to be set at $2500.[23]

Daniel kept the mails full pushing this legislation. He sent several letters to President Van Buren encouraging him to support the bill, and he kept in close touch with Rives. He blasted the whole system of paying judges "like day laborers by the quantum rather than for the quality of what they are to perform," which he said was "grossly absurd." [24] He puffed the amount of his labors a little to Rives, claiming that he was on the bench for ten weeks out of the year and was subject to call in his chambers for various orders at other times; [25] and in a burst of a vainglory he told Van Buren about the fine income he would have were he to return to his practice and about the more lucrative positions he might have taken if he had not accepted the district judgeship on the assumption that it was to be put upon a proper salary.[26]

At the same time, Daniel did not truckle. His relations with Rives in particular were typical of his unyielding integrity. He was almost desperately dependent on Rives to get the legislation through. Yet he chose to make it absolutely clear that in the current dispute within the Democratic party he stood with Van Buren on the opposite side of the fence from Rives. In the very midst of their correspondence on the salary question, Daniel wrote his senator, "I must say to you in candor, that our views of these evils [division in the party] or of the origins of them, rather, differ most essentially . . . It appears to me that the positions assumed and enforced by the President's message are the true, the *old fashioned* (if the phrase may be allowed), the safe Republican doctrines; the only doctrines, indeed, which can either render or continue us as a free, prosperous, virtuous, and happy people." [27] Daniel was in no wise discourteous to Rives; he conceded that the senator's views had been formed fairly after full deliberation. But in none of the salary correspondence did he pretend that their positions were anything other than diametrically opposed. His record in that respect is a good — and a typical Daniel — record.

The salary legislation did not pass. Senator Prentiss of Vermont fought and defeated the bill on the ground that the increases would put the Federal salaries ahead of state court salaries and would thus drain off the best state judges into the Federal system.[28] His argument apparently persuaded his fellow senators and Daniel thus lost his increase as a result of a states' right argument that could scarcely have appealed even to him. Similar legislation was brought forth again and again during Daniel's term, but nothing ever came of it. Perhaps kept on by continuing hope, he did nothing about his threats to resign.

Chapter IX

THE SUPREME COURT APPOINTMENT

PRE-CIVIL WAR judicial ethics did not exclude judges, even Federal judges, from local politics. The great Marshall himself set the pattern for Virginia by being first a conspicuous Federalist and then a conspicuous Whig, freely participating in political conventions. After one state convention the Richmond *Whig* attacked the presence of the judges at the Democratic meeting, not on the ground of their being judges, but rather on the ground that they were bad judges without qualifications for their judicial offices.[1]

Hence nothing in the nature of his position barred Daniel from a political life, and the new leisure of his unexacting position gave him even more time than before for such activities. He campaigned for Van Buren in the election of 1836 and remained an active supporter during the severe political difficulties which beset the new administration. As Van Buren's banking problems intensified with the depression of 1837, he upheld the President incessantly with newspaper letters.

The honeymoon period of the Van Buren administration lasted approximately one month. About three weeks after the inauguration the Democracy of Richmond and the state legislature held a victory party at the Eagle Tavern. The 110 Democrats present heard a two-hour speech by Senator Rives, the guest of honor.[2] Daniel, one of the presiding officers at the affair, had the pleasure of hearing himself toasted: "Peter V. Daniel — the firm and able advocate of Republican prin-

ciples — the faithful and impartial arbiter of the judiciary."
Within thirty days rifts were so deep that such a gathering
could not have been duplicated during Van Buren's administration.

Daniel's last major campaign role came in Van Buren's
fight for re-election in 1840, when there were more conventions than there were terms of court. As a proxy member for
an absent legislator he attended the state legislative caucus
for the last time. He was on the main committee on organization and was a member of the committee to prepare the party
platform. There followed the usual labors of party work, the
encouragement of county organization, the distribution of
literature. The central committee presented its cause as one
of adherence to the principles of Jefferson, Madison, and John
Taylor of Caroline, and Daniel supported the committee with
another series of political letters.[3]

The campaign was in no way a replica of that of 1836.
Henry Clay, with his great political perception, realized that
his party would always be in the minority unless it could, to
the necessary extent, take both men and measures from the
Democrats. Within six years in Virginia the Whigs had acquired two strong Democratic leaders, both United States
senators, Leigh and Rives. In 1840 they set about to acquire
the Democratic technique as well, and nominated General
William Henry Harrison, who could be presented to the
voters as a real man of the people. Using their press and their
orators to turn Van Buren into a dandy gorging himself on
gold plate in the White House while the people hungered,
the Whigs presented their candidate as the man of no very
obvious principles but of great homespun integrity. All the
class prejudice against aristocracy which the Democrats commonly used against the Whigs was now used against the
Democrats in the famous log cabin and hard cider campaign.
To the earnest Daniels of the Democracy the Whig refusal to

debate issues was utterly infuriating. The task of the Virginia Democrats was made all the harder by the Whig nomination of John Tyler of Virginia for the vice presidency. The central committee was left with the general charge that Harrison was both a federalist and an abolitionist, and with the bare assertion that the depression was the fault of the Bank of the United States.[4]

Daniel's political activities were usually hard work but could be a social pleasure. A regional gathering in Hanover County was a veritable orgy. Daniel accepted his invitation in print, his response reflecting his fervor. Of course, he said, he would be present to do his bit in this struggle by the Democratic party in behalf of political and moral integrity, the rights of men, and prosperity against the danger of extremist abuses of Federal usurpation and abolitionist fanaticism. He broadly hinted that a Harrison victory would lead to a slave insurrection and the murder of women and children.[5] Daniel was showing that he too could steal enemy tactics, forgetting, perhaps, that in 1836 he had thought the Whigs wicked to raise the abolitionist scare.

The Hanover meeting was a robust affair of belligerent speeches and *one hundred* toasts at dinner. The delegates went home with a good feeling toward each other, their cause, and their tavernkeeper, rightly toasted as "a most comfortable provider." Daniel's own toast was a maudlin offering to good old Hanover County: "She will be neither hoaxed, coaxed nor fuddled into an abandonment of her Democratic integrity." He himself was hailed as the "firm, bold and fearless champion of the rights of the states and the sovereignty of the people."[6]

The Hanover convention, for all its jollity, was only a local spirit raiser. The big affair was the Democratic state convention at Charlottesville in September 1840, where Daniel presided over 500 delegates. The party platform there adopted represents the essence of Daniel's political thought at the time that he stood on the threshold of his final office.[7] From the many thousands of words emerge these central principles which Daniel carried with him to the Supreme Court:

1) The old Federalist party opposed liberty. Its major work was the Alien and Sedition Acts. The Virginia and Kentucky Resolutions were still "the best commentary upon the constitution and the ablest defense of our reserved rights."

2) The Bank of the United States was the "master heresy of federalism," from which the people had been saved only by the "heroic chieftain," Andrew Jackson.

3) "We believe, that the constitution is a compact between the States, and that the Federal government is invested with those powers only which are given to it in expressed terms."

4) "We believe, that no money should be levied from the people, which is not required for the legitimate purposes of revenue."

5) "We are utterly opposed to . . . a national bank, extravagant schemes of internal improvement by the general government, and an oppressive tariff for protection." All three violate the principle of strict construction of the constitution.

Although the Charlottesville convention presented its argument as an appeal to reason, both the Democrats and the Whigs promptly abandoned that elevated goal. It is doubtful if a less inspiring experience than the 1840 campaign is to be found in the history of the county. The Whigs, carefully avoiding any issues, organized a great parade in Richmond in which a log cabin was drawn by six mules and many speeches were made, not one of which mentioned the bank, the tariff, or internal improvements. The Democrats of Richmond decried this as a shabby substitution of an appeal to passion for an appeal to reason, and at the same time the *Enquirer* edified its readers with the charge that General Harrison had become

insane and was wandering about the countryside like a blub-
bering child.[8]

When the last epithet was in, William Henry Harrison
was President of the United States. He had not, however,
carried Virginia. Though Richmond went heavily for Harrison, Van Buren had a 1500 statewide lead in a total vote of
35,000. The Democratic party in Virginia had suffered the
loss of some of its most prominent figures, but even with a
Virginian on the other ticket and depression still in the air,
the party had nonetheless prevailed at home.

In the period between the election and the inauguration
the Supreme Court was tending to its usual business in Washington. Justice Barbour of Virginia had a little indisposition
early in February which kept him in his room for two weeks,
but his fellow Justices helped him while away the time, and
on the evening of February 24 he was back at his duties, attending a meeting until 10:00 o'clock. He died in his sleep
that night.[9]

Thus as of the morning of February 25, 1841, there was
a Supreme Court vacancy. Van Buren was to be President for
nine days more and Congress was in session. Van Buren had
a strong desire not only to fill the vacancy, but to fill it in a
fashion that would give the Whigs a maximum amount of
trouble. There was no time for correspondence or lengthy
consideration, for every day's delay increased the possibility
that the Whigs might defeat a nomination by preventing a
vote until mandatory adjournment on March 4. Van Buren
quickly canvassed the possibilities, and on the twenty-seventh,
two days after Barbour's death and a week before the end of
his term, he appointed Peter V. Daniel as a Justice of the
Supreme Court of the United States.

This was an almost indecent speed, with Daniel appointed
before Barbour could be buried. The Democrats in Virginia
were as surprised as anyone else. Recommendations from

that state had not even been drawn up before the vacancy was filled. Moreover Daniel would not have been their unanimous choice. Still ignorant of the appointment, Dr. Brockenbrough, for example, recommended Henry St. George Tucker of the Virginia supreme court of appeals as the Democrat who would be most satisfactory in the position,[10] and the Democrats in the legislature recommended state judge John Y. Mason, who only two months before had been defeated by Rives for the Senate seat.[11]

The Whig reaction was one of unlimited fury. The fair rewards of office were slipping out of their hands, and that the recipient was one of their extremest adversaries made them no happier. The Richmond *Whig*, whose hatred for Daniel could be matched only by his for it, declared that not one human being in Richmond except for Daniel's few friends approved of the nomination, and it described as an act of "naked indecency" the appointment of anyone "to fill the seat just warm with the person of the deceased." [12] This was scarcely honest piety, as the same editorial showed; its solution would have been to leave the seat open for a few days, until General Harrison took office. Democrats on the other hand were delighted. They were confident that Daniel had the necessary ability, and were more than confident that his tough-minded adherence to Democratic principles would be an asset in the administration to come.

The Whigs were not without experience in such a situation, and their leaders in Congress quickly lit upon a scheme. The Democrats had enough votes to confirm Daniel's appointment if they held together, but they would have only until March 4. If a rift could be created in the party that majority could be broken.

A device to this end was ready at hand. It will be recalled that at this period of our judicial history each Supreme Court Justice had trial as well as appellate duties. Each had a circuit for which he was responsible. Barbour's, to which Daniel would succeed, was the fourth or Virginia and North Carolina circuit. Judges were appointed normally from the circuit over which they would preside. If the circuit itself could somehow be broken up, there might no longer be a Virginia vacancy. The Whigs whereupon promptly lined up in support of a bill to abolish the fourth circuit, putting Virginia in the circuit to the north and North Carolina in the circuit to the south, and creating a new western circuit in its place.[13] If the western Democratic senators and representatives should rise to this bait, Daniel would automatically be undone.

The decision to take this course was made by the Whigs immediately upon the appointment. Senator Smith of Indiana, a Whig, sanctimoniously observed that Providence had now permitted a long overdue adjustment of the circuits of the country in recognition of the actualities of the judicial business, and thereupon announced the new proposal.[14] Happily for Daniel, the Junto's influence was widespread, and the senior senator from Virginia, William Roane, was an old intimate associate. Roane was probably genuinely staggered by the surprise which he professed at this sudden proposal to abolish his home circuit. In his protest he spoke of the venerable nature of the circuit, of the long association of the two states. He stressed that it was the circuit of John Marshall himself which some now proposed to abolish.

The essential weaknesses of Roane's position were that the fourth circuit did not have much business, and that there should have been a new western circuit. These facts were clear, and the Whig sponsor of the bill made the most of them, twitting Roane on his greed for a judicial seat at the expense of the public interest. Roane retorted that the comparative unbalance of the judicial business was temporary, connected with the depression, and gravely assured the Senate that no considerations of office affected his judgment on the question. He good-naturedly asked whether the Whigs could make an equally sincere disclaimer.

Missouri's Thomas Hart Benton, the leading Democrat on the floor, opposed the change as unfair to the East and inadequate for the West. He proposed increasing the size of the Supreme Court to twelve, giving all three of the new circuits to the West; he directly challenged Whig sincerity, asserting that if the measure were passed they would probably repeal it as soon as Harrison was in office. Benton was answered by another good Democrat, James Buchanan of Pennsylvania. Buchanan met Benton and Roane head on, asserting that a circuit that had outlived its usefulness should not be maintained for sentimental reasons, and that nine justices were enough if not too many for the Supreme Court. He was sure that Chief Justice Taney could easily add Virginia to his small circuit, and that Associate Justice Wayne of Georgia could as easily add North Carolina to his.

It was left to Senator Rives to close the debate. Rives's choice was not easy. He could only hope to defeat Daniel by sacrificing the interests of Virginia. But the desire to defeat Daniel was greater than the desire to keep a Virginia seat on the Supreme Court, and so, taking high ground and asserting that he stood by the national interest, Rives supported the measure. It thereupon passed by the heavy vote of 34 to 13. The Whigs had successfully split the Democrats.

Whether the Whigs ever seriously expected this measure to become law is doubtful. It was freely noted on the floor that passage at this session was almost impossible. The measure passed the Senate on the twenty-seventh and the twenty-eighth was Sunday. There were thus at most only four days to pass the bill in the House, where Democratic discipline was stronger than in the Senate. But to the wily Whigs, the actual passage of the bill was of no great consequence. So long as there was a *prospect* of its passage, the vote on Daniel might be delayed until it was too late.

Hence on March first no relevant action was taken in the Senate. Finally late in the day of the second it became apparent that the prospects of the legislation in the House were hopeless, and Daniel's appointment was called up.[15] It was moved that the nomination be tabled, and two or three senators argued that the House might yet pass the Redistricting Act. The western senators were torn between their regional and their party allegiances; most of them concluded that it was Daniel or nothing, since their bill would in any case not pass. The critical motion to lay the nomination on the table lost by a vote of 21 to 25. A motion to refer the nomination to the Judiciary Committee lost by a similar margin. Whig strategy turned to delay. This was before the day of the filibuster, or Daniel would undoubtedly have been defeated. But there were delaying tactics, and Henry Clay, the Whig leader, knew them all. The gentleman from Kentucky started to fight and his supporters made speeches against Daniel running on into the evening.

The first opponent was Senator Southard of New Jersey. Southard had known Daniel since his Princeton days and considered him wholly unqualified for the Supreme Court. He made a great show of his personal friendship for Daniel, at the same time denouncing him as a political partisan unduly active in the recent election and as one who had been "pursuing these controversies to blood."

Roane at once took the floor in Daniel's behalf and indignantly inquired what Southard had meant by his allusion to blood. According to Roane, Daniel was a man of the purest character and he added, in a burst of enthusiasm which may have twinged his conscience, that there was "no man more free from any vindictive feelings than Daniel." Southard, who obviously did not know of Daniel's one duel, quickly withdrew his assertion saying that it had been made in the heat of debate and all he meant to denounce was Daniel's partisanship.

This debate, including two roll calls, had dissipated much time, and finally in the evening Senator Clay himself took the floor to ask that action be postponed, particularly since Senator Rives had been compelled to leave. When Clay's proposal was rejected, he looked about the Senate floor and, seeing how little filled it was, ostentatiously picked up his hat and said to the presiding officer, "I bid you goodnight." As the Democrats contemptuously echoed, "Goodnight," all of Clay's well-disciplined crew marched out behind him, except for two Whig senators who, obviously operating under a prearranged plan, walked off the floor and around to a point behind the chair of the Vice President.

The retirement of Clay and his followers broke the quorum and made it impossible for the Senate to proceed. If only Democrats had been left, no one would have pointed this out. But the two Whig Senators were present to enforce the rules, and the Democrats had no immediate recourse but rage. One of them angrily denounced the Clay tactics as dastardly, treacherous, and faithless to the public duty. This outburst may have relieved his disposition, but it scarcely furthered the cause. Senator Benton determined that if he could not confirm Daniel, he could at least embarrass the Whigs. In that era appointments were considered in closed sessions of the Senate. Benton moved that the Senate abandon that rule for the moment and let the people see that the Whigs had stopped the public business of the country by running out on it. Putting his considerable bulk into a chair, he proclaimed that he would sit there until the absent members returned, and that the morning sun would reveal to the world the sorry straits to which the Whigs had reduced the government of the United States.

This was magnificent drama, but it did not help Daniel,

and in any case Benton's proposal to change the rules could not itself be acted on in the absence of a quorum. Senator Silas Wright of New York, Van Buren's floor leader in the Senate, made the better suggestion that the Senate interrupt its business long enough to round up the absent Democratic members who were still in the city and who if present would make a quorum. And so the Senate stood in interrupted session while the homes and, doubtless, the taverns of the city were quickly combed for absentees. By approximately 11:00 o'clock at night on the second, twenty-seven Senators had been rounded up. This was exactly the number necessary for a quorum. Twenty-six were Democrats, and one was the Whig Senator Smith of Indiana. The other Whig left behind had disappeared. Smith faced a terrible dilemma. If he left, there would be no quorum, but there would be no Whig left on the floor to make the point and hence its absence would not be legally noticed. If he stayed he would serve to make up the quorum. The rules of parliamentary procedure had never worked with a more superb irony. Smith made his choice and stayed. If he could not defeat Daniel, he could at least have the pleasure of voting against him. A vote was quickly taken, and by a vote of 22 to 5 Daniel was confirmed. The five included Smith and four Democrats who, though they were against Daniel, were not enough against him to block confirmation by breaking the quorum.

Thus, shortly before midnight on March 2, 1841, Peter V. Daniel became an Associate Justice of the Supreme Court of the United States. As might be expected, the Whigs writhed,[16] and the Democrats took comfort.

Ten days later Martin Van Buren, by then a week out of office, reported on the close of his administration to his great predecessor, Andrew Jackson. "I had an opportunity," said the Little Magician to Old Hickory, "to put a man on the bench of the Supreme Court at the moment of leaving the government who will I am sure stick to the true principles of the constitution, and being a Democrat *ab ovo* is not in so much danger of a falling off in the true spirit. The Federalists have railed about the selection of our old friend Daniel of Va., but that did not distress me as much as some supposed it would do." Replied Jackson, "I glory in the firmness of the pure Democrats in the Senate in defeating this wicked and unprincipled attempt of this vile and wicked demagogue" (Clay), who had made so unscrupulous an attempt to defeat "that pure Republican, Mr. Daniel." [17]

The appointment of Daniel to the Court presents the perfect example in politics of the clash between the immovable object and the irresistible force. The most conspicuous quality of the new Justice was firmness in resistance to change — bullheaded intransigence, if one wishes to be uncharitable about it. Yet change was the most conspicuous quality of the country he was chosen to serve.

Daniel in 1841 was an embodiment of the Virginia and Kentucky Resolutions of 1798, of a spirit of earliest vintage Jeffersonianism, of the philosophy of John Taylor. To Daniel the economy of eighteenth century Stafford County or of pre-1812 Richmond represented the highest possible economic order. Resistance to the Bank of the United States had been for him the simplest kind of act of faith because he was opposed to all banks, and all the more to a federal one. Indeed, in his view, the entire form of corporate business enterprise was subject to sharpest suspicion, and a class of merchants of greater substance than a grocer or a haberdasher was of distinctly marginal economic utility.

The point of view Daniel brought to Washington was a sort of high-church agrarianism. It was with great pride that he chose to sign one of his letters to the editor "an old fashioned man." He saw the country as being utterly subverted by the influence of corporations which were a menace to the intelligence, morality, and sturdy independence of a people who would somehow drive back this threat. He feared the great corporate monopolies, spreading like a plague throughout the country, with the banks as the most vicious among them. He saw as a great menace what he described as the "mercantile community in New York," a class which he felt thoroughly deserved "the strictures of the celebrated Adam Smith." [18]

To Daniel, the rise of great cities in itself threatened sound morals and sound political principles. He rejoiced that his own Virginia was not caught up in the expansion of the times; it never occurred to him that perhaps the nineteenth century was passing Richmond by. In his own state, happily, the towns were still small; "We are yet an essential agricultural people, still jealous of mercantile and corporation power, and therefore nothing would sooner put in peril the popularity of any man with the body of our people, than to convince them that he is the partisan or the creator of that power." [19]

He believed that the Federal government existed to protect the people against enemies foreign and domestic. Even the state government he thought should be largely limited to maintenance of the status quo. For Daniel was not merely a Virginian but a tidewater Virginian and was prepared to make no concessions to the spirit of rebellion within his own state.

In Daniel's time the United States was truly "busting out all over." In no period of its history was the country to grow so fast as in the almost two decades of Daniel's Court membership. The national population in 1840 was seventeen million. By 1860 it had reached thirty-one and one half million, increasing at the rate of 35 percent per decade. Florida and what remained of the Midwest — Wisconsin, Minnesota, Iowa — came into the Union during this period. The Mexican War resulted in the addition of more than a third of the continental United States. When Daniel took office, gold had not yet been discovered at Sutter's Creek, and Fremont and Kearny had not yet headed for the west coast. Yet within ten years of his oath of office California was a state, and within another ten Oregon joined.

The expansion was far more than geographical. In 1841 the railroad had but shortly before been introduced. By the time Daniel died, it fairly covered eastern United States and within another ten years it would reach the west coast. In 1841 the telegraph had not yet been invented. By the time of Daniel's death it reached everywhere.

The spirit of change was even more dramatic than a shift of space and things. Ideas were everywhere on the march in this greatly fertile era in the intellectual life of the United States. The years around 1841 saw the beginning of such movements as abolition, women's rights, social reform, communal life, labor unionism and widespread public education. By 1860 these ideas were common enough, and all on their way to various degrees of real acceptance.

These were days of infinite hope and infinite potential, and yet also days of sadness and despair. The rise of manufacturing in the 1840's and 1850's brought hideous slums, and the migration of an immense and oppressed people from Ireland gave the northern cities their first experience with what appeared to be an indigestible minority. The coming of the Irish and of the Germans, who were more easily assimilated, affected the cities primarily, but the rural areas as well.

Of all the intellectual changes to come between 1841 and 1860, the most important was the rise of abolitionism. What appeared to be still a crackpot eccentricity when Daniel took office was in ten years to become a major political force in the United States. Its effect on Daniel's own intellectual life was to make even more rigid an outlook which had no flexibility to start with. Daniel took office in 1841 as an exemplar of nationalism within the Democratic party, the southern anchor of an Albany-Richmond axis. Within ten years, under the impact of abolitionism, his entire intellectual orientation was to turn south, and his passionate extremism made him one of the earliest and most willing secessionists. By 1851 he could blame even the weather on the wickedness of the North. When the wind was cold, he said, "Ah! That vile north. It infects and spoils even the very atmosphere we breathe." [20]

Daniel's firm set of social values and political principles was coupled with a realization that his Supreme Court seat gave him the power to do something to carry his principles into effect. As he saw it, the permanence and stability of the court enabled that body to give direction to the whole government. Hence he saw each day's work, each new case, as a vital opportunity to spread the sound principles of old Virginia. [21]

Van Buren had described Daniel at the moment of his appointment as a "Democrat from the egg." This indeed he was. He thought of the Whigs as the "federal corporation party." [22] Months after his appointment, when he perceived the spread of banks and corporations to every hamlet, he still hoped that they might be weeded out of society altogether. [23] To the end of his life Daniel subscribed to the early attitude of Thomas Jefferson that the best result for the country would be the total suppression of banks. [24]

To meet the evils of his age, Daniel relied upon what he proudly conceived of as the "old Democratic doctrine." As he saw it, government was created for the "protection of life, property, and reputation," and, except for the national defense, for no other purpose. [25] While he had learned to swallow Van Buren's protectionist views, he never learned to like them or to accept them as constitutionally valid: "My own notion is, and ever has been, that in strict political justice government has no right to discriminate between the pursuits of private enterprise." [26] Since a protective tariff necessarily aided selected industries, it was a discrimination and hence unconstitutional.

This principle applied also to the enjoyment of privileges in the territories of the United States. Congress, he contended, had no constitutional power whatsoever to restrict slaves in the territories, and the Missouri Compromise which attempted to do so was wholly unconstitutional and void. In Daniel's view, Congress had no power to "deprive one person of the United States or of the citizens of the United States, of that which belongs to the United States collectively, and as a whole, and is arbitrarily bestowed upon another and favored portion of the union, or of the citizens of the union." Indeed he regarded even the suggestion of such a possibility as a plain outrage.[27]

If the Daniel who came to Washington in 1841 had been an agrarian philosopher of gentle and contemplative manner, he might have viewed the passing scene with some sorrow, done his best to resist the course of events, and resigned himself to facts. But Daniel brought with him all the ferocity with which he had enlivened the endless disputes at home. Neither the passage of time nor the elevation to high office calmed Daniel's political hostilities. In 1847 he found in a Mississippi newspaper that the Whigs in Richmond had given a party for Daniel Webster. He boiled at a distance of eight hundred miles as he wrote his daughter that he had heard of the affair for this "most depraved and immoral creature." It was all in character. He added: "I am rejoiced that the company was very small, and that no man for whose principles I have the slightest respect was present at the unhallowed meeting." [28]

For Daniel in a bitter mood, not even the grave could end a quarrel. When he returned from the funeral of former President John Quincy Adams in 1848, he wrote his daughter thus:

I have just returned from the Capitol from the funeral of Mr. Adams, in which the court were a part of the pageant . . . What may be the feelings of his immediate family, I know not, but it is probably that few men ever lived whose public life had attracted to them less of personal partiality. There was nothing kind, much that was harsh and violent in his public intercourse. I have held no surprise that the Whigs should attempt to magnify him in highest degree — that is part of their strategy . . . all their partisans are magnified into great men. But 'tis strange the Democrats should commit themselves as they always have to be used as instruments in the creation of influences to be wielded against themselves. What still more surprises me is that [we] should actually aid in such dishonest purposes. For example in the proclamation of the President ordering homage to be shown both by the civil departments of the government and by the military toward a man whom I have every reason to believe was regarded by the President as a perfect instrument of mischief. This conduct perhaps may be excused by some as charity for the dead; but in this as in other instances (at least of all perhaps in instances like this which affect the public) charity should not be indulged at the expense of honesty.[29]

This was a part of the Daniel who took the bench in 1841. Happily it was not all of him or he would have been an unendurable horror to those compelled to live and work with him. Daniel loved Lucy and gave devoted attention to any of the problems of his three children. He concerned himself with his slaves and their welfare. And he got along well with those colleagues who were in a substantial degree like-minded. He and these brothers of the bench lived together, worked together, and dined together in true harmony, and with many evidences of real affection.

This, then, was the Daniel who came to the Court in 1841. He was a man of controversy, ferocious, unyielding, and utterly humorless in dispute. Yet his rough and always cutting edge had spots of true softness. His whole being cried out for an agricultural country, a land of farms and small shops, in which no man would own more than he could him-self control and in which there would be no aggregations of capital larger than a simple partnership. His dream was of a Stafford County become national, a nation whose business was done by men of unhurried rectitude, protected by a government which was occupied with patrolling of the bor-ders, preferably far at sea. He took up his new duties in the spirit of dedication. Indeed, "an old fashioned man" had come to Washington.

Chapter X

DANIEL TAKES HIS SEAT ON THE COURT

WHEN DANIEL'S APPOINTMENT was confirmed in March, the 1841 term was about over and it was too late for him to take his seat in Washington for that year. His actual working time as a Supreme Court Justice began in January of 1842 and lasted through the 1858–59 term, so that his active years on the Court were 18. The first case in which he heard argument, *Watkins v. Holman*, began on January 11. It is a fair measure of the leisurely approach of the times that the argument lasted for two and one-half days.[1] The first case to be actually decided by the Court after he joined it was *Swift v. Tyson*,[2] certainly the most famous opinion of the term. The case was submitted on briefs on January 14, and the opinion was handed down on January 25. This very famous decision, one of the most nationalistic of all of Daniel's years, held that in a case dependent upon the law governing commercial paper, the law to be applied by the Federal courts should be general commercial law as formulated by the Federal courts without any particular regard to the law of the state in which the case arose. Justice Story prepared the draft of Court opinion between the fourteenth and the twenty-fourth; it was accepted by his colleagues with a qualification from only one Justice which was apart from the main point.

Swift v. Tyson is a perfect illustration of the error which lies in reading the views of one generation back into the views of another. In 1938 this case was overruled, on the ground, among others, that it was severely incompatible with the right of the states to make their own law.[3] In short it was found that a strongly states' rights Court had given too much power to the Federal government. The opinion of Justice Brandeis to the effect that the Constitution requires application of state law appears to be precisely what Daniel would have said — if he had thought of it. As Daniel did not dissent there could not have been much of a states' rights issue in the case as originally conceived.

On January 20 the Chief Justice assigned to Daniel his first opinion, and on February 2 it was handed down.[4] The issue was whether a judge of a probate court in Mississippi had the power to appoint a temporary clerk, the question arising because an interest in property depended upon an act of a clerk the legality of whose appointment was at issue. The problem was an unexciting one, but its disposition was workmanlike and thoroughly worthy. Daniel wrote three more times for the Court in matters of no great moment before it adjourned in March of 1842.[5]

The Court to which Daniel came had but recently been raised in number from seven to nine, a number which has been maintained, except for a brief time, ever since. The expansion in 1837 had given Jackson two extra appointments, and the result was that Daniel came to a bench with a workable Jacksonian majority. The solid core of that majority consisted of five, including Daniel, and of these, four remained together for the two decades of Daniel's service. Of this group John McKinley of Alabama, who had been appointed at the beginning of Van Buren's administration and served until 1852, most consistently shared Daniel's views. Two others of the group were James Wayne of Georgia, who frequently disagreed with the other Jacksonians, and John Catron of Tennessee. Each of these two served longer than Daniel. Each was a figure of real if not great ability, and Catron in particular had a workmanlike quality which much appealed to Daniel. Head of the Court and of the bloc was Chief Justice Roger B. Taney, far and away the strongest intellectual and personal force in Daniel's life for the remainder of his public service.

Justice Henry Baldwin had also been a Jackson appointment but went his maverick way. Also a Jacksonian, after a fashion, but one who had been kicked upstairs to get him out of the Cabinet, was John McLean, a Justice who for thirty years on the Court was preoccupied with his attempts to get elected president of the United States on any ticket which would nominate him. He was an unsuccessful Republican aspirant against Lincoln in 1860. McLean was consistently opposed to Daniel on important matters. The remaining Justices were Smith Thompson, a Monroe appointee who died in 1843, and, finally, the most distinguished associate, Joseph Story. Story had been appointed by Madison in 1811, and resigned and died in 1845.

Daniel came onto the Court at a time when the institution's entire direction was changing. The death of the great Chief Justice Marshall in 1835 and his replacement by Taney marked the end of an era, and the mass of Jackson and Van Buren appointments within a six-year period radically changed the Court's goals and values. This change was for Story, the last of the long-time Marshall associates, a matter of great gloom, all the more so because he resisted the national tide of Jacksonianism with a passion only slightly more restrained and urbane than that with which Daniel advocated it. His attitude was summarized in a letter of 1844 to his only likeminded colleague, Justice McLean: "You will know that I have for a long time desponded as to the future fate of our country. I now believe that we are too corrupt, imbecile and slavish, in our dependence upon and under the auspices of demagogues, to maintain any free constitution, and we shall sink lower and lower in national degradation." [6]

The Jacksonian Court had very little patronage to dispense, but shortly after Daniel's appointment it put the spoils system to work on what there was. One of the few principal officers of the Court was its reporter, Richard Peters, who had served for fifteen years. Peters had long been an intimate of Story but was personally unsatisfactory to Justice Baldwin. Early in 1843, with only seven Justices present, the Court by a vote of four to three removed Peters and replaced him with General Benjamin C. Howard of Maryland.[7] This callous discourtesy to Story was magnified because he was absent on account of illness. Had he been present there would have been no majority to remove his friend. Justices Baldwin, Wayne, Catron, and Daniel voted for removal; Taney, McLean, and Thompson dissented; McKinley was also absent. The vote was taken one evening and Peters was informed the next day.[8] Peters attributed the action to Baldwin's spirit of revenge, discounting Wayne, Catron, and Daniel as so many party hacks without the training or talent to perform their jobs. Story was deeply wounded by the incident.

What is more important about the Peters affair than the result to one or another of the reporters is its reflection of the group spirit. The Jacksonians could, on the whole, be expected to stay together. There were bound to be moments of difference in particular instances; as we will see they dissented from each other. But the dominant mood was one of cooperation. McLean, who was thoroughly outside the group and whose only close tie was with Story, thought of the bloc as a regular working political caucus. As McLean reported to Story early in 1843, during Daniel's second term, "everything is carried by caucus, our friend Wayne being chief manager. He has managed to control Thompson, who with himself, Catron, and Daniel, constitute a majority of the Court." In this letter he described in detail the manner of the Peters action and his own suggestion of Charles Sumner, another Story protégé from Massachusetts, as a replacement. However, once McLean saw that "the whole matter had been previously arranged" he declined to have anything further to do with the election at all.[9]

As an aftermath the Court drifted into a large and a small camp. In Marshall's time the Justices had usually lived together in a boardinghouse while in Washington; but in 1843 McLean suggested to Story that their two families take quarters apart. "I do not believe you will enjoy yourself with our brother judges," he dryly added.[10]

McLean's remark must be regarded as a momentary burst of ill-temper, because fundamentally it was simply not true. Moreover, McLean's whole description of the bloc which he found against him for a moment between 1842 and 1844 was by no means a description of the Court as a going institution. In the first place, this was a Court whose members were, an overwhelming part of the time, renowned for their exemplary courtesy toward one another and toward others. These were men of strong feeling, but Taney, Catron, Wayne, and Daniel were also southern gentlemen. Wayne in particular was known for an elegance of manner. Taney, an immensely strong-willed and powerful figure, had a famous quarrel with Justice Curtis over the publication of the opinions of the *Dred Scott* case in 1857 and occasional lesser moments of friction with others, but by most accounts his leadership of the interminable Court conferences was a triumph of personal relations. From at least some of his colleagues, including Daniel, he earned a deep and abiding affection.

Moreover, Wayne did not generally have the influence in the Court which McLean attributed to him. Wayne was not really consistently of a mind with his fellow southerners. Whereas Daniel was the first secessionist on the Court, Wayne was an abiding unionist; and in his intellectual outlook he was often a strong federalist as well. Justice Curtis, when he came to the bench in 1852 as the real inheritor of the Webster constitutional tradition, described Wayne as the most high-toned federalist on the bench. On many vitally important matters, McLean and Wayne were to be together much more often as the years went by than Daniel and Wayne.

Taney was the real leader of this Court. During Daniel's years of service there were several competent judges on the bench, of whom Daniel was one. But there were, apart from Story for a brief time, only three Justices who are commonly regarded as possessing exceptional talents: Taney, Curtis, who served only from 1852 to 1857, and Campbell, who came to the bench in 1853 and stayed on the Court until after Daniel's death, when he resigned to go with his seceding Alabama. Campbell did with genius what Daniel did in a work-a-day way, and the two were basically likeminded.

The Court to which Daniel came was an institution whose members worked immensely hard. In this respect a more radical switch from the leisurely life of a Virginia district judge would be impossible to imagine. Basically each Justice had two jobs, the first as a member of the Supreme Court sitting in Washington, and the second as a trial judge sitting on circuit in some assigned area of the country. At the beginning of Daniel's service the Supreme Court convened in January of each year and sat until March, the Justices then scattering to their trial assignments. Congress very soon moved the opening back to December, an extension which was to be repeated in subsequent years up to the present time, when the Court begins its annual term in October and sits until the following June.

While it was sitting, the routine of the Court was extremely taxing. Arguments were heard from 11:00 to 4:00 each day. From 4:00 to 5:00 the Justices were at leisure. Then they had dinner and came together in conference at 7:00 in the evening. These conferences frequently lasted for many hours. The procedure was described by Justice McLean:

> Before any opinion is formed by the Court, the case after being argued at the Bar is thoroughly discussed in consultation. Night after night, this is done, in a case of difficulty, until the mind of every judge is satisfied, and then each judge gives his views of the whole case, embracing every point in it. In this way the opinion of the judges is expressed, and then the Chief Justice requests a particular judge to write, not his opinion, but the opinion of the Court. And after the opinion is read, it is read to all the judges, and if it do not embrace the views of the judges, it is modified and corrected.[11]

In the mornings they examined the records, wrote opinions, and studied law.

Usually the Justices dined together, for a good number of them continued the habit of maintaining a common mess in their boardinghouse. During Lucy's lifetime Daniel never had the means to set up an independent house in Washington; so she remained in Richmond while he was sitting. He missed his domestic routine and he frequently visited the Waynes and the Catrons during the years in which they maintained homes in Washington.

The Justices who lived together achieved a friendly and affectionate intimacy. The little illnesses of one or another were the subject of common concern, with Taney exercising an almost elder-brother dominion over Daniel in this regard. As Daniel wrote his daughter one time when he was suffering from influenza, "The Chief Justice laid his positive command on me and forbade my going out at all." [12] Taney's home was the closest, being only a few miles away from Baltimore, and on occasion he took others of the Court over for entertainment.

Daniel, when he could, contributed to the common table.

It gave him great pleasure to turn up something which would delight his fellow Justices, as for example a cheese or vegetables from Spring Farm. When he received excellent asparagus from home he gave some to the Catrons and served some at the common mess. It was a real coup for him to be able to report at home that "the Chief Justice, who rarely touches vegetables, ate most heartily of the asparagus." [13]

This cozy atmosphere undoubtedly relieved somewhat the intensity of Court work, in which Daniel immersed himself. He allowed himself little leisure. His only exercise was his walk to the courtroom in the Capitol and an occasional brisk walk in his neighborhood.[14] He rarely attended social events. With the realization that his womenfolk at home would be considerably more interested in these matters than in his cases, he told them about such affairs when they occurred. In 1843 he attended a ball given by William Carroll, the clerk of the Supreme Court, which he described to his daughter thus:

Anticipating the usual labors of our nightly conference, I had sent my formal apology to the lady in whose name the invitation was sent, and went to the conference at the usual hour. The other judges also came, but in a short time they determined on an adjournment and insisted that I should go with them to the ball. I had then all the preparation plans (which with me you know is no trifle) to make. All this was gotten through, however, and to the ball I went, where I found a great deal of fashion, and what was no doubt considered a quite brilliant assembly. It was to me however somewhat irksome for I was quite a stranger — not a lady in the company was known to me, except the wife of my brother Catron. She however is quite a civil and cheerful lady and seemed disposed to take me under her care, and I was very much indebted to her kindness. She expressed her regret that I had not my daughters with me and said she should be very much pleased to have the care of them. She inquired, also, kindly, about your mother . . . Amongst the company at the party were Mr. and Mrs.

Webster . . . His wife is an unusually tall thin woman with no beauty though with all the expense of apparel — she wore a velvet dress. After the history of my participation in this festivity your mother will think I have turned out for frolic when she shall be informed that I have accepted an invitation for dinner at Col. Benton's on Wednesday next, the dinner to take place six days after the invitation.[15]

If Lucy thought her Peter was "turned out for frolic," she could set her mind at rest. Daniel went to an occasional dinner and attended the President's New Year's reception — some years. His willingness to be seen at the White House depended rather considerably on his attitude toward the occupant. He did attend a dinner given by President Zachary Taylor, taking away from the table a souvenir bonbon for his daughter.[16] But Fillmore, successor upon Taylor's death, was very nearly too much for him. Throughout December of 1850 Daniel took the position that he simply would not pay any respects to Fillmore regardless of the tradition. Finally he gave in. As he reported to Elizabeth,

after a resistance of a month, I was controlled by the persuasion of my friends, particularly by that of the Chief Justice, to visit the de facto President. I went strongly against my own opinions and feelings, for I have a deep contempt and disgust of the creature who by an unfortunate accident has been placed at the head of the Government; but everyone said that such a visit was an accustomed deference paid to the *office* of Chief Magistrate, and that my omission would be thought singular; especially as others professing the same feelings and opinions with myself did not omit the ceremony.[17]

The next year, one may rather expect to his delight, he got as far as the White House door but found the crowd much too great to permit his entrance. He cheerfully turned away.[18]

If a Justice went to Washington to have a good time he could find one, but this was not Daniel's way. Usually he enjoyed the work, though occasionally he kicked hard against the burdens. "This office of Judge of the Supreme Court may be, and I presume it is, an office of honor, but I feel most impressively that it is a slavery of the most absolute character," he said. As the years went by and the work piled up, the burdens became heavier and heavier and he had a genuine and well-warranted complaint when he reported that, "as the end of the term approaches, I have scarcely time to eat or sleep and have barely left my desk today." [19]

From the standpoint of the sheer comfort of living, the greatest blessing of all to Daniel as a Supreme Court Justice was the improvement in his financial condition. The salary, $5000 a year, was scarcely princely; but it was so great an improvement that the note of want and of desperation disappeared altogether from Daniel's voice for the rest of his years.

And there was the reward of significant work to be done. Daniel's opinions for the Court during his first term, that of 1842, have been mentioned. None of them was of any great moment in the life of the time. But at the 1842 term there was one case which was genuinely exciting and genuinely important by the standard of the day, and in this Daniel acquitted himself very well.

The case was *Prigg v. Pennsylvania*.[20] The gravity of the matter as the Court itself saw it was summarized by the veteran Justice Story, who delivered the opinion of the Court, thus: "Few questions which have ever come before this Court involve more delicate and important consideration; and few upon which the public at large may be presumed to feel a more profound and pervading interest."

The underlying issue in the *Prigg* case was the proper relationship of state fugitive slave laws to the Federal law on the same subject. Under the Constitution no fugitive slave could, upon reaching a free state, be released from his slavery by the law of that state. Rather, by the express language of the Constitution, such a slave "shall be delivered up, on claim of the party to whom such service or labor may be due." The Constitution did not specify by what law the person was to be delivered up. If a slave passed into a free state, someone had to apprehend him, someone had to decide that he in fact had been a slave and was not simply wrongly charged with being a runaway, and someone had to turn him over for deportation back to the state of his origin. All of this took a process of law; self-help might do in some cases, but certainly not in all.

The Federal Fugitive Slave Law of 1793 provided for particular procedures for recapturing fugitive slaves. A Pennsylvania statute on the same subject required somewhat different steps, and provided a penalty against anyone who should take a slave without following the state law. Prigg came into Pennsylvania from Maryland and there captured a runaway slave and her infant child by the simple device of taking her, without compliance with the Pennsylvania law. He was charged with having violated that law, and the issue before the Supreme Court was whether the Pennsylvania law on the subject was valid.

For the Court majority, Justice Story held that this was a matter within the exclusive power of the Federal government, and that any state law on the same subject was invalid. He held that the states could neither help nor hinder the recapture of fugitive slaves — that this was an exclusive Federal power.

Daniel and three other Justices agreed that the Pennsylvania act was unconstitutional, but for wholly different reasons. In this, his first completely individual expression in the Supreme Court, Daniel's opinion was temperate, well reasoned, well presented, and only a little prolix. He did not believe that because certain powers "potentially existed in Congress they were therefore denied to the states." As he saw it, "the prosperity, the necessities of the country, and the soundest rules of constitutional construction, appear to me to present a decided negative to this inquiry."

With Daniel this was a matter of sensible and sound doctrine and the passage of time makes it appear that, in logic, he had by far the best of the arguments. But it was also a practical matter.

> Let it be declared that the rights of arrest and detention, with a view of restoration to the owner, belong solely to the Federal Government, exclusive of the individual right of the owner to seize his property and what of the consequences? In the first place, whenever the master, attempting to enforce his right of seizure under the Constitution, shall meet with resistance, the inconsiderable number of Federal officers in the State, having their frequent remoteness from the theatre of action, must in numerous instances, at once defeat his right of property, and deprive him also of personal protection and security. By the removal of every incentive of interest in state officers, or individuals, and by the inculcation of a belief that any cooperation with the master becomes a violation of law, the most active and efficient auxiliary which he could possibly call to his aid is entirely neutralized.

Based on the fact that Prigg had won, the immediate popular reaction was that the finding was a victory for slaveholders. Former President John Quincy Adams savagely derided all of the opinions in his diary, saying they caused "the transcendent omnipotence of slavery in these United States, riveted by a clause in the Constitution." [21] Since some of the northern laws had in fact been impeding the recapture of fugitive slaves, their invalidation was viewed with shock by those who were opposed to the fugitive slave laws.

Story himself saw his opinion as "a triumph for freedom," and so it in fact proved to be for precisely the reasons which were anticipated by Daniel. The states hostile to any recapture of fugitive slaves proceeded to repeal their own laws and to withdraw any form of cooperation with Federal enforcement, and the practical effect was a decline in recapture which led to a new Federal fugitive slave law in 1850.

By March of 1842, Daniel was thoroughly immersed in his new job. He had participated in his first really big case, and had acquitted himself creditably.

Chapter XI

DANIEL'S ROLE, IN GENERAL AND
ON EXCLUSIVENESS

DANIEL SAT as a Supreme Court Justice from the beginning of the 1842 term until the beginning of the December 1859 term, with an absence of one term in 1846 because of illness. During his years on the bench the Court disposed of about 800 cases. A one-ninth share of this number would have been about 89; Daniel in fact wrote 74 majority opinions. Occasionally he concurred specially, and in about 10 percent of the cases he dissented, filing written dissents some fifty times.

In short, Daniel wrote almost as many dissents and concurrences as majority opinions. To borrow Taft's phrase about another Justice, he was an "off horse." His proportion of dissents increased over the years as the majority of the Court moved ever further from his views. Before 1851 about two thirds of Daniel's opinions were for the majority; after that time he was in dissent appreciably more often than he was the spokesman for the Court.

The accompanying table shows the approximate distribution of his opinions through the conventional fields of law. This tabulation makes clear the following facts.

1) Daniel spoke most often for the Court in matters of land title, procedure, and equity. Fifty percent of his majority opinions were in these fields.

2) Daniel's constitutional opinions for the Court were relatively few. Partly this was because his Court had many fewer constitutional cases, both in number and in proportion, than the present-day Court. Seventy-nine constitutional cases were decided in the eighteen years of his active service, and this was about 10 percent of its total business. Today's Court hears more constitutional cases in one year than Daniel's heard in ten, and the proportion of such cases to the total business of the Supreme Court is now about three times as high as it was in Daniel's day. In addition, Taney assigned more of the constitutional cases to himself and to Grier, and later to Curtis, than to the other Justices. Finally, Daniel so frequently dissented in constitutional cases that he obviously could not be writing for the majority at the same time.

3) Daniel never spoke for the Court in an admiralty case. He was a thorough dissenter, disagreeing almost invariably with his colleagues on the existence of admiralty jurisdiction.

4) Similarly, Daniel was predominantly a dissenter on matters of Federal jurisdiction. This was particularly because of his belief that corporations should not be permitted to sue and be sued in the Federal courts.

5) There is no field in which Daniel was not at least occasionally against the Court. However, he was more often against it than its spokesman in matters of constitutional law, Federal jurisdiction, admiralty, and patents.

Unhappily, the majority of Daniel's "Opinions of the Court," like those of most other pre–Civil War Justices, must be put aside as of no great legal or historical significance. They indicate nothing except that a good many trifling cases have come to the United States Supreme Court in the course of its history. They are primarily useful in evaluating Daniel's style, or for depicting the general scope of the Court's work.

In the opinions concerned with land title, procedure, bills

Distribution of Daniel's Supreme Court opinions by subject

Subject	Percent of all Daniel's opinions	Number of Daniel's majority opinions	Percent of Daniel's majority opinions
Constitutional law	16%	7	10%
Federal jurisdiction	21	9	12
Procedure	8	11	15
Admiralty	12	0	0
Land title	11	15	20
Equity	8	12	15
Administrative law	5	7	10
Bills and notes	5	5	7
Patents	4	1	1
Contracts	2	3	4
Tariffs	1	2	3
Wills	2	0	0
Miscellaneous	5	2	3
TOTAL	100	74 [a]	100

[a] This figure does not include concurrences in cases in which there was no majority opinion.

and notes, contracts, tariffs, and miscellaneous matters, opinions which constitute about one half of his majority work, the subjects are so minute that it is impossible to wring any integrated philosophy out of them. A great number of these cases today would be decided, probably finally, by a state trial judge. It would be sheer antiquarianism to detail most of them. From the day the first pleadings were filed, they could have been of interest to no one but the litigants. A sampling of the least important of Daniel's decisions might include the matter of the validity on its face of a particular tax deed; a problem of the rights of one with equitable title under the Missouri practice; a question concerning a District of Columbia tax deed; a question of the sufficiency of title in a particular fact situation.[1] In the aggregate, these four opinions by Daniel have since been cited by the United States Supreme Court fewer than ten times.

About half of Daniel's cases in the general area of real property are of this type. The other half, dealing with basic problems of protection of the public domain, are more meaningful and will be separately discussed. The procedure cases were also frequently trifling. Of Daniel's eleven majority opinions in this field, seven have been subsequently cited by the Supreme Court a grand total of eleven times, and almost as seldom by the lower Federal courts. His three contract cases have since been cited a total of twice in the Supreme Court; and three of the bills and notes cases have been cited some four times in all. One of the tariff cases has never been heard of since, and neither of the two "miscellaneous" majority opinions has been subsequently mentioned in the Supreme Court, although one of them has had some appreciable state court currency.[2]

What has been briefly outlined is in no sense a disparagement of the quality of Daniel's work, but a comment on the nature of the Supreme Court's business in the 1840's and 1850's. Perhaps a third to a half of Daniel's work went into the vast ocean of law as pebbles, without even a ripple. To find the truly significant portion of his labors of two decades, one must cut to a fairly small core.

At that core was one great issue which has been a constant, serious constitutional problem for 150 years and to the partial solution of which Daniel made some contribution. This was the great question of the exclusiveness of Federal power. In such issues, both economic and political, Daniel was invariably on the side of state as against purely national power.

The problem turns on Article I, Section 8, of the Constitution. This section gives to Congress its powers — the power to regulate commerce, the power to regulate bankruptcy, the power to regulate patents, for example. The general issue drawn from these clauses was: Did the grant of these powers to Congress *exclude* the states from regulating in the same fields?

In this section of the Constitution there are seventeen power-granting clauses, plus the eighteenth catchall which empowers Congress to do what is "necessary and proper" to carry out the other seventeen. Of the seventeen, some are patently exclusive, such as the power "to exercise exclusive legislation" over the District of Columbia, or the power to coin money, expressly forbidden the states by Article I, Section 10. The war power in various forms, including the Army and Navy clauses, are also made exclusive by the express provisions of a later section. On the other hand, certain powers clearly were not exclusive, such as the power to collect taxes. Of the seventeen clauses, eleven were either obviously exclusive or obviously not exclusive because of explicit wording, other provisions of the Constitution, or the imperative implication of their content. There could be argument about the remaining six. The proponents and opponents of exclusiveness settled down for the fight, both sides armed with the abstractions of Hamilton's *Federalist* paper number 32. (Article 1, Section 8, excludes state action only where such state action is "totally contradictory and repugnant" to Federal action, said Hamilton.)

Of the six contestable clauses, those granting the power to promote science and the useful arts and to punish piracy and offenses against the law of nations did not come up for consideration before the end of the nineteenth century; and Congress so early exercised its patent power and its postal powers that questions of exclusiveness simply did not arise.[3]

Three clauses remain. Two of them, the commerce clause and the bankruptcy clause, were of enormous economic significance; and the third, the power to punish counterfeiting, was an important pawn protecting the doctrinal king and queen. A similar problem arose in connection with the separate fugitive slave clause. All four issues were before Daniel's Court, and on all four his position was vigorous and clear — to him, the clauses were not exclusive.

There are two ways of attacking the concept of exclusive Federal power. One is the frontal attack — to hold that the powers are concurrent, and that the states are free to regulate the same subject matter so long as their laws do not directly conflict with Federal regulation. The other way can achieve very nearly the same result by indirection. An extremely narrow construction of the scope of a Federal power would eliminate conflict with a particular state regulation even if the Federal power were exclusive. Daniel used both devices to uphold the position of the states.

Daniel took up the question for the Court for the first time in connection with the problem of punishment of counterfeiting. Article I, Section 8, Clause 6, of the Constitution gives to Congress the power to punish the "counterfeiting of securities and current coin of the United States." Ohio passed a statute which did not specifically forbid counterfeiting, but which did forbid passing counterfeit money. Daniel upheld a conviction under the Ohio statute against the defense that the statute was invalid because the congressional power was exclusive.[4] Counsel were in flat collision. The defense contended that Congress unquestionably had the exclusive power to authorize the coinage of money; the prosecution, that the power was concurrent.

The Ohio counterfeiting case was first argued in 1845, prior to the resignation of Justice Story. At that time, no majority could be made, and the case was set for reargument.[5] Daniel solved the problem, if not to the satisfaction at least to the acquiescence of eight of the Justices, by ducking the question of exclusiveness altogether. He dug out of the common law of England two separate offenses, one the offense of counterfeiting money, and the other the offense of passing counterfeit money. The first, he declared, was an offense against the state. The second was simply a private cheat among citizens. He held that the Federal government had not been given power to deal with the passing of counterfeit, and that therefore this was left to the states with no issue of exclusiveness to be decided. This approach satisfied Justice Wayne, who believed in exclusiveness as much as anyone. Only Justice McLean dissented, resting on the ground of exclusive power and taking comfort in his loneliness by invoking the shade of the departed Story as having agreed with him when the case was first presented.[6]

A far larger problem was whether the states could pass local bankruptcy laws. Article I, Section 8, Clause 4, gave to Congress power to pass "uniform laws on the subject of bankruptcy." Congress showed no inclination to act. Could the states exercise the function meanwhile?

Here another clause of the Constitution came into play. Article I, Section 10, forbade the states to pass any laws impairing the obligations of contracts, and the whole function of a bankruptcy law was to do precisely this by relieving persons unable to pay from the necessity of meeting financial commitments. If the bankruptcy clause itself were not exclusive, the contract clause, by possible interpretation, might make it so.

These questions arose for the first time during Marshall's tenure, and received answers which remained fairly clear until Congress, by passing its own bankruptcy act in 1841, momentarily ended the exclusionary problem. The issue was deadly serious, for the situs of the bankruptcy power was of vital concern to the most respectable classes in the community. In *Sturges v. Crowninshield* Marshall had held in 1819 that debts contracted prior to a state insolvency law could not be discharged by a state statute.[7] However, in 1827 the Court, through Justice Johnson and over one of Marshall's rare dissents, held that a debtor could be discharged under state law from a debt entered into after the passage of the state act if the contract from which the debt arose had its situs in the state and was between citizens of that state.[8]

In 1847, on the one occasion on which Daniel had an opportunity to express himself on this issue, he took a far stronger position than Johnson in favor of the state power. In concurrence he declared that nothing in the bankruptcy clause prevented the states from creating any insolvency system they wished; to him the clause was completely nonexclusive: "The mere grant of power to Congress while that power remained dormant would leave the states in possession of whatever authority appertained to them at the period of the adoption of the Constitution."[9]

The sole limit on the state's insolvency power, he said, was the contract clause. This meant that a state could not relieve debtors from contracts existing prior to its adoption of an insolvency law, but in all cases of contracts entered into subsequent to the adoption of a state insolvency law the state had complete power. In Daniel's view the statute became an implied term or condition of every contract entered into after its enactment. Daniel, like Taney in the same case, would not draw back at Johnson's stopping point — to both Daniel and Taney the state law was perfectly effective against citizens of other states, so long as the contract was made and was to be performed in the state which had enacted the insolvency law.

This was strong and important doctrine, for had it been accepted by the rest of the Court, the states would have possessed a really effective method of alleviating economic distress within their borders. Since the Federal act of 1841 was repealed in 1843, state law was the only bankruptcy legislation available for essentially all of Daniel's life. In its assumption that a contract is subject to the law concerning amelioration of debts in existence at the time it is entered into, Daniel's position foreshadowed the modern, completely accepted view.

The largest issue of exclusiveness before the Court at this time was the interpretation of the commerce clause: "Congress shall have power . . . to regulate commerce among the several states." If this were construed as an exclusive congressional power the states would be prevented from regulating their most important domestic concerns. If it were held that the commerce power reached the normal business affairs of life such as transportation, buying and selling, or even production, and if only Congress could regulate these things, the states as regulatory bodies could virtually close up shop.

The law when Daniel came to the bench can only be described as chaotic. Marshall had dabbled in the theory of exclusiveness, and had been tempted by it. There is language in two of his opinions, *Gibbons v. Ogden* and *Brown v. Maryland*, that has given comfort to those believing in the theory of Federal exclusiveness. But when the pinch came, Marshall was never quite ready to accept the doctrine. In these two great cases he finally found some other basis of decision so that in each case the regulated industry was freed of the burden of its regulation by the state, but not on such a broad basis as the general theory of exclusion. When he finally met a situation in which state regulation of commerce seemed imperative, he did uphold the state power.[10] At Marshall's death the constitutional law on this point was ambiguous.

The prospect for legal certainty did not improve in the few years between Marshall's death and Daniel's appointment; and the confusion was destined to become considerably worse before it improved. In *New York v. Miln*,[11] Daniel's predecessor, Barbour, expressly declared the question of the exclusiveness of Federal power to be open.

At the very moment Daniel's name was before the Senate for confirmation the Court had another inconclusive word on the subject.[12] Daniel Webster reviewed the Marshall opinions and contended that the great Chief Justice had upheld the concept of exclusiveness, and Justices McLean and Baldwin accepted Webster's interpretation of Marshall. Chief Justice Taney, on the other hand, felt that this was still an open question. Daniel thus came to a divided Court. Justices McLean, Wayne, and Story were then or later champions of the total exclusion theory. Taney was soon to reveal himself as its firm opponent; and Daniel stood even more firmly than Taney on the same ground.

The issues came before Daniel in four cases or groups of cases. The *License Cases* in 1847 constitute the first group.[13] These involved the validity of liquor control laws in Rhode Island, Massachusetts, and New Hampshire. In attempting to find the answer six Justices wrote nine opinions. Taney was able to divide the three cases into two groups. In the Rhode Island and Massachusetts situations, the liquor was already in the state and had been through its first stage of distribution before the state law took hold. Hence Taney could conclude that the laws of these two states did not involve a regulation of commerce at all. But the New Hampshire statute put the really hard question. In that state the law affected the first importer of the liquor while the liquor was still in the original package in which he received it. The process of intrastate distribution at this point had not yet begun. Hence the New Hampshire law was the clearest possible regulation of interstate commerce. In upholding the power of New Hampshire, Taney held flatly that "The mere grant of power to the general government cannot . . . be construed to be an absolute prohibition to the exercise of any power over the same subject by the states." [14]

As Taney saw it, the states, for the safety or convenience of trade or for the protection of public health, might wish to make many regulations of commerce. "Such regulations," said Taney, "are valid unless they come in conflict with a law of Congress." Reviewing all of the decisions on the other clauses of Article I, Section 8, Taney concluded that none of these was exclusive of state regulation of the same thing unless some language in the Constitution clearly and expressly made it exclusive. Nelson, Catron, and Woodbury agreed essentially with Taney's view that the clause was not exclusive, and the other Justices scattered into highly individual positions.

Daniel's vote went with these four of his fellows, and so there were five to make a majority. Thus for a fleeting and confused moment in American history the law of the United States was that the commerce clause was *not* exclusive — and Daniel's position was the most extreme of all. His colleagues had attempted to reason around the dicta of Marshall. Daniel would overrule them. The Marshall theory of immunity of imported goods from state taxes and regulation while they remain in "the original package" Daniel thought quite wrong. He poked fun at the ambiguous concept that imports were immune until "broken up and mingled with the mass of property." Suppose, said Daniel, the import were a telescope, a piano, or a horse — must these be "broken up"? To Daniel there was a higher good than this forced immunity from taxation — the citizen who received the protection of the state should "contribute to the support of the government which yields this protection, whether he shall have imported that property, or purchased it at home." [15] In short, to Daniel all imports are subject to state regulation as soon as title vests in someone within the state, "whether he is the first, second, or third proprietor." Once the goods are out of the customs house and are the exclusive property of the importer or the importer's customer they are taxable, said Daniel, and this whether purchased "by cargo, package, bale, piece, or yard, or by hogsheads, casks or bottles."

The Court fully understood that the question before it was the power of the states to regulate business and the power of the states to raise money by taxation. When Daniel asserted that the goods should be taxed because it was the duty of every citizen to "contribute to the support of the government" which makes it possible for him to live and carry on his business, he was asserting in the bluntest possible fashion what has become very close to a majority point of view today. But clearly the issue was far from settled: a vote of five to four to uphold the power of the states to tax was a wobbly majority, and particularly where the subject was liquor, likely to be regarded by all as particularly subject to regulation. A shift of position or a death or a contrary-minded replacement could reverse the rule. In a sense both came; for the next case was decided if not by a shift by a wobble; and when the next case after that came along, death had changed the composition of the court.

The *Passenger Cases* constitute the second group.[16] During the periods of flooding immigration in the nineteenth century many shipping companies were in the business of carrying immigrants. Pennsylvania imposed a tax measured by the number of immigrants. The ostensible purpose was to provide money to care for the indigent and ill who became public charges when they left the boat. Whether this was in fact the purpose or whether the tax was for general revenues, the Court had no way of knowing. But for commerce purposes, the case was essentially the same as the *License Cases* for in each case it involved a tax on something — in the one case a unit of liquor, and in the other an immigrant — crossing the state line.

The *Passenger Cases* were kept before the Court for four years, and argued and reargued while the Court attempted to make up its mind. Finally, in 1849, with eight Justices issuing opinions which took seven hours to read, the cases were decided. The net result was to invalidate the state laws by a vote of five to four. The nonexclusive bloc (Taney, Catron, Daniel, Woodbury, and Nelson) of the *License Cases* had been depleted by one; Catron swung to the other side, while the remaining four stood together.

Catron's stand did not mean that he had forsaken his doctrine; he merely found here a different problem. For a network of Federal treaties and statutes concerning immigration permitted the conclusion that Congress had deliberately intended to exclude the states from levying such a tax. If so, there was no question of the power of the states to tax where Congress had *not* acted, for in this view Congress had taken hold of the field and the states must leave it alone. Grier agreed with this ground of decision as did McKinley and Wayne.

McLean went further. For him the issue never changed — as he saw it, the states had no power to regulate in this area whether Congress had done so or not. Wayne and McKinley, having accepted the narrower ground of Grier, also agreed with the broader ground of McLean. The principal obstacle to this position was the opinion of Justice Barbour in *New York v. Miln*,[17] in which the Court had said that the power of the states to regulate was "open." Wayne pushed *Miln* aside in a few amazing paragraphs in which he purported to reveal that a majority of the Court had been quite taken by surprise by Barbour's opinion. When that opinion was read on the last day of the term, said Wayne, they had never agreed with parts of it, and there had been no previous opportunity in these eleven years to reveal that remarkable fact. In response, Taney scolded Wayne for talking out of Court and attempting to undermine, by conference room gossip, the entire stability of the opinion system.

Daniel was keenly aware that the issue and the case involved "an important statewide question." [18] He dissented as a prophet of doom. To him the majority was "trampling down . . . some of the strongest defenses of the safety and independence of the states." He restated himself on the exclusiveness theory, rejecting it entirely. Reviewing all of the other cases involving the exclusiveness question under any part of the Constitution, he demonstrated — quite conclusively — that there was no real precedent for the exclusive point of view. He concluded in a gloomy mood, applicable not only to this precise issue but to the whole complicated subject matter, that for the states, "the march of abuse will be onward and without bounds."

The sharp collision between Taney and Wayne had some side effects on Daniel. Shortly after the opinion came down he wrote his daughter that he had recently called on Mrs. Wayne, of whom he was fond, and continued,

> I regret that the remoteness of her residence has caused me to see so little of her. I cannot help fearing that this may have been in some way affected by another cause. An unfortunate collision has occurred between Wayne and the Chief Justice in which there is some approach even to bitterness. And although I have no part in it, it seems to me that this may be suspected [*illegible word*] my being an [intimate] with the latter, and that there has been less cordiality of manner to me than I have formerly experienced. Certainly I have not been so much pressed to visit the family as I have been. I regret this very much and have certainly done nothing to cause it.[19]

The great central issue of the distribution between the Federal government and the states, of power over commerce was no more settled than before. In this frightful welter of extended opinions, the bar of the country had no real answer. One can only say that in the middle of the nineteenth century the Court was hopelessly divided on whether the states retained the power to regulate commerce, with a thin and barely discernable majority in favor of the proposition that they could.

And then, on September 4, 1851, at the worse conceivable moment from the standpoint of the Taney-Daniel camp, Justice Woodbury died. His death was sudden. Daniel greeted it both as a personal misfortune and a national calamity, since the seat could now be filled by a Whig. He anticipated the worst.[20] Thus coincidence made policy, for Woodbury's death came during the only term between 1828 and 1860 in which a genuine Whig occupied the White House.[21] Had it come but two years before or after, Taney or Daniel might have influenced the appointment. But at this one moment the power to influence fell to another — Daniel Webster. And Webster had supported a broad philosophy of commerce-clause exclusiveness from the time of his first argument before Marshall — in what had been Marshall's first commerce-clause case — until his most recent presentation before Taney in the *Passenger Cases*.

President Fillmore asked Webster for his views. Webster concurred in Fillmore's own thought that Benjamin R. Curtis of Boston would be a wise choice, and on September 22, 1851, Fillmore appointed Curtis.[22] The 1851 term opened with memorial proceedings for Woodbury. Taney began his remarks by observing that "The Court is very sensible of the loss it has sustained in the death of Judge Woodbury." For the Taney-Daniel Democratic group of Justices this was certainly true. Only a few days later the Court heard argument in *Cooley v. The Wardens*,[23] which has been the leading precedent on the power of the states in respect to commerce ever since.

The issue in the *Cooley* case was the validity of a Federal statute which permitted the states to regulate pilotage in their harbors, and a Pennsylvania statute, subsequently passed, which required either the use of local pilots or the collection of a fee for the benefit of the Society for the Relief of Distressed and Decayed Pilots. If the commerce clause vests power to regulate commerce exclusively in the Federal government, argued taxpayer Cooley, Congress cannot delegate this power to the states, and Pennsylvania may not exercise it.

The case was argued before a bench of eight, Justice McKinley being absent on circuit. Had the Court of two years earlier been present, decision might have been easy — if the states and the Federal government both had constitutional power to regulate commerce, the tax was certainly valid, and five Justices would have said as much. But it was not the old Court, and the time had come for compromise. Taney assigned the writing of the majority opinion to Curtis in order to let the new Justice try his hand at a solution.

Curtis, one of the ablest Justices in the history of the Court, approached his problem with a loyalty to his mentor Webster. (He wrote Webster at approximately the time of his appointment saying, "I am not given to profession, but I can say with truth, and it gratifies me to say it, that your relation to the great interests of the country has been such, and is such, that I would suspect my own patriotism, if I were not disposed to serve you when I can." [24]) At the same time Curtis had every desire to solve his problem and thus to give the country a rule it could live with. His solution was to divide the whole field of commercial regulation into two zones, both described abstractly: some parts of commerce "imperatively demanding a single uniform rule . . . some, like the subject now in question, as imperatively demanding that diversity, which alone can meet the local necessities of navigation." And how were these to be distinguished? "Whatever subjects of this power are in their nature national, or admit only of one uniform system, or plan of regulation, may justly be said to be of such a nature as to require exclusive legislation by Congress." Pilotage was not in that category.

This was the exact doctrine originally advanced by Webster before Marshall in the first commerce-clause case of *Gibbons v. Ogden*. There Webster had said that not all commercial matters were exclusively of Federal concern, but that most were — "The powers should be considered as exclusively vested in Congress, so far, and so far only, as the nature of the power requires." [25] What Webster could not achieve by himself, he had achieved through his disciple. Of the bench of eight, Taney, Grier, Nelson, and Catron concurred with Curtis. McLean and Wayne dissented. To them the commerce power remained absolutely exclusive and no exceptions could be made.

Daniel was left alone. A Whig had captured his allies. He concurred in Curtis' result that the Pennsylvania act was constitutional, but for quite different reasons. Regulation of pilotage, he said, was not regulation of commerce at all. This was so inherently the prerogative of the states that he doubted whether the Federal government could take away the regulatory power if it wished to.

Thus, by compromise, the Court put aside its most difficult problem. As Curtis himself saw it in his private correspondence, his opinion would "excite surprise because it is adverse to the exclusive authority of Congress and not in accordance with the opinions of McLean and Wayne, who are the most high toned Federalists on the Bench. But it rests on grounds perfectly satisfactory to myself and it has received the assent of five judges out of eight, although for twenty years no majority has ever rested their decision on either view of this question, nor was it ever directly decided before." [26] With this compromise, the Taney Court had spent its creative strength. The infinitely more difficult problem of sorting out the "national" matters which could only be regulated by Congress and the "local" matters which could be regulated by the states remained to perplex other

Courts, all of which for the past century have had a consistently difficult time with their inheritance.[27]

The fourth case involving the exclusiveness theory was *Pennsylvania v. Wheeling Bridge*.[28] From the political and economic standpoint as well as the legal, this was most important commerce case before the Court in the early 1850's. Wheeling believed that the bridge, which crossed the Ohio River, would make the river and thus Virginia the natural outlet for all trade from Ohio and the West. The stakes were tremendous. More than $25,000,000 had been expended in building transportation facilities between Pittsburgh and Philadelphia and some $40,000,000 to $50,000,000 a year flowed annually from Ohio through Pittsburgh to the East. The bridge, which was the biggest construction project in the West, had been dedicated with thousands of candles and with marching girls. At the dedication Henry Clay had cried defiantly, "You might as well try to take down the rainbow."

Pittsburgh contended that the bridge blocked river traffic. Her steamship captains ostentatiously hauled in their chimneys as they approached it. Pennsylvania, in behalf of Pittsburgh, sought an injunction against the operation of the bridge. The majority of the Court was willing to require that the rainbow at least be moved a little, Taney and Daniel dissenting.

Justice McLean wrote for the Court. With his eagle screaming somewhat ungrammatically ("In a country like this where there would seem to be no limit to its progress, the injury complained of would be far greater in its effect than under less prosperous circumstances."), McLean held for the majority that the bridge as it stood conflicted with a Federal statute and with congressional policy by impeding river commerce and that its level must be raised.

Taney dissented tersely, directly, and persuasively. Daniel, his spirit imbued with a strong loyalty to his home state, settled down to do prolix justice to the issues in a twenty-page dissent. He denied that the state had power to bring an action in behalf of a local interest such as this and in any case he thought the bridge no nuisance. He denounced the majority for preferring river commerce to railroads. "The obvious superiority of the railroad, from its unequalled speed, its greater safety, its exemption from dependence upon the wind or on depth of water, but above all, its power of linking together the distant and extended regions interposed between the rivers of the country, spaces which navigation never can approach, must give it a decided preference." Instead of raising the bridge he would have the boats use shorter smokestacks or have them constructed so that the smokestacks could fold back.

Far from believing that the bridge conflicted with the congressional exercise of the commerce power, Daniel believed that Congress could not interfere with such a bridge if it wanted to, for it could not cripple commerce by putting arbitrary, unjust, and oppressive limitations on it. The Justice had a fair vocabulary of legal invective, and in the course of this opinion he used most of it. For once in his life he became something of a hero in the West.[29]

Chapter XII

REGULATION OF BUSINESS

THE MOST IMPORTANT restriction upon the legislative regulation of business before 1890 was the contract clause of the Constitution. As interpreted by Marshall, the phrase "No state shall pass any law impairing the obligation of contracts" gave full opportunity to the judges to supervise the legislators. This interpretation was modified but continued by subsequent courts. Most state regulatory legislation in some manner affects contracts — a tax reduces profits on contracts, a rate regulation does likewise, an exercise of the power of eminent domain may affect many contracts, and so on. The problem before the courts was essentially this: How much of the states' routine legislation should it supervise under this clause, how far should it restrict the power to govern?

There were two essentially different relationships which, if the court desired, could be construed as covered by the contract clause. One was the relationship of individuals or corporations among themselves. The other was the relationship of the individual or corporation to the state. The first is the situation the founding fathers had most clearly in mind; they were attempting to prevent legislation aimed at relieving debtors of the unpleasant necessity of paying their debts. But Marshall, in two daring opinions, added the other category to the purview of the contract clause. In *Fletcher v. Peck* [1] he held that a land grant from a state was a "contract." Such a contract based upon legislative act could not be subsequently set aside by the state even where the proof was overwhelming that the grant had been obtained by fraud. In the *Dartmouth College* case [2] he added a capstone by holding that a corporate charter was also a contract with the state.

This latter decision was for many years of the most enormous economic importance. In the early nineteenth century the corporate form was comparatively unfamiliar, and charters were obtained by special acts of the state legislatures. The *Dartmouth College* decision added to the charter an implied protection from subsequent state regulation. As Mr. Webster is reputed to have said, it was "a small college but there are those who love it." There were bridge companies, turnpike companies, and banks which were loved by somebody, too, and all came slipping into the shelter of the Constitution along with the small college.

Daniel was a consistent and inveterate foe of the application of the contract clause to corporate charters. He never wrote an opinion invalidating a state law on contract-clause grounds. Prior to 1846 he concurred in four such opinions; [3] but thereafter he never agreed with such a finding.

There were essentially three different ways of narrowing the reach of the clause. One was to hold that the particular relationship on its facts was not a contract. Another was to hold that assuming that there was a contract, the particular subsequent law did not impair it. The third was to hold that for jurisdictional reasons the aggrieved party could not raise the issue in court. Daniel was an effective user of all three.

Daniel only once saw an impairment where a corporate charter was involved — and the record in this instance is open to question. In *Gordon v. The Tax Court*,[4] the Court held invalid in part a Maryland statute taxing the stockholders of a bank, on the grounds of violation of contract. The opinion was by Justice Wayne, and Daniel either joined in it, or dissented without a record having been kept of his dissent, or was absent without record. Normally the presumption would

be that he joined in the opinion; but the doctrines announced
are so flatly in conflict with everything he later said on the
subject that it seems more probable that his apparent acquiescence may be an erroneous report.

In the remaining corporation cases Daniel's views were
strongly and clearly set forth. In the first place, he believed
that a corporation could not be treated as a "citizen" and therefore was not eligible to sue or be sued in Federal courts under
that clause of the Constitution governing cases between citizens of different states. This view is considered in detail elsewhere; suffice it to say here that under it Daniel could dispose of all cases not arising from state courts. However, since
many of the cases did come from the state courts, he made
use of other means of limitation as well.

The foremost limitation on the Marshall doctrine when
Daniel came to the Court was Taney's opinion in the *Charles
River Bridge* case.[5] Taney limited the *Dartmouth College* rule
to situations in which the particular right claimed by the corporation had been clearly and explicitly granted in its charter;
unless this were the case a subsequent statute would not be
considered as an impairment of the grant. Mere implication of
right would not be enough — the opportunity for inferences
favored the state.

The first case in which Daniel had an opportunity to apply
this principle involved the Planters Bank of Mississippi. In
1830 Mississippi had chartered a bank with power to receive
deposits and make loans. The bank also had power, like the
other banks of the time, to issue notes of its own which circulated as paper money. If the bank was undependable, or if
evil times came, the notes issued by it and circulated as money
would depreciate, frequently being worth considerably less
than 100 cents on the dollar.

In 1840 Mississippi passed an act which forbade banks to
transfer to other institutions notes received from persons who

had borrowed money from them. The object of the law was to prevent evasion of another Mississippi statute which required the banks to accept their own possibly depreciated currency in payment of debts to them. For a person to whom such a note was assigned could refuse the bank's currency. The bank could thus evade the consequences of the depreciation of its own paper.

Woodbury, speaking for seven of the Court, held the 1840 act unconstitutional on the ground that it impaired the 1830 charter, which was a contract. Taney and Daniel dissented, Daniel filing a pointed, clear opinion. The occasion called for the expression of his deepest convictions. Here, in his view, a rascally banking corporation was fleecing the people of Mississippi by sharp practices. The plaintiffs, said Daniel, were corporations, owing their every power to the state which had created them. They had never been explicitly given the power to transfer bills and notes; the state of Mississippi had permitted them to be bankers, not brokers. Indeed, banks are supposed to be depositories and lenders: "The practice of becoming brokers for the sale of their own paper or the paper of their customers, to put themselves in funds, is not, therefore, one of their regular functions, and can flow only from an abuse of these functions, and is a perversion of the legitimate ends of their creation." He was particularly indignant at the injustice of permitting the banks to pay their own debts in depreciated paper, while they received their income in good coin. That the banks should be allowed "to appropriate to themselves or their favorites" these unjust gains was "subversive of justice." For him the 1840 Mississippi act needed no vindication or apology, for its purposes were "to prevent, if possible, the paper of the corporations, spread over the community by them, from utterly perishing on the hands of the noteholder, and to disappoint dishonest combinations to set the public laws at defiance, and, further to oppress and ruin the noteholder by taking his property, and leaving him the worthless and false and simulated representatives of an equivalent."

In the *Planters Bank* case Daniel relied essentially on two grounds. In part he simply followed Taney's precedent of the *Charles River Bridge* case; the corporation had not been explicitly given this power. But on the other aspect of the case Daniel was fumbling toward a position which was never fully accepted until long after his death. His emphasis on the real evils which the 1840 act was supposed to correct was not just so much oratory; it was his first expression, not clearly articulated here, that the contract clause was not an absolute. Rather, it was subject to the police power, to the power of the state to correct real evils. Before he was done, Daniel would be able to carry into a majority doctrine his deeply held conviction that even the sanctity of contract must yield where the public good overwhelmingly demands it; it is not overdrawn to say that the modern understanding of the contract clause, which is radically different from Marshall's, really begins with Daniel's position in the *Planters Bank* dissent.[6]

Decisions such as *Woodruff v. Trapnall*,[7] in which Daniel also dissented, gave every incentive to corporate interests to corrupt the legislatures that granted their contracts. If a bank could buy out one legislature, it could collect back its expenses from the people in the form of high rates and service charges for as long as it desired, and nothing could be done about it. Chief Justice Taney in this case very candidly described the practice of pushing corporate charters through the legislature in the last days of the session.

A most colorful influence case arose because one A. J. Marshall had offered to lobby a right-of-way bill through the Virginia legislature for the Baltimore and Ohio Railway for $50,000. He was successful, and sued for his pay. The Marshall proposal as made in writing to the railroad contained shrewd observations on the realities of political life. He said:

> The mass of the members in our legislature are a thoughtless, careless, lighthearted body of men, who come there for the 'per diem', and to spend the 'per diem'. For a brief space they feel the importance and responsibility of their position. They soon, however, engage in idle pleasures, and on all questions disconnected with their immediate constituents, they become as wax, to be molded by the most pressing influences. You need the votes of this careless mass, and if you adopt efficient means, you can obtain it. I never saw a class of men more eminently kind and social in their intercourse. Through these qualities they may be approached and influenced to do anything not positively wrong, or which will not affect prejudicially their immediate constituents. On this question of the 'right-of-way', a decided majority of the members can vote either way without fear of their constituents. On this question, therefore, I consider the most active influences will ever be the most successful.[8]

Marshall's plan was a simple one: "The railroads should send down a corps of agents, stimulated to an active partisanship by the strong lure of a high profit."

Justice Grier gave the opinion of the Court holding that Marshall's contract was unenforceable: "The use of such means and such agents will have the effect to subject the state governments to the combined capital of wealthy corporations, and produce universal corruption, commencing with the representative and ending with the elector." [9] Judicial virtue in the face of fraud thus exposed was easy enough. But more commonly the fraud was not exposed, for usually the corporations paid their agents and the thieves did not fall out. When the fraud was not apparent, when the state had merely been taken advantage of, the Court held that a later legislature could not correct the errors of its predecessor.

This was a problem of first magnitude in Ohio, where the

legislature had originally granted widespread tax exemptions to banks and then sought to withdraw them. First by statute and later by the state constitution itself, Ohio sought to undo its original excessive generosity. All its efforts were held invalid by the Supreme Court. In the Ohio cases, of which *Piqua Branch Bank v. Knoop* and *Dodge v. Woolsey* were principal,[10] Daniel had another and abler colleague to write the principal dissent; it was sufficient for Daniel to concur briefly with Campbell.

In the Ohio contract cases as in the commerce cases, Daniel's principal opponents were McLean and Wayne. On the central issue of whether a state was capable of divesting itself of a power so vital as that of taxation, they held in the affirmative. As McLean saw it, "The exemption of property from taxation is a question of policy and not of power . . . inducements must be held out to capitalists to invest their funds."

The dissent attacked these principles from every quarter. Campbell, Catron, and Daniel set as their task the analysis of the economy of their country. Strengthened by their analysis, they attacked the whole principle of corporate tax immunity. To Justice Catron, the problem was essentially one of sound public administration. The fifty banks involved, valued at some $18,000,000, accounted for about one fortieth of the taxable property of Ohio. It was impossible for the states to give away their power to tax such substantial assets.

Campbell plunged even more expressively to the fundamentals of power in government. To him it was simply unthinkable that "a careless or corrupt legislator" could thus cripple a state. He described the manner in which in the Turkish Empire religious and charitable properties were immune from taxation, declaring that there the country was dominated by the interested and benefiting class "just as the corporate moneyed interest is dominant in Ohio." He saw the opinion of the Court as imposing just such an incubus upon the resources and growth of the United States. The dissenting objection he put forcefully and pungently thus:

> Should it be that a state of this union had become the victim of vicious legislation, its property alienated, its powers of taxation renounced in favor of chartered associations, and the resources of the body politic cut off, what remedy have the people against the misgovernment? Under the doctrines of this court none is to be found in the government, and none exists in the inherent powers of the people, if the wrong has taken the form of a contract. The most deliberate and solemn acts of the people would not serve to redress the injustice, and the overlooking speculator upon the facility or corruption of their legislature would be protected by the powers of this court in the profits of his bargain . . . the court, therefore, becomes the patron of such legislation, by furnishing motives of incalculable power to the corporations to stimulate it, and affording stability and security to the successful effort.[11]

These views, which Daniel completely shared, were iconoclastic in his day. It is no wonder then that Daniel almost never spoke for the majority in a contract-clause case. The leading exception is *West River Bridge Company v. Dix*,[12] Daniel's foremost constitutional opinion.

In 1795 the Vermont legislature granted a charter to the West River Bridge Company to build a bridge over the West River in Brattleboro. The tolls were fixed for forty years subject to a revision thereafter, provided the company continued to make a profit of at least 12 percent. The bridge, a covered wooden structure after the fashion of the time, was thereupon built, and with it a toll house, gate, barn, and other buildings. It operated for many years.

Almost fifty years later Joseph Dix and 54 other inhabitants of the region became unhappy enough about the bridge to protest it. It was a "sore grievance," they alleged, and a reflection upon the proud name of Brattleboro. Why should our "wealthy town," they asked, be less able than its neighbors to maintain a free bridge across the West River? Taking advantage of an 1839 statute, they petitioned the county court to order the bridge condemned and to require Brattleboro to pay the cost of the bridge.

The county court appointed three commissioners, who assessed the property at $4000. The court accepted these findings and ordered the bridge made free on June 1, 1844, upon payment of the declared amount. The company appealed to the state supreme court, alleging among other things that its charter was a contract which could not be abrogated by condemnation. The state supreme court held that the contract clause was not violated by the exercise of the power of eminent domain.

The company then appealed to the United States Supreme Court, and both sides retained new counsel. The company secured the services of Daniel Webster, foremost exponent of the rigid contract clause, and retained with him Jacob Collamer. Samuel S. Phelps of Vermont represented the state. The case was argued for three days, January 5, 6, and 7, 1848.

Webster's argument was his usual analysis of fact and law culminating in his inevitable prediction of impending doom for the country and its financial interests if his advice were not followed. (There is no evidence that any distinction between these two sets of interests ever occurred to Webster.) The case was extremely complicated because at this early date the power of eminent domain was much less clearly defined than it is today. The first exercise of a Federal eminent-domain power to be considered by the United States Supreme Court was still thirty years in the future.[13] We understand today, to put it loosely, that governments may take whatever property interest they need for the purposes of government so long as they pay just compensation. They may confiscate for virtually any rational purpose, and they may confiscate any property, whether it is tangible or intangible. Our present legal controversies turn not on the what and when but on the extent of taking.

But though this is clear today, it still remained to be established in 1848. Hence Webster's argument ran through these principal premises: (1) A corporate franchise such as that held by the West River Company was not "property" at all, and hence not subject to the eminent-domain power. The eminent-domain power reaches real and personal property but not a "franchise, a pure franchise." (2) The eminent-domain power, if it reaches the franchise at all, is subject to and controlled by the contract clause. The franchise is a contract immune from the subsequent power of sovereignty. Otherwise "there is an end of public faith." Here the name of Chancellor Kent was invoked as authority. (3) The damage was underestimated. The company was entitled to all that it would receive as tolls, less expenses of operation. On that basis condemnation would be prohibitively expensive.

Of these contentions, it was the second that was the heart of the case. One of two constitutional powers must dominate the other. Was the contract clause subject to or superior to the power of eminent domain? Here Webster was ready to offer attitude as well as citation. In the last analysis, the issue was one of policy: the power of eminent domain, he said, was new to our Constitution. It was adopted from arbitrary governments. The Supreme Court must keep careful confines over this new power or it would become the means of despotism. Rules such as that sought by Vermont would lead to "the most levelling ultra-isms of Anti-rentism or Agrarianism or Abolitionism."

Phelps in opposition quickly brushed aside the details and came to the serious question. Of course there was a power of eminent domain, and equally certainly the Federal provision in the Fifth Amendment requiring just compensation applied only to takings by the Federal Government and not to takings by Vermont. Hence the question of amount was not before the Court. The real question was whether the contract clause limited the eminent-domain power.

Phelps admitted that the contract clause put some limits on the eminent-domain power. Specifically, since the Vermont constitution itself required compensation, there must be compensation, for this right was implied as part of the original grant. Moreover, there must be some rational necessity for the taking. This latter question, however, was one wholly for the state to decide. On the merits, said Phelps without flourish and with dry citation, franchises too were within the power of the state.

Preparation of the opinion fell to Daniel and he wasted no time in elaborate research. He could not say his say as though he spoke only for himself. But his two foremost intellectual opponents did speak for themselves, McLean in concurrence and Wayne in dissent, and he was therefore free of the burden of walking the tightrope so as to conciliate their views to his own. He made the best of this opportunity.

Daniel's opinion began with acceptance of the view that the corporate charter was a contract; but, he said, the contract contained unwritten as well as written terms. All contracts were implicitly subject to the state's power "of guarding its own existence, and of protecting and promoting the interests and welfare of the community at large." All property stems in some fashion from the state: "But into all contracts whether made between state and individuals or between individuals only, there enter conditions which arise not out of the literal terms of the contract itself; they are superinduced by the pre-existing and higher authority of the laws of nature, of nations, or of the community to which the parties belong."

This is the clearest expression in our early law of the

conception of the police-power limitation on the contract clause. For Daniel did not mean to say that contracts were subject only to the power of eminent domain. Far from it. Every contract, he said, is subject to inherent conditions of the type he had mentioned. And then to the instant case: "*Such* a condition is the right of eminent domain." To Daniel at least, the "such" is vital, for in his philosophy the eminent-domain power was only one of the limitations on contractual immunity from state supervision.

The question then became whether the eminent-domain power, this implied reservation in the original contract, reached franchises. This, said Daniel, was obvious. There is no difference for eminent-domain purposes between corporate and unincorporated property. The founding fathers would never have held a contrary notion; indeed no one would "until the opinion seems to have obtained, that the right of property in a charter corporation was more sacred and intangible than the same right could possibly be in the person of the citizen." A franchise was property, no more and no less, and the whole structure of Webster's argument was shoved aside with an annoyed gesture and a few citations.

In this view the only question was one of power of the state. If the state had power to take, there was nothing for the Supreme Court to decide concerning the adequacy of the payment. Hence Daniel did not consider at all whether the payment should be more than the $4000 allowed.

Wayne dissented outright. McLean, seeing the drift of the tide, was satisfied to try to slow its progress. He argued that Vermont could take the bridge, but attempted to restrict the doctrine to its facts. In his view Vermont could not have taken over a corporation and run that corporation itself. Particularly, it could not condemn and operate a bank, or even a toll bridge, unless it made the bridge free. Nor, said McLean, could the state condemn the bridge and give it to others. In these attempted limitations, it must be added, McLean has never been followed in any subsequent opinion.[14]

West River Bridge carried into majority doctrine the view Daniel had expressed in dissent in *Planters Bank*, the doctrine that to some undefined extent the contract clause was subject to the police power. The solid core of the opinion is that the sanctity of contract may have to yield before imperative public necessity. The doctrine grew and expanded to become, along with the *Charles River Bridge* limitation, one of the two greatest limitations on the contract clause. In the 1930's when Chief Justice Hughes needed leading authority to sustain the mortgage moratorium legislation of the great depression, it was to the *West River Bridge* case that he went.[15]

Chapter XIII

THE STATE AND THE NATION

DANIEL'S DETESTATION of internal improvements financed by the Federal government was as great as his hatred of banks, and he could as easily claim that they were unconstitutional. For Daniel internal improvements were the very core of political evil, for they led to expenditures which in turn led to the necessity of ever higher tariffs to raise revenue. In no respect did Daniel more completely represent the landowning class of eastern Virginia than in this view; and not even his travels in the West gave him the sympathy for improved roads and canals which hardship might have bred. If these projects were to be undertaken, they should be done by the states and not by the nation. Let Pennsylvania pay for its own roads — Virginia should not contribute.

With a burning fervor Daniel leaped at an opportunity which one less fanatic might not have seen. The leading Federal internal improvement was the Cumberland Road. Daniel found a pretext to call the whole road unconstitutional.

The Cumberland Road, or the National Road as it was sometimes called, is the present Highway 40 which runs from the east to the west coast. Originally it was begun as a Federal highway, the first great "internal improvement." Starting in Maryland, it crossed Pennsylvania and Ohio, passing through Columbus. In 1837, when it had already reached Ohio, the road was turned over to the states concerned, with the agreement that the United States would not be required to pay tolls for carrying the mail over the road.

The words of agreement actually exempted from toll the carriages hauling the mail. Shrewd holders of mail-carrying contracts, being also engaged in the transportation of other property, began to mix the mail shipments with private goods, claiming exemption for the whole load. Pennsylvania retaliated by taxing the carriages hauling mail and other commodities. Taney, for the Court, held this levy to be a violation of the agreement.[1]

Daniel dissented on two grounds. He thought the compact between Pennsylvania and the United States permitted the tax. This should have been enough, but it was not. He also declared that Congress had no power to authorize internal improvements of any kind. It followed that Congress had no power to acquire the Cumberland Road and hence had no power to limit state taxation of it. Therefore, in his view, the Federal portion of the compact was void, and Pennsylvania could tax at will.

A more extreme dictum can scarcely be found. The agreement was open to the interpretation Daniel gave it; there was, therefore, no necessity for questioning the right of the government to make the agreement. That Daniel, normally cautious in respect to the superfluous, broke his customary bounds here is indicative of the depth of his feelings. Yet he did not explain his constitutional theory in any great detail. This theory, developed in a later opinion on a similar case, consisted of these points: (a) Congress can acquire property only for constitutionally specified purposes, of which a turnpike is not one; (b) the power to establish post roads given Congress by the Constitution is the power to select among existing roads, not the power to create new ones; (c) considerations of advantage are irrelevant; let those claiming the power amend the Constitution.[2]

The dissent in the Pennsylvania case is worth quoting because it may well be the narrowest conception of the powers of the Federal government ever expressed by any justice in any opinion, and the essence of the point of view permeates all of Daniel's judicial work:

> I hold, then, that neither Congress nor the Federal Government in the exercise of all or any of its powers or attributes possesses the power to construct roads, nor any other description of what have been called internal improvements, within the limits of the States. That the territory and soil of the several States have pertained to them by title paramount to the Constitution, and cannot be taken, save with the exceptions of those portions thereof which might be ceded for the seat of Federal Government and for sites permitted to be purchased for forts, arsenals, dock yards, etc., etc. That the power of the Federal Government to acquire, and that of the States to cede to that Government portions of their territory, are by the Constitution limited to the instances above adverted to, and that these powers can neither be enlarged nor modified but in virtue of some new faculty to be imparted by amendments of the Constitution . . .
>
> In accordance with the principles above stated, and which with me are fundamental, I am unable to perceive how the Federal Government could acquire any power over the Cumberland Road by making appropriations, or by expending money to any amount for its construction or repair, though these appropriations and expenditures may have been made with the assent, and even with the solicitation of Pennsylvania. Neither the Federal Government separately, nor contractly with the State of Pennsylvania, could have power to repeal the Constitution.[3]

Daniel's fight for the supremacy of the states in the Federal system also touched the field of Federal jurisdiction. In the middle of the nineteenth century the settling of disputes was, in relative proportion to the entire work of government, a far greater assignment than it is today. The power to decide even minor quarrels was to a very large extent the power to govern, particularly since under the philosophy of the time, the power to decide carried with it the power to make the rules of decision, or, in short, to make the law.

Most of the questions involved a short section of the Constitution which gave the Federal courts jurisdiction in controversies between citizens of different states. The statutes of Daniel's time implemented the constitutional provision, giving to the Federal courts as their principal subject of business these so-called "diversity cases," cases in which the parties were of different states and the amount involved was above a prescribed minimum.

The dominant principle of Daniel's jurisdictional policy was to keep as many cases as he could out of Federal courts and in state courts. Usually, he made no elaborate effort to spell out the reasons for this philosophy, but occasionally he gave a hint. In the last opinion of his life, filed in March 1859, the issue was whether a wife who had been given a qualified divorce, or a divorce from bed and board, in a state court, and had been awarded alimony by that court, could sue in Federal court to collect the alimony. The jurisdictional issue was whether a wife with a qualified divorce could be said to live in a state other than that of her ex-husband. The Court, through Wayne, held that the jurisdiction existed. Daniel dissented, as did Campbell and Taney. Daniel's argument was technical: At common law a husband and wife were one; if they were one they could not be living in different states; a qualified divorce did not totally dissolve that unity. But his policy considerations were far less technical. He said, "It is not in accordance with the design and operation of a government having its origin in causes and necessities, political, general, and external, that it should assume to regulate the domestic relations of society and, with a kind of inquisitorial authority, enter the habitations and even enter the chambers and nurseries of private families, and inquire into and pronounce upon the morals and habits and affections or antipathies of the members of every household." In short, the whole business of divorce and everything about it was local business.[4]

There were numerous ways of making it difficult to get cases into Federal courts, and Daniel tried a good many of them. One device was the rigorous insistence on complete diversity of all parties. This is the requirement that all parties on one side of the lawsuit be citizens of states different from those of all parties on the other side. Marshall's Court had held that diversity must be complete, that if even one defendant and one plaintiff were from the same state, the Federal court could not proceed. But this left the question of the necessity of complete diversity among nominal parties, parties who were listed in the lawsuit only because of some quirk of the law and who really had nothing to do with the case. In a whole series of cases, Daniel as a dissenter took the narrowest possible view of Federal jurisdiction.[5]

The greatest and most fruitless controversy in which Daniel engaged in his effort to limit the Federal jurisdiction was over the constitutional right of corporations to sue or be sued in Federal courts. The language of the Constitution opens the Federal courts to "citizens" of different states. A corporation is at law "an artificial person," but it is not a "citizen"; and the diversity clause of the Constitution does not speak of "persons" as do some other clauses. Insofar as words have meaning, corporations, therefore, cannot have access to the Federal courts on the basis of diversity of citizenship. They simply are not citizens. Why the Constitutional Convention should have failed to deal with jurisdiction in corporate cases, we do not know. The delegates were sufficiently familiar with that form of enterprise so that the problem certainly should have occurred to them. But as the country's economic system altered, as the banks and railroads and manufactories began more commonly to function, corporations more and more sought access to Federal courts. One of the major needs of the Court of Daniel's time was to find a way to let them in.

The first to take a hand with this difficult problem had been John Marshall. When the Bank of the United States, a Pennsylvania corporation, sought to collect a debt from a Georgia debtor named Deveaux, Marshall as the architect of a businessman's world was ready to find a way to use the Federal courts for the purpose.

In so doing he made one of the greatest errors of his life. For, far-seeing though he was, Marshall could not anticipate the rise of the gigantic stock corporations in the United States. In 1810, when the bank brought its suit, he permitted it to proceed in Federal court on the theory that in such cases one must ignore the corporation itself, pierce the corporate veil, and look to the citizenship of the stockholders who made up the corporation. Since all of the bank's stockholders were citizens of Pennsylvania, said Marshall, it is as if this were a suit between Pennsylvanians and Georgians. Therefore, diversity is complete, and the suit would lie in Federal court.[6] The trouble with the Marshall theory was that while it served the commercial world of 1810, it was a millstone around the businessman's neck within thirty years. The number of national corporations with shareholders in many states was steadily increasing. Under Marshall's interpretation these could never sue or be sued in Federal courts.

It fell to the Taney Court to devise a new means to the end. In 1845, in *Louisville Railway v. Letson*,[7] Wayne for the Court achieved the new result. He overruled the theory of the *Deveaux* case and substituted a new one: thereafter a corporation was to be "deemed" a citizen of the state of its incorporation for jurisdictional purposes. Thus by wave of a hand, Wayne "deemed" the word citizen out of the Constitution.

In the next two decades the Court polished the Wayne

theory, trimmed its appearance, and finished with the most remarkable fiction in American law. A conclusive and unrebuttable presumption was established that all stockholders of a corporation were citizens of the state in which the corporation was chartered. With reiterated assertion that the corporation is not a citizen, the Court has by this fiction put all its stockholders into one state. By operation of this fiction, every one of the shareholders of the General Motors Corporation is a citizen of Delaware despite the fact that there are more shareholders than there are Delawareans.

To all this, Daniel dissented. He did not participate in the decision of the *Letson* case.[8] Repeatedly and to the end of his life he denied jurisdiction in every diversity case in which a corporation was involved. In his last term in 1859 he dissented in six cases on this ground.

When Daniel began the course of these dissents he had the company of Catron and Campbell. Catron had joined in the *Letson* case, as he was later careful to explain, only because in that case the directors and officers of the corporation were of states different from the adverse party; and he did not consider himself bound by Wayne's opinion.[9] Campbell, who was appointed after the *Letson* decision, at first attacked the whole notion of corporate entry into Federal courts. But only Daniel stuck to his guns to the end. Campbell and Catron eventually acquiesced in the majority view and Campbell finally wrote an opinion of the court sustaining jurisdiction in such a case on precedent.[10]

Daniel was not one to yield to any majority, and he scored Campbell as sharply as his other colleagues when Campbell ultimately yielded. Daniel said:

> If the soundness of those arguments [once made by Campbell] is still regarded as a regular deduction from Constitutional principle, and from fealty to the Constitution, then a relinquishment of those arguments or the failure to assert them

on every occasion similar to that first calling them forth, however justifiable in the view of others, would in myself, by myself, be felt as a compromise of a sacred and solemn duty. The vindication of truth, whenever we shall be called on to speak or to act, can never, in my opinion, be properly shunned; I, therefore, am bound to reassert all which I have endeavored earnestly, however feebly, to maintain, and which I still believe.[11]

The rationale of the objection to corporate access to Federal courts was spelled out largely in dissents in six cases, four by Daniel and two by Campbell, in one of which Daniel concurred.[12] As always, Campbell's opinions are somewhat sharper and clearer than Daniel's. The composite of the arguments made in these opinions runs as follows.

1) The simple argument: A corporation is not a citizen, and no possible logic can make it one. At most, and this is a very undesirable most, one could follow Marshall's device of looking through the corporate structure to the citizenship of its shareholders. With national corporations this would still keep most of them out of the courts.

2) The argument from authority: The *Letson* case is recent error, in conflict with the *Deveaux* case.

3) The second argument from authority: Our cases repeatedly require explicit averments of citizenship. We make a mistaken exception for corporations.

4) The argument from the nature of government: This broadening of jurisdiction reduces the states to subservience to Federal power. The Federal government is foreign to the states, a lion which will devour their powers. "For myself I would never hunt with the lion." [13]

5) The argument of economics: Once we permit the corporations to claim that they are citizens for purposes of this clause, they will claim it for purposes of others. This will enlarge the power of "wealthy, powerful, and ambitious cor-

porations" and of "the commercial states." [14] These corporations will become more powerful than the states in which they exist and will, if given access to Federal courts, control or influence them.

The arguments were unavailing, and the corporations went their way. Having acquired access to the Federal courts, their next need was an efficient procedure for using the Federal judicial power to set aside state legislation regulating them. The principal difficulty was the Eleventh Amendment, which handicapped suits directly against states. But ingenuity found a way. In *Dodge v. Woolsey*, a shareholder sued his corporation to enjoin it from obeying a state statute. The object was to secure diverse citizenship, and for this purpose the legal fiction could be used only to a point. The corporation was deemed to be a citizen of Ohio, and its shareholder was recognized as a citizen of Connecticut. Campbell dissented from Wayne's opinion, and Daniel concurred with Campbell. This was as far as the corporate manipulation of Federal jurisdiction could go, and before the end of the century the gain was largely reversed.[15]

Daniel's other great rear-guard action was in resistance to the admiralty jurisdiction. This time he was pitted flatly against his chief, for it was Taney who carried the torch of the revolutionary.

The issue was where cases concerning ships and shipping should be tried. If there were, for example, a collision between vessels on the high seas, the case might be tried, according to the Constitution, in the Federal courts under an appropriate act of Congress. In such an instance the case would be heard by a Federal district court which would sit without a jury, and which would apply the law of admiralty. On the other hand, under the then traditional law, if the same collision should occur on the inland waterways, the case would be heard in a state court, presumably with a jury. The general rule was that admiralty jurisdiction in all matters concerning shipping extended only to the high seas and the tidewaters — the Great Lakes and the inland rivers were wholly subject to state jurisdiction.

This was a genuinely important matter in the early nineteenth century. In the first place, prior to the development of the railroads water shipping was for practical purposes all the transportation there was. Legal problems relating to such shipping thus bulked large in the total law business of the country.

Resistance to the spread of admiralty jurisdiction was extremely keen. Primarily it was based on the absence of a jury, but it also involved both the strong states' rights feeling of the time and a resistance to the law of admiralty which, because of its special origin, still seems strange and different to many lawyers.

Prior to 1825 it was not clearly established whether admiralty jurisdiction would follow the spreading population of the United States into the inland waters. Between 1821 and 1825 Congress seriously considered legislation to limit admiralty to the high seas and the tidal waters. Kentucky congressmen in particular feared that they might find admiralty courts on the Ohio, and they were determined to resist. Limiting legislation passed in the Senate but failed in the House. Then in 1825 the Supreme Court, in an opinion by Justice Story, unanimously held in the case of *The Thomas Jefferson* that admiralty jurisdiction was limited to the high seas and to the tidewaters.[16] In that case it was suggested that if Congress wished to extend admiralty jurisdiction to the inland waters, it should do so through use of its commerce power.

Rarely has a principle established for the ages by a grave Supreme Court decision been overthrown so quickly. There continued to be strong pressure to let both accident or collision cases and contract cases concerning shipping go into the Federal admiralty courts. There were many reasons for this pressure, including a preference for uniform law, the shippers' familiarity with general admiralty principles, and a desire on the part of the steamboat interests to subject their crews to Federal mutiny and desertion laws, which applied wherever there was admiralty jurisdiction.[17] The Court began chipping away at the rule of *The Thomas Jefferson* in 1847 and 1848 and overthrew it in 1850, with Daniel resisting all the way.[18] In addition to the strictly legal arguments, Daniel's opinions in these cases outlined the policy considerations which made him desire to hold down admiralty jurisdiction: first, he felt that the actual law of admiralty was "less congenial with our institutions" than the common law; second, he objected to the loss of jury trial; third, he objected to letting into the Federal courts disputes between citizens of the same state; fourth, he objected to the procedure of the admiralty courts, which he felt less calculated to get at the truth than the rules of the law courts; and fifth, he objected to the inconvenience to the people, noting that unlike the local courts, the Federal courts might be a long distance from their homes.

In 1851 the Court went the rest of the way and overruled *The Thomas Jefferson*.[19] The main question was: Did the admiralty courts of the Federal government have just as much jurisdiction on the lakes and rivers of the country as on the high seas? Taney for the Court answered this question in the affirmative, thus rejecting *The Thomas Jefferson* altogether. In an opinion which has ever since been commonly regarded as a classic in jurisprudence as well as in the particular subject matter, he pleaded the necessities of an expanding country as grounds for taking a new look at the whole subject. On the basis of that look, and of the obvious unreasonableness of a rule which may have made sense in insular England but not in continental United States, he held that "there is certainly nothing in the ebb and flow of the tide that makes the waters peculiarly suitable for admiralty jurisdiction, nor anything in the absence of a tide that renders it unfit." So far as the majority was concerned, if the speedy remedies of the admiralty courts were an aid to the transportation industry of America, they ought to be just as available to the shippers of Detroit as to the shippers of Boston. *The Thomas Jefferson* he rejected as a decision "made in 1825, when the commerce on the rivers in the West and on the lakes was in its infancy, and of little importance, and but little regarded compared with that of the present day."

By this time Daniel was the lone dissenter. A matter more appealing to his stand-pat approach to the Constitution could not be found. He stressed that by the decisions in England and by the previous decisions of this very Court, it had been clear that there was no jurisdiction; "and although it is admitted that the power was once clearly understood as being limited to the ebb and flow of the tide, yet now, without there having been engrafted any new provision on the Constitution, without the alteration of one letter of that instrument, designed to be the charter of all Federal power, the jurisdiction of the admiralty" is to be vastly extended.

But what of the argument that the practical necessities of life required a broader view? Daniel responded exactly as Daniel could be expected to respond; this was the Daniel who in 1812 would not advance a few pence of the public funds to purchase trousers for a shivering militiaman at the barricades. As far as he was concerned, the Constitution was to be interpreted exactly and precisely and at all times as it was intended by those who wrote, and according to their vision: "My opinions may be deemed to be contracted and antiquated, unsuited to the day in which we live, but they are founded upon deliberate conviction as to the nature and objects of limited government." He sharply stressed the novelty of the majority position: "I have at least the consolation — no small one it must be admitted — of the support of Marshall, Kent, and Story in any error I may have committed."

As with the matter of corporate access to the Federal courts, Daniel maintained his resistance to the end. The issue did not have for him the burning quality of high urgency which made him almost savage in the corporate cases, and in one of the later decisions he was satisfied simply to tease his brothers a little. He pointed out that a tributary of the Potomac crossed Pennsylvania Avenue. "Upon the return of the tide," he wrote, "there may be seen on this water numerous boys bathing or angling, or passing in canoes. Should a conflict arise amongst these urchins, originating either in collision of canoes or an entangling of fishing lines, or from any similar cause, this would present a case of admiralty jurisdiction fully as legitimate as that which is made by the libel in the case before us." [20] Right up to his last week as an active member of the court, he objected to any exercise of jurisdiction in an admiralty case beyond that which had been traditional.[21]

Daniel thus opposed the first two great overrulings of constitutional doctrine in the nineteenth century: the overruling of Marshall's decision in *Bank of United States v. Deveaux* and the overruling of *The Thomas Jefferson*. (I speak now not of new departures, of which there were many, but of flat overrulings or rejections of earlier doctrine on the ground that the times had outgrown it.) What these two have in common is that in each a radically changing national economic scene made imperative a re-examination of an earlier policy. That re-examination might have been achieved by either judicial reconstruction of the law or by constitutional amendment. In the early nineteenth century the country might have chosen either method. If they had chosen Daniel's way, we would doubtless now have a much more amended Constitution than is the case. But Taney's Court chose, over Daniel's objection, to meet new situations by judicial reconsideration. Thus began the national tradition of keeping constitutional questions open to a greater degree than other issues. For the Daniel who thought of himself always as "an old fashioned man" the other way would have been better.

Chapter XIV

PERSONAL RELATIONS

THERE WERE three women in Daniel's life, and tragedy marked the end of his relationship with each. They were his first wife, Lucy Randolph; his elder daughter, Elizabeth; and his second wife, Elizabeth Harris.

Lucy was the major influence toward sweetness and kindness in Daniel's adult life. Until he went to the Court in 1841 the two were almost never separated by anything more substantial than his business trips around Virginia. But from 1842 to 1847 Daniel's absences became extensive by virtue of his sessions in Washington and his travels on circuit, and these were very hard for both to bear.

Lucy's life revolved around her husband, her children, her church, and always her health. The nature of her ailment is unclear, but whatever it was, it robbed her of her strength. She was never really sturdy and she had few adventures. Excitement for her consisted of occasional excursions around Virginia, as for example a trip to Daniel's home area in Stafford County.

The timidity which Daniel first noticed in Lucy stayed with her throughout life. This was never a *grande dame* of Virginia society. She was truly a fluttering bird in a little cage of a world, hopping about in constant concern, with no ability to tell the large problems from the small ones. What is probably her last letter to her husband tells her story:

> I did not expect dearest to write to you again, before your return; but finding I have made you uneasy, I only write, to

say, that you know all the events of the winter, but you cannot know, how entirely our son's marriage contributes to my comfort, by seeing the increase of his happiness — and the more I know of my dear Mary, the more am I convinced she is qualified to make this beloved son happy.

I always feel doubly anxious in your absence, and this winter, knowing we should have an increase of expense, I allowed myself to be very anxious. Change of servants, from those I was willing to keep, for strangers, first disturbed me. [*Word illegible*] now, then the bacon gave me much uneasiness. When I let matters of this sort trouble me, I am sure, I cannot expect anyone to care for my troubles. I have seen around me suffering of every sort, and it has not come near me, yet I have allowed myself to be anxious about trifles. I acknowledge this to be wrong, but excuse myself, on account of feebleness of body that allows my great sensitivity to overcome me.

I am sad at the thoughts of dear Margaretta leaving us. She is indeed a most charming inmate. She goes on Tuesday. If you should be coming out of court when the boat comes in, or the cars go out rather, you might chance to see her, as you pass.

You do not acknowledge the receipt of the money Peter sent in my letter. Charlotte has the measles so mildly that I have sent for George only to decide the fact of her having it, and to say that my treatment was right. Goodby darling till we meet —

Your wife.[1]

On the night of November 14, 1847, at about ten in the evening, someone started a fire in a building being used as a school on Grace Street near the Daniel home. The fire never reached the Daniel property, but the excitement did. The shock and strain were too much for Lucy, who had a stroke and died. The surprised and horrified community gathered at the Episcopal Church next morning and heard her minister, the Reverend Mr. Norwood, report her death. Norwood spoke of her delicate health, noting, however, that she had lately been better, and of the loss sustained by her family and by Richmond society.[2]

Lucy's death after 37 years of marriage left a desolate husband and a truly bereaved family. Daniel finally sought refuge in writing, as he always did when strong emotion gripped him, and attempted to prepare for the children a memoir of their mother.[3] He wrote "To my dear children, from their father. I have performed a work both of duty and affection — very imperfectly performed I know; still it is a relief to my heart to have executed it even in this imperfect way. And I trust it may yield both gratification and advantage to my dear children by enabling them more fully to contemplate an example of almost unequalled excellence, and by aiding their efforts to form their own characters from that high model placed before them."

Daniel thought back to the happy beginnings. He recollected for the children when he had first met their mother, recalling "the striking loveliness of her person, mind and habits." He recollected their courtship and their marriage, their happy life together, and her devotion to the Episcopal Church. There follow some pages of the sentiment of the occasion, culminating with, "Let us then, my beloved children, endeavor to bow in all humility to the will of God . . . perhaps it may be permitted that she whom we mourn may be commissioned our guardian angel."

With Lucy's death, however, Daniel himself took over even more firmly than before the task of guarding his family. In his family relationships Daniel was clearly a well-meaning fussbudget. He kept an eye on every detail of his own life and on that of everyone around him. He needed socks — Elizabeth would find them in such and such a place and send them. New shirts should be made — pleats should be just so; and later the shirtmaker had to be reproved because they were unsatisfactory.[4] The chimney should be cleaned in a particular manner; the horse sent to meet him should be run at a particular gait; the windows of the house should be marked in a particular way; scalded bran should be given the horses; the girls should stay out of the sun; Elizabeth should ride for her health, she should walk for her health, she should go to bed early and rise early for her health; the bacon should be hung properly. And so it went. This constant flow of instructions does not reflect willful tyranny, but affection without common-sense restraint.

Of the three children, Daniel's keenest relationship was with his older daughter, Elizabeth. His son Peter, Jr., was a source of pride. Peter succeeded to Daniel's property interests and succeeded as well to some of his positions in Democratic state politics in the 1840's. The son was a lawyer who eventually became a railroad executive as well.[5] But Peter had a life and family of his own and the two were not in a position of regular daily need of each other. The same is true of his second daughter, Anne, who married into a North Carolina family and went there to live. Daniel stayed in touch with Anne and was interested in her and fond of her, but there was no substantial mutual dependence between the two.

Elizabeth, on the other hand, never married. She had been her father's regular confidante even during her mother's lifetime and when Lucy died Elizabeth succeeded to her position as lady of the house. The two kept up an astonishingly constant correspondence with each other, and though the letters from Elizabeth to her father are lost, many of those from Daniel have been preserved. During the 1847–48 Court term, for example, there is an average of two long letters a month from father to daughter which have been preserved, and there may perfectly well have been others. To Elizabeth, and a little less often to Anne, he told whatever he hoped would interest them about Washington life and his part in it. He talked some politics with Elizabeth, though never with Anne, whom he regarded as a light-headed miss interested only in the social life of the capital.

The six years from 1847 to 1853 were acutely lonely. When the Justice was at home, he had the companionship of Elizabeth and doubtless of old friends, although even this circle shrank. Ritchie, his companion-in-arms in the battles for the Jackson administration, had come to Washington to edit a national Democratic paper; but the deterioration in their personal relations which had begun during the Van Buren administration reached a point of decisive split about 1850. When the Justice was on circuit, he had such limited and highly sporadic social contacts as Arkansas and Mississippi — his circuit — could then afford. When he was in Washington his fellow Justices were his dominant company. As has been noted, he was not much in the Washington social whirl. He received the usual number of formal invitations, but regularly declined them, very nearly restricting his social life to a small number of almost required official functions. Daniel's recreation was not a party, it was a walk, and his favorite destination was the Douglas greenhouse.[6] Wherever he traveled, his first interest was in growing things — from the watermelons and peaches on Van Buren's New York estate to the flowers of Mississippi. His preoccupation with the produce of his own farm was a pleasant agrarian's monomania.

Daniel's relations with all of his colleagues was courteous [7] — his failure to acknowledge the retirement of Curtis in 1857 was a very rare exception. But he was only intimate with Democrats; the others he largely ignored. In almost a hundred letters written between 1843 and 1853, letters in which the names of Taney, Grier, Catron, Wayne, and Woodbury are constantly recurrent, the names of Story, McLean, and Curtis do not appear even once. In a correspondence in which he records even casual visits, there is no evidence that he ever took one meal or had one common social experience with any of these Justices — and the pleasure with which he recorded that he and Wayne had been invited to a dinner at which no

Whigs were guests suggests that he saw as little of these political adversaries as possible.

Between 1847 and 1853 Daniel shared a boarding house in Washington usually with Wayne, Grier, Catron, and Taney. At times General Howard, the court reporter, was also with them, though Daniel's dissatisfaction with the reporting of one of his dissents led to some unpleasantness with Howard in 1855.

The Howard incident arose in connection with *Northern Ind. R. Co. v. Michigan Cent. R. Co.*[8] In this case Justice Catron concurred and Justice Daniel dissented, these opinions following each other consecutively in the report. However, due to an error, Daniel's name was not inserted at the beginning of his dissenting opinion, so that the Catron opinion appears first to concur and then to dissent. This was an 1853 opinion. When the bound volume of the reports came out, someone brought the error to Howard's attention, the reports being his precise responsibility. He put an erratum note at the beginning of the next volume.

It is not clear when Daniel first heard of the blunder. In any case, he saw fit not to mention it to Howard until January of 1855, at which time he precipitated a completely unreasonable correspondence. He wrote Howard saying that the clerk of the Court had just asked for a copy of his dissenting opinion in a recent case. He had informed the clerk that he wished to think for a time as to whether he intended to have any of his dissents included in the reports of the Court henceforth. So far as he was concerned, he wrote, accurate reports were more important for dissents than for majority opinions. There had been other errors of which he had not complained, but the incident of the *Indiana Railroad* case made both Catron and him look ridiculous.

Howard was duly and politely contrite, but the mistake had been more Daniel's fault than his. Today all opinions are printed even for working purposes within the Court, but in those days each Justice wrote out his opinions by hand. He then gave it to the clerk of the court, Mr. Carroll, for filing. Sometimes the Justices neglected to put their names at the head of their opinions, so that when the opinions passed to the reporter from Carroll the only way he had of knowing the author was either his recognition of the handwriting or a possible notation by Carroll himself.

Howard explained this system: "The last thing which I do before making up the package for the printer, is to go carefully over it in a final review to see that all is right. In this case, I must have omitted to notice the absence of your name at the head of your opinion, and, of course, the printer continued his unbroken page. If you had placed your own name at the head of the opinion, or if I had noticed the absence, the mistake would not have happened." Howard went a little further, noting that occasionally in the past there had been problems with Daniel's handwriting and proposing that if Daniel would have his opinions copied by someone in the clerk's office and checked over before they were sent to the printer, greater efficiency would result.

If Daniel was angry in the first place, the reply made him furious. To have Howard suggest that the error in the *Indiana Railroad* case was his fault seemed to him grossly unreasonable. Certainly the reporter and the clerk should at least want to know whose opinions they were recording and reporting and any failure in this respect was their own fault. So far as having the opinions copied by the clerk, he knew of no legal authority for the clerk's office to perform this service, and in any case, careful proofreading would be equally required. So far as handwriting problems were concerned, if those charged with printing would use simple intelligence, they would not convert words into nonsense. In the future he would not have his dissents printed in the reports at all.[9]

This exchange with Howard reflects the weaknesses of Daniel's character. He was sadly subject to the vices of pettiness and arrogance and to an insufferable self-righteousness. Perhaps it was too much bother for him to have his opinions copied so that he could check them over before printing; a busy Justice could reasonably enough say that this was what staff was for. But certainly only a person overly impressed with himself would insist upon being emancipated from the necessity of writing his name on his opinions, and would assume that his opinions would be easily recognized by all.

The one invariably delightful relationship of Daniel's Court experience was with Taney. This friendship, unparalleled in Daniel's life, was marked by affection and respect coupled with reasonable difference of opinion. These differences were comparatively moderate — there was nothing like the gulf between Daniel and McLean — and Taney was skillful at minimizing them. Though Daniel kept his complete intellectual independence, Taney's behavior toward him was almost paternal. This is the more odd in that only seven years separated their ages. But Taney was older in service to the common cause. He had borne the brunt of withdrawing the deposits from the Bank of the United States, he was senior of the Court, and he had the prestige of his position. For whatever reason, Daniel in every respect but that of intellectual subservience followed his Chief Justice's lead. When Daniel had a runny nose Taney told him to stay in bed and he dutifully did it.[10]

The two men saw each other both in term and out. In 1851 Daniel went for a short vacation to a Virginia spa. Taney at the time was vacationing at Old Point Comfort, Virginia, and asked Daniel to join him, which he promptly did. There the two Justices, Daniel aged 67 and Taney aged 74, had a gay and friendly time. Taney aroused his companion at 11 o'clock one night for a two-mile walk on the beach. The dinners they attended lasted until midnight. The pace was too fast for Daniel — he was stricken with gout and returned in pain to Richmond where a still energetic Taney came by for a sick call.[11]

Like many Justices, Daniel in moments of boredom or fatigue toyed with the notion of leaving the bench. His daughter Elizabeth encouraged the impulse. Daniel once went in to see the Chief Justice with a letter from her suggesting some plan of retirement. He reported the matter back to Elizabeth thus:

> I have been puzzling myself to conjecture what can be your scheme for releasing me from the labors of the bench. True, I hate the very [*word illegible*] of the court, and would gladly never put my head within one if 'twer practicable to avoid so doing. I fear it is beyond your power, or any other power save that which may end my days, to accomplish such an emancipation. The amusing part of the matter is that upon reading your letter I went to the room of the Chief Justice, and with some appearance of gravity, said to him, what do you think of my leaving the bench? He looked up to me with a face of astonishment and exclaimed, What! When you leave the bench I shall follow you. I would not remain without you. You were never more needed than at this time. I then laughed and read to him the passage from your letter. Whereupon he said jocularly, present my best regards to Miss Elizabeth, and say to her, that if there was danger of her accomplishing anything of the kind, I should try to invent some process to prevent her from effecting her end.[12]

To some extent the nature of Daniel's intellectual alliances on the bench can be reduced to a pattern and can be suggested statistically. The following table shows the number of times each Justice joined in dissent with every other Justice throughout the period of Taney's service as Chief Justice, which is to say from 1836 to 1864. Daniel sat for a long middle portion of those years. The Justices who sat with him for most of this time were Taney, McLean, Wayne, Catron, and Grier. He was in agreement in dissent with his fellow southerners and fellow Democrats Taney and Catron twenty times each, and with Grier, with whom he served 25 percent fewer terms, eleven. With Campbell, who was on the court for only seven of Daniel's terms, he agreed in dissent twelve times — these are predominantly the contract clause, corporate citizenship, and admiralty cases. On the other hand, with McLean and Wayne he joined in dissent only seven and three times respectively. Most striking of all is the record of lone dissents. Daniel dissented alone, forty-six times, more than twice as often as any other Justice. Daniel had approximately three times as many lone dissents as Taney, Catron, and Campbell put together. This was indeed an independent man!

The table also shows something of the intellectual pattern of the Court. Taney, Daniel, Catron, and Campbell rarely joined in dissent with McLean or Wayne. Lone dissenters were most likely to be either McLean (who dissented alone twenty-one times) or Daniel, which is to say either the extremest federalist or the extremest agrarian of the Court. Indeed, McLean and Daniel represent the points of the pendulum within whose arc the Court swung for many years.

As time passed Daniel's world became not larger but narrower. His life in the 1830's had been a composite of national politics, law practice, and his wife and family. Later he had added to this the duties of a Federal district court judge. But his life changed considerably when he went on the Supreme Court. Within a few years he had terminated his relationship with Van Buren and with it his liaison to any part of the northern Democratic party. Moreover, Supreme Court judging took him out of politics. As time went on and new faces occupied the national scene, he drifted farther and farther away. It is inevitable that this should happen to any Supreme Court Justice as he outlasts the administration which appointed him. In Daniel's case the tendency was more marked because he

Number of times each Justice joined in dissent with every other Justice and number of lone dissents, 1836–1864[a]

	Taney	Story	Thompson	McLean	Baldwin	Wayne	Barbour	Catron	McKinley	Daniel	Nelson	Woodbury	Grier	Curtis	Campbell	Clifford	Swayne	Miller	Davis	Field	Lone dissents
Taney	—	0	0	8	0	5	1	15	2	20	11	3	8	0	1	2	0	0	0	0	3
Story	0	—	2	4	2	1	0	1	2	0	—	—	—	—	—	—	—	—	—	—	2
Thompson	0	2	—	0	2	0	1	2	0	0	—	—	—	—	—	—	—	—	—	—	2
McLean	8	4	0	—	2	21	0	1	8	7	6	7	8	9	2	1	—	—	—	—	21
Baldwin	0	2	2	2	—	0	1	1	0	0	—	—	—	—	—	—	—	—	—	—	17
Wayne	5	1	0	21	0	—	0	5	7	3	6	4	14	4	0	2	0	1	0	0	5
Barbour	1	0	1	0	1	0	—	3	0	—	—	—	—	—	—	—	—	—	—	—	0
Catron	15	1	2	1	1	5	3	—	1	20	8	0	13	1	13	1	0	1	0	0	8
McKinley	2	2	0	8	0	7	0	1	—	1	0	1	3	0	—	—	—	—	—	—	2
Daniel	20	0	0	7	0	3	—	20	1	—	6	4	11	4	12	1	—	—	—	—	46
Nelson	11	—	—	6	—	6	—	8	0	6	—	4	5	2	2	2	0	1	0	0	4
Woodbury	3	—	—	7	—	4	—	0	1	4	4	—	1	—	—	—	—	—	—	—	4
Grier	8	—	—	8	—	14	—	13	3	11	5	1	—	1	3	1	0	1	0	0	8
Curtis	0	—	—	9	—	4	—	1	0	4	2	—	1	—	4	—	—	—	—	—	1
Campbell	1	—	—	2	—	0	—	13	—	12	2	—	3	4	—	0	1	1	—	—	5
Clifford	2	—	—	1	—	2	—	1	—	1	2	—	1	—	0	—	1	2	0	0	4
Swayne	0	—	—	—	—	0	—	0	—	—	0	—	0	—	1	1	—	2	2	0	0
Miller	0	—	—	—	—	1	—	1	—	—	1	—	1	—	1	2	2	—	0	0	3
Davis	0	—	—	—	—	0	—	0	—	—	0	—	0	—	—	0	2	0	—	0	1
Field	0	—	—	—	—	0	—	0	—	—	0	—	0	—	—	0	0	0	0	—	0

[a] This table was prepared in 1948 by Charles Alan Wright, now professor of law at the University of Texas Law School.

was appointed at the very end of an administration. The situation did not change when his own party returned to power with the election of 1844. President Polk was a stout Jacksonian and a protégé of the Old Hero, but Daniel scarcely knew him; [13] and insofar as Daniel could do anything from the sidelines prior to the nominating convention of 1844, it had been as a friend of Van Buren rather than of Polk.

Daniel was so completely a stranger to Polk that when he wanted to make one suggestion for an appointment in the Polk administration, he did it through General Jackson; and by this time he had been out of touch with Jackson for a long interval.[14] Daniel thereafter overcame his sense of delicacy and made occasional direct suggestions to Polk. Shortly after the inauguration he reported to Polk that the Whigs in Virginia had been utterly ruthless in their destruction of the Democrats, and he asked that one of the victims of Whig proscription be given the post of surveyor of the Port of Richmond.[15] But his various efforts in this regard were of little effect. He never achieved any real intimacy with the Polk administration, and was for practical purposes virtually a stranger to all succeeding administrations.

The result was that in the bleak period after Lucy's death in 1847 Daniel's Washington life was largely circumscribed by the bench, the bar, and the cases before him. It was a brilliant bar, and there were occasional displays of real interest to the public as well as the Court. To this Court came what Daniel thought of as the great Yankee lawyers such as Ames, Whipple, Webster, and Rufus Choate. He reported that one of Choate's "high rhetorical speeches" was "quite entertaining and some portions of it very pretty, but in the main too ambitious of display, to which argument is not infrequently sacrificed." At the same term Henry Clay made one of his parting appearances before the Supreme Court and while there paid a formal visit on Daniel. He told Daniel that this was his last appearance in the Court and broadly hinted that he would never again seek the presidency, saying that he never expected to come East from Kentucky again. Daniel politely, and quite sensibly, disbelieved.[16]

Daniel set out to write up the Clay argument for the amusement of his daughter Anne:

I can give you an account of the scene in our courtroom yesterday. You have heard already that the great Whig idol, Mr. Clay, has been here for some weeks or fortnight. He had a cause on the docket, though it was thought that the object of feeling the political pulse, at this great seat of intrigue was as much the purpose of his coming as anything else. The attention and even adulation which has been shown him here has been excessive — and what seems more remarkable to me when I reflect on the very exceptional course of this man's affairs, that this following in almost servility has been more extreme on the part of women (ladies I suppose they must be called) than on the part of the men. Every day the expectation he was to speak has drawn a crowd [which upon seeing that] other advocates, and some of them abler than he occupied the floor at once dispersed. On yesterday it was known that he was to address the court and in consequence the courtroom was crowded to suffocation, chiefly by females, scarcely one of whom could comprehend the mere legal questions to be discussed. This crowd I am told began as early as nine o'clock in the morning. As to his argument of this law question, it was tolerable, nothing extraordinary and certainly inferior much to that of his opponent, Mr. Sargeant. Finding himself surrounded by this crowd of admirers I presume he thought himself bound to say something to flatter them, so he began by telling of his having been in the Parliament of England and in the Court of King's Bench in neither of which were the speakers or judges surrounded by such brilliance, sparkling eyes and elegant female forms; and with some such other flummery — but the singular part of the scene was the endurance of the crowd in heat for three and one half hours by the females, several of whom were compelled to remain standing during the whole time.[17]

There was some minor entertainment value in the *Gaines* case. This can only be described as the most incredible long-term litigation ever to be before the Supreme Court.[18] A rich New Orleans merchant named Daniel Clark had an illicit liaison with a Creole woman named Zulime Desgrange, by whom he had a daughter Myra. The result was a will controversy presented to the United States Supreme Court eleven times between 1836 and 1891, involving for Myra (then Mrs. Gaines) some thirty lawyers and the better part of a million dollars in fees and costs. The case was of great fascination to Justice Wayne, who carried the judicial torch for Myra with earnest ardor, but it was only of passing interest to Daniel. Mrs. Gaines ran a social lobby in connection with her case and in February of 1848 gave a dinner at Brown's Hotel to celebrate a recent success to which she invited Taney, Wayne, and Daniel. Daniel again had dinner with her and the Waynes during the next term. Daniel was to hear the case again in 1852, when the Court gave ten days to its argument. Daniel found it very offensive that ladies ("in appearance at least") should have crowded the courtroom to hear talk of the by now very old indiscretions of Mr. Clark. Chief Justice Taney was probably thereafter dropped from any of Myra's intimate little dinners, if such there were, because he joined the majority on this round in deciding against Mrs. Gaines, though Wayne and Daniel stuck with her.[19] The case did not come back again in Daniel's lifetime.

In the years after Lucy's death, the relationship between Daniel and Elizabeth became inevitably closer. At one point Elizabeth misunderstood a question from her father as some kind of a criticism, and felt called upon to justify certain expenditures. Daniel replied once to set his daughter straight: "Now and for all time let me say, that I desire no more such explanations. My wish is that my house should be liberally provided; that it should be the resort of cheerful, genteel company; that my daughter who is the head of my household should have health and cheerfulness to enable her to receive and enjoy such associates; that she should always be well, and on proper and suitable occasions, elegantly dressed." [20]

Daniel realized he needed this kind of a home because he perceived for himself that he was sinking into a dejected state. In the only moment of true introspection of which we have any record, he proceeded to reveal himself to Elizabeth with deeply accurate insight. He told her that a happy home was essential to keep him from utter despondency. "It may surprise persons who look at the mere surface of things," he said, "to be told, that the prevailing tendency of my disposition has always been to deep melancholy. Like many of the same idiosyncracy, I am excitable, and capable of quick and strong impressions, even of mirth and joy; but that was never the predominant trait in my temperament. On the contrary, I can well remember how often in my youth and even in childhood (and without any assignable cause) I have felt as if I must die from mere depression."

This melancholy and depression Daniel could keep in control during his years of practice and politics; but even then his mental stability had basically depended upon Lucy, "the soothing influence of that tenderness and unlimited sympathy and confidence which can exist in only one relation in life." With nothing but the tedium of the Court, and with the happy influence of Lucy irretrievably gone, "that darkness which to some extent obscured the morning of my life seems to be settling more thickly upon its evening." [21]

There was only one thing inaccurate in this moment of self-revelation. The "tenderness and unlimited sympathy and confidence" was not restricted to only one relationship. In 1853 Daniel married Elizabeth Harris of Philadelphia.

Of Elizabeth we know little. She was about 31 years of age at the time of her marriage to Daniel, who was then 67.

She was the daughter of Dr. Thomas Harris, the chief of the Bureau of Medicine and Surgery in the Navy Department, and a sister of Navy Lieutenant Thomas Harris, Jr. After the marriage in October of 1853 Daniel took her to a home on Franklin Row in Washington and there began to establish again the family and social life which he enjoyed.

Almost the only facts known about Elizabeth are that she was "interesting," at least in the view of Justice Curtis; that she was nearsighted, a fact which later was to prove to be of considerable importance; and that she was prolific. For Daniel, who had three children as old as his second wife, soon became the father of two more, a daughter Mary and a son Travers. Whatever else is to be said of the life of the Justice hereafter, with two babies in the house it at least could not again have been dull.

Chapter XV

SECTIONALISM AND SLAVERY

When Daniel came to the Court, he came as a liaison between North and South. He had won his preferment, built his entire career, on the construction and maintenance of the alliance between the Democratic parties of New York and Virginia. But this he was able to do because in the 1830's abolitionism was only beginning to strain North-South relations. The immense momentum of the antislavery movement carried the strain to the breaking point in the decade of the 1840's, and Daniel's own thinking moved rapidly with the shifting scene. Thus, in 1832 Daniel had been a staunch supporter of Jackson and a passionate opponent of Calhoun and nullification in South Carolina. The rising tide of abolitionism drove him off these positions, pushing him to the most complete extremism. By 1844 he was ready for secession if necessary — the old firebrand who in 1812 was willing to take on both France and England was one of the first public officials in America ready to see the South take on the North. For the last dozen years of his life, after the election of Taylor and Fillmore in 1848, he was a Southern sectionalist of the most extreme sort, his hostility to the North becoming a passion.

During his first years on the Court Daniel remained a loyal Van Buren lieutenant. As he traveled about the country on his circuit, he kept Van Buren informed of political developments which might affect the New Yorker's opportunity of returning to the White House in 1844 after having been ejected by the voters in 1840. Whether this was valuable advice is unimportant; certainly it was well intended. The critical issue on which Van Buren was caught in 1844 was whether to annex Texas, which had recently revolted from Mexico. In a general way the South favored annexation because, among other things, it would permit the extension of slavery. For this very reason the North was generally opposed. Van Buren was against the annexation but he evaded the issue in the hope of winning his seat in the White House again. Daniel reported to him candidly that he was suffering in Virginia because he drew back from annexation. As for Daniel himself, he was unsympathetic to annexation and thought it simply a Calhoun scheme to hurt Van Buren. As Daniel saw it, many southerners opposed the annexation for fear of the effect that the addition of so large a new territory would have on the price of land in the old states of the South.[1] When Polk was nominated in 1844, Daniel was distinctly disappointed, regarding him as a nonentity. At the same time, Daniel had already fully developed his belief that the South should secede if the North attempted to interfere with slavery in any way whatsoever.[2]

Daniel's last trip to the North came in the early fall of 1847. He and Lucy went to Boston and New York, fuming a good share of the way ("I can scarcely imagine a greater slavery, or any condition more absolutely vulgar, unrefined and unrefining than the scuffle and the selfish contention for accommodations infinitely inferior to our daily comforts at home, which make up the chief part if not the whole of a journey to *The North*.") He found Saratoga Springs, the usual Southern rendezvous in the North, acceptable but nothing else. However, he and Lucy did go to West Point and to Kinderhook to call on Van Buren. There he passed two days in pleasant conversation tarnished only by sadness at the recent death of Van Buren's principal supporter, Senator Silas Wright of New York. Daniel duly praised the gardens, the peaches, the watermelon, and the company.[3]

Thus ended the idyl. A month later, in October, a New York State Democratic convention approved the Wilmot proviso, which provided that all territory obtained from Mexico should be free. Van Buren was thought to have backed it, but his role was not clear. Daniel wrote in great alarm. He assured Van Buren that he was telling everyone that Van Buren could not possibly have committed such a heresy because "your own fidelity to the Constitution has been such that I would not believe that without your express statement that you are about to depart from the course of your previous life and to sunder forever your connection with true democracy of the Union."

For Daniel, as he told Van Buren, this was a pure constitutional question: Congress had no power whatsoever to deal with slavery in the territories. He emphasized that so far as the Wilmot proviso was concerned, "There is no true Southern man from the schoolboy to the octogenarian who is not prepared for any extremity in order to repel it." [4]

Van Buren replied evasively.[5] Daniel responded with dignity and with a double sorrow. He had but recently lost his wife Lucy in most tragic circumstances, and now he was losing the principal political friend of his life. He stated firmly that he could never accept the view that territory acquired by joint resources and exertion of the entire nation could be used for the benefit of a part of it only. If this was Van Buren's view, then "I shall have lived to witness a development, that even the great overwhelming and stunning personal calamity which has come upon me cannot prevent me from contemplating with deep sorrow and alarm. I shall have been constrained to perceive on the part of those, on whom of all the public men in this nation I imposed the greatest trust, what my deliberate convictions compel me to view as the overthrow of the great national compact; as the extreme of injury and oppression; oppression in its most galling form, because it declares to me that I am not regarded as an equal." He reminded Van Buren that Virginia was the home of Washington, Jefferson, Madison, and Monroe. Were all to be regarded as of an inferior caste? He ended on a formally hopeful note: "I would not, however, my dear sir, mean that any political differences of opinion should disturb our long cherished personal relations."[6] The hope was vain. The friendship was over.

The remaining thirteen years of Daniel's life were marked by fanaticism. As has already been illustrated, he blamed even the bad weather on the North, and was severely offended that respectful funeral rights should be given to antislavery former President John Quincy Adams. When some oranges were sent to him from the Deep South he was triumphant at this evidence of southern accomplishment, wondering "when *The North* . . . would ever produce anything like these oranges! or indeed anything else that is good and decent."[7] He resolved never to go north of the Delaware River again and believed that the southern people should not cooperate with the northern states in the selection of a President or, for that matter, in any political activities at all. As far as he was concerned, every northerner was an abolitionist and an enemy of the South. If his course of withdrawal and isolation were to lead to dissolution of the Union, then, as he saw it, this was something which the North had brought upon itself by its repeated violations of the Constitution.[8]

These were the views of Daniel a good ten years before the Civil War, during the lowest and unhappiest phase of his adult life, after the death of his first wife and before his marriage to his second. They were expressed at a time when he was down on everything; when he thought all of Washington to be the home of "profligacy, roguery, and humbug"; when he hoped that some dictator might throw out the incumbent Whig government — for he had "long been convinced that ours is at this time the most corrupt government in the Christian world at least." [9] The old unionist of 1832 had really reversed positions. When John C. Calhoun died in 1850 Daniel went to the funeral with all proper respect. "An unpracticable man," he said, but "a most exemplary one in his character and life." [10]

It was in this frame of mind that Daniel dealt, on occasion, with problems of slavery before the Court. In his first decade of service this was a relatively slight problem because the Court managed to stay, most of the time, fairly far from the slavery controversy. Two genuinely difficult cases, one of which severely agitated the country, were decided during the 1841 term in the days in which Daniel was up for confirmation; but thereafter there was comparative calm. [11]

In his first term Daniel heard *Prigg v. Pennsylvania.* Other cases involving the movement of slaves followed. The Court in a unanimous opinion by Justice Woodbury gave a broad and comprehensive interpretation to the Federal fugitive slave law. [12] The defendant Van Zandt had been found with nine Negroes who had escaped en masse into southern Ohio from nearby Kentucky. After an exciting chase, his wagon had been caught. Van Zandt defiantly proclaimed that his escapees were "by nature, as free as you and I," and that given an opportunity he would do it again. He was sued for damages under the Federal statute. Two men who were later to be in Lincoln's cabinet, Salmon P. Chase of Ohio and William Seward of New York, represented Van Zandt. They made a comprehensive attack on the validity of the fugitive slave law, an attack which the Court brushed aside.

The next case seriously treating slavery policy was *Strader v. Graham,* [13] a case involving what may well have been the first traveling Dixieland Band. A Kentucky slaveowner named

Graham owned two young Negro musicians named Henry and Reuben whom he assigned to one Williams, a bandleader, for the purpose of permitting them to play at dances and other public entertainments in Louisville, Cincinnati, and southern Indiana points. On the occasion of their escape these two and a third slave named George boarded a boat out of Kentucky. They were taken to the Ohio shore, and there escaped to Canada. Graham sued the boatowner for wrongful transportation of his slaves. A prime point in the defense was that the Negroes were not slaves at all, but rather had become free by virtue of having been voluntarily allowed to go into free states. The argument in their behalf was, as put by the counsel for the defendant, "As soon, then, as they touched the soil of Indiana or Ohio, with the consent of their master, the quality of freedom attached to their persons, and could never afterwards be disassociated from them."

In this case Daniel kept silent. Chief Justice Taney's opinion held that the Court had no power to decide whether the musicians had become free as a result of their performances north of the Ohio River. It was up to Kentucky to decide the nature of "the status, or domestic and social condition, of the persons domiciled within its territory." Therefore, the Kentucky determination on this point was final and there was nothing for the Supreme Court to review. It should be noted that the principle thus established would apply to the *Dred Scott* case, for that case would also turn on the effect on the slave of temporary sojourn in free states. There was some criticism of the *Strader v. Graham* decision, but it was generally accepted.[14]

Throughout these years the Court was, like all the other institutions of government, a part of a system which perpetuated and administered slavery. The whole conception and relationship was one to which all of the Justices were thoroughly accustomed. Any national court dealing day in and day out with problems of property would inevitably deal with all kinds of property, and one of the kinds was slaves. For example, a Mississippi planter gave a mortgage to the Commercial and Railroad Bank of Vicksburg for $130,000 secured by the "Negro slaves Nancy, and her child, Milley and her child, Viney and her child, Tempey and her child, Mary, Louisa, Juliana and Charlotte." A problem arose in connection with the foreclosure of this mortgage. The Court's unanimous opinion was written by its then most antislavery member, Justice McLean.[15] The rule of law announced would have been absolutely identical if the property had been good farm land in Vermont instead of prolific slave women in Mississippi.

All of which is to say that in Daniel's time there were two types of slave cases, those which were routine and which did not involve any sectional friction, and those which were of the utmost tension. The tension cases were consistently those which involved conflicts of policies between two states, and the fugitive slave cases were the prime example. The next of these was *Moore v. Illinois*,[16] in which the issue was the validity of the Illinois law punishing someone for harboring a fugitive slave. The defense was that the Illinois law was unconstitutional on the ground that this entire subject was committed to the hands of Congress, the contention being that this had been the holding of the majority in *Prigg v. Pennsylvania*.

The contention would appear to be exactly right. The essential difference between the majority opinion of Story and the opinions of Chief Justice Taney and of Daniel in the *Prigg* case was that Story asserted that the Federal power to enact laws relating to fugitive slaves was exclusive, while the other two contended that it was concurrent. In upholding the Illinois law in 1852 Justice Grier restated the rule of the *Prigg* case — in terms of the Taney-Daniel position. The Federal power was not exclusive, he said, so long as the state laws were in aid of capturing the fugitive slaves and did not interfere in any way with Federal power. Taney and Daniel, whose views had now prevailed altogether, discreetly stayed silent. McLean held to his original position of ten years before that the Federal power was exclusive.[17]

When the *Dred Scott* case came to its final decision in 1857, Daniel was a fifteen-year veteran of a court which had managed for all that time to keep on the outside edge of the slavery controversy. While some involvement was inevitable, it had stayed as far away from the center as possible. The *Dred Scott* decision put the Court directly into the middle.

Between 1847 and 1857 the issue of whether slavery should exist in the territories had become the largest single question in the United States. The Compromise of 1820 had attempted to settle this question for the Louisiana Territory, providing that all territory north of the southern border of Missouri, except Missouri, should be free. The Compromise of 1850 made provision for the territory obtained from Mexico. The Kansas-Nebraska Act of 1854 had repealed the Compromise of 1820. The career of every significant public man in the United States hung on the issue. Franklin Pierce went out of the White House in 1856 as much because of dissatisfaction with his Kansas-Nebraska policy as any other reason. Lincoln and Douglas in Illinois would soon stage their final struggles on this issue. Men died in battle in Kansas over whether that territory should be slave or free.

In 1857 the Supreme Court, in what is universally regarded as the gravest single miscalculation ever made by the American judiciary, concluded that it could settle this vast controversy by issuing its opinion. The Court misapprehended its powers. But it was pushed into the situation, in part at least, by the endless political aspirations of Justice McLean.

The story of the *Dred Scott* case does not need retelling, but we should review it briefly in order to examine Daniel's role.[18] Scott was a Negro who instituted a suit in 1846 in the state courts of Missouri against his master, alleging that he had become free because he had been taken into free territory. The Missouri state courts held that his return to Missouri re-established his slave status. If Scott were a citizen, he would be a citizen of Missouri, and his owner, a woman, was a Missourian. Since to enter Federal court the suit had to be between citizens of different states, his owner, who had during the long battle married a Massachusetts abolitionist congressman, set about to create diversity. She sold Scott to a New Yorker, Sanford, thus giving the Federal court jurisdiction. The suit was then brought by Scott, claiming to be a citizen of Missouri, against Sanford, a New Yorker. The case was decided against Scott in 1854 and was appealed to the United States Supreme Court.

At the moment of its appeal, which was in May of 1854, a decision might reasonably have passed on the validity of the Missouri Compromise. But later in the same month Congress repealed the Missouri Compromise, providing by the Kansas-Nebraska Act that the territories could decide the question of slavery for themselves. Thus the *Dred Scott* case no longer necessarily involved any great issue. These three questions might be, but did not all need to be, decided: (a) Whether Scott's status was settled by Missouri law, which had already been determined against him. On essentially identical facts the Court had held in *Strader v. Graham*, a few years before, that the legal effect of a return to a slave state was to be determined by the law of that state. (b) Whether Scott was a citizen of the United States. Scott brought his case in Federal court claiming to be a citizen of Missouri suing a citizen of New York under that clause of the Constitution which permitted the Federal courts to hear cases between citizens of different states. If Scott were not, in the constitutional sense, a citizen of the United States, the

Court would have no jurisdiction. (c) Whether as a matter of Federal law Scott's passage into territory which had been declared free by the Compromise of 1820 gave him his freedom.

If either of the first two questions were decided against Scott, there would be no necessity or utility in reaching the third. Indeed, if one of the first two questions were decided against him, there would be no point in going to the other. If the Court had no jurisidiction, then it should have no authority to discuss the subject any further. When the case was argued in February of 1856, the common impression was that the case would be decided against Scott on the authority of *Strader v. Graham*, although soon a notion spread abroad that the Court might instead hold that he was not a citizen and that therefore it had no jurisdiction. On April 8, 1856, Justice Curtis wrote his uncle in Boston that the Court had decided not to determine the issue of the validity of the Missouri Compromise, since this was unnecessary. As Justice Campbell remembered the matter almost twenty years later, in the spring of 1856 five Justices (Taney, Wayne, Daniel, Nelson, and Curtis) thought that the case could be disposed of on the jurisdictional ground. However, according to Campbell, since Nelson was in doubt, the matter was set for reargument, which would have the effect of carrying it over until after the election of 1856.

Meanwhile the Court was subject to a certain amount of extrajudicial pressure. Alexander Stephens from Georgia, then a member of the House of Representatives and later a vice president of the Confederacy, reported that he had been "urging all the influences I could bring to bear on the Supreme Court" to decide the Missouri Compromise issue. On the other hand there was some contrary pressure and some attack on the Court because of fear in the House of Representatives that the Court might invalidate the compromise.

On February 15, 1857, after the second argument, the Court met in conference and decided to settle the issue on the authority of *Strader v. Graham*, holding that the matter was to be settled by Missouri law, and reaching no other question. The opinion was assigned to Justice Nelson.

There the matter should have rested. But either McLean and Curtis or McLean alone determined to dissent, opening up the whole Missouri Compromise question by declaring in favor of its validity.[19] At this point, whether egged on by the impending McLean dissent or for independent reasons, Justice Wayne began strongly urging his colleagues to deal with all of the questions in the case, thus disposing of the slavery issue once and for all.[20] By February 19, only four days after the majority had concluded to dispose of the case on a relatively noncontroversial basis, Wayne, Taney, Catron, Daniel, and Campbell had agreed that instead it should be decided on the broader ground. On February 19, Justice Catron wrote President-elect Buchanan telling him that the Court was ready to decide the constitutional question and asking Buchanan to urge Justice Grier to join in deciding the largest instead of the smallest possible question in the case. Grier was persuaded, replying to Buchanan that he, Taney, and Wayne "fully appreciate and concur in your views as to the desirableness at this time of having an expression of the opinion of the Court on this troublesome question." Grier told the incoming President that since the other five Justices who had resolved to determine the constitutional question were from south of the Mason-Dixon line, he was inclined for the sake of the Court to go along with them: "I am anxious that it should not appear that the line of latitude should mark the line of division in the Court." [21]

In consequence Buchanan was able to give to the country in his inaugural address on March 4 the smug assurance that he was prepared cheerfully to abide with whatever decision the Supreme Court might give on the constitutional question. Two days later the Court began the reading of its opinions.

Alas for any appearance of judicial solidarity, there were nine Justices and nine opinions. They took essentially three approaches. The first encompasses the opinions of the Taney bloc of six, holding generally that Scott was not a citizen and that the Missouri Compromise was unconstitutional. The second is the opinion of Justice Nelson, originally contemplated as the opinion of the Court, but which that Justice now used as his own with the adjustment of a few words. This opinion, the only one justifiable on precedent, held on authority that Scott's status was determined by Missouri law and that under Missouri law he was a slave. The third approach is that of the separate dissents of McLean and Curtis, which upheld Scott's citizenship and his freedom in consequence of the Missouri Compromise, the validity of which they also upheld.

The six opinions on the majority side varied in length. That of Justice Grier was only a few words, noting his agreement with both Justice Nelson and the Chief Justice. The opinion of Justice Wayne was not a true separate opinion, but only a few paragraphs intended to rebut some of the dissenters' attacks on the Taney opinion. The opinions of Justices Campbell and Catron on the majority side were, at a minimum, full-length affairs. Campbell's was some twenty-six pages of rather overelaborate scholarship. The Catron opinion was made to depend upon certain legal consequences supposed to flow from the treaty with France by which the Louisiana Territory was acquired, an argument which had not much appeal to anybody but himself.

As between the Taney and Daniel opinions, the Taney opinion was given first, had the prestige of the Chief Justice behind it, and was joined without qualification by Justice Wayne and almost without qualification by Justice Grier. It thus came closer to being the "opinion of the Court" than

Daniel's. However, from the standpoint of a generally effective presentation of the issues and a resolution of them, one may fairly claim for the Daniel opinion the distinction of being the best of the majority opinions. Its conclusions were at one with those of Taney, and any differences were in execution and style.

For Daniel the case presented no intellectual issues which he had not long since decided. He had never doubted the invalidity of the Missouri Compromise from the day it was passed. Hence there was no issue for him as to how the question should be decided; the only problem was getting to it.

Here he lumbered a little. It took him six pages to get through the facts and to sift out the pleadings so as to satisfy himself that the jurisdictional issue was in the case, but from this point on he had smooth sailing. He noted "that the African Negro race never had been acknowledged as belonging to the family of nations; that as amongst them there never has been known or recognized by the inhabitants of other countries anything partaking of the character of nationality, or civil or political polity; that this race has been by all the nations of Europe regarded as subjects of capture or purchase; as subjects of commerce or traffic; and that the introduction of that race into every section of this country was not as members of civil or political society, but as slaves, as property in the strictest sense of the term." Thus all Negroes came to the United States as slaves. In that capacity they had no relationship of any kind with the state. The slave "is himself strictly property, to be used in subserviency to the interest, the convenience, or the will, of his owner." As property he cannot be a citizen.

Daniel then reached the more difficult question. Granting that property cannot be a citizen, can emancipation grant citizenship? In other words, does the slave who is not a citizen become a citizen by being made free? "It is difficult to perceive by what magic the mere surcease or renunciation of an interest in the subject of property, by an individual possessing that interest, can alter the essential character of that property with respect to persons or communities unconnected with such renunciation." According to Daniel's argument, which was based upon Roman authority, an owner could by his own act make a freed man, but he could not make a citizen — only the state could do that.

It followed, in this view, that Scott was not a citizen and that the Court therefore had no jurisdiction. This could have settled the case, and it is at this point that the Daniel opinion has the advantage of candor over that of Taney. Taney, having reached the same point in a somewhat different way, proceeded to argue that the question of the validity of the Missouri Compromise was necessarily and properly to be decided on principles of law. Daniel, on the other hand, recognized that no further discussion was necessary. But he too was caught up in the great Wayne illusion that the Court could settle the difficult central issue and so he continued: "But as these questions are intrinsically of primary interest and magnitude, and have been elaborately discussed in argument, and as with respect to them the opinions of a majority of the Court, including my own, are perfectly coincident, to me it seems proper that they should here be fully considered, and, so far as it is practicable for this Court to accomplish such an end, finally put to rest." He proceeded to declare the Compromise of 1820 invalid for very much the same reasons which he had advanced in his letter to Van Buren ten years earlier, and over and over again in the course of his life. As he saw it, in its management of the Federal territory the government had no power to discriminate between the citizens of one state and the citizens of another, to say that a citizen of Maine could take his property into a territory but that a citizen of Virginia could not. The territories were the common property of all, and all must have equal rights in respect to them. The Compromise of 1820 was nothing but "a means of forfeiting that equality of rights and immunities which are the birthright or the donative from the Constitution of every citizen of the United States within the length and breadth of the nation . . . Congress could not appropriate [the territories] to any one class or portion of the people, to the exclusion of others, politically and constitutionally equals."

Once the opinion was down Daniel was involved, though only a little, in a nasty quarrel between Taney and Curtis. The Curtis and McLean opinions were released to the press as given and were thus accurately reported in the North before the majority opinions. In order that the Curtis opinion might be more widely publicized, but in conjunction with the Taney opinion, Curtis asked the clerk of the Court for a copy of the Taney opinion. Taney, under the written endorsement of approval from Justices Wayne and Daniel, the only two Justices then in the city, directed the clerk not to give a copy to Curtis. Curtis was thus in the position of not being able to obtain a copy of an important opinion of the Court of which he was a member. The resultant personal tension was a factor — though only one — in his resigning shortly thereafter.

But these personal matters were remote from Daniel, as was most of the *Dred Scott* controversy; for he was immersed in his own tragedy. On the evening of January 3, 1857, a month before the *Scott* reargument, the Daniels had been out to dinner and returned to their home at about 10 in the evening. The Justice went to his library. Mrs. Daniel retired to her room. Perhaps she had lighted a candle and placed it on her dressing table, and it fell off; or perhaps a candle was burning on the hearth and, because she was nearsighted, she did not see it. From whatever source, a flame touched her calico robe and it ignited. She screamed in terror and ran into the hall outside the bedroom. There a burst of air caused the whole thing to flare up. Daniel heard her scream and rushed from his study, but before he and a servant who heard her cries could reach her she was severely burned. They quickly rolled her up in the carpet to put out the flame, but it was too late. After hours of the most extreme agony she died. All she was able to say as to the manner of the accident was "The candle, the candle." [22] Daniel himself was somewhat burned in the effort to put out the flames.

The next day when the Court sat, the Chief Justice said, "Gentlemen of the Bar, you are already, I presume, apprised of the calamity which has befallen our brother, Judge Daniel, in the sudden and painful death of his wife. Our respect and regard for him, as well as our sense of what is due to him as a member of this tribunal, will prevent the Court from proceeding with the business of the term. The funeral of Mrs. Daniel will take place tomorrow, which the members of the Court will attend." Daniel did not return to the Court until mid-February.

Elizabeth was interred in the Oak Hill Cemetery, in Georgetown. The President, members of the cabinet, Judges of the Supreme Court, and many officers of the Army and Navy as well as personal friends were in attendance. The couple had been married a little over three years. Daniel never had any real happiness again.

Chapter XVI

ROUTINE COURT BUSINESS

JUDGING IN THE pre-Civil War years was not always, or even frequently, a matter of settling great disputes over commerce, contracts, corporations, or slavery. There was as well the routine business of the Court, the settling of private disputes and occasionally the making of broader social policy. This work is so diverse that it defies integration. Yet it requires discussion because this is what occupied most of the Justices' time. Even today, when the Supreme Court selects for its determination what it regards as the most important matters in a nation of 180 million people, 90 percent of the business of any term is workaday stuff which will not be of much interest to the historians of the twenty-first century.[1] This was far more true in Daniel's time, when many factors contributed to the making of a far less exciting docket than we have today.

Daniel tended to his share of this business. As has been shown, he wrote a fair share of the majority opinions during his years on the Court and considerably more than his share of dissents. It could scarcely be said that he bore the burdens of the ever increasing Court docket uncomplainingly, but he bore them, and stood up under them. For the load on the Court was becoming impossible. In 1840 a total of 92 new cases were filed. In 1850 the number of new filings was 253, and in 1860 it was 320.[2] The Court did what it could; in 1849 it cut the interminable oral arguments; and by sheer hard work and longer terms it increased its output. By the end of

Daniel's tenure the Court disposed of almost twice as many cases per term as it had twenty years before.

Nonetheless, the Court fell farther and farther behind in its docket, for there could be no long-range cure until it was relieved of its circuit duties and its members were permitted to apply themselves exclusively to the work in Washington. Daniel himself was completely aware of the necessity of eliminating these duties, an awareness heightened by his own severe distaste for the circuit assigned to him. Where he could, he urged that the Supreme Court be made into an exclusively appellate tribunal with long enough terms to be able to dispose of the country's business. The circuit system clearly misapplied judicial time. Moreover Daniel thought it purposeless to have the Justices hearing appeals from themselves. He feared that if the country were to cling to the circuit system, as the nation's territory expanded the Court would have to be increased to an impossible number.[3] But as the years went by he became acutely aware that though there was always talk about correcting the circuit system, nothing was likely to be done about it. And indeed during his lifetime nothing was.

This meant, then, that as a practical matter throughout Daniel's years, nine Justices sitting between December and March of each winter were called upon to dispose of more business than they could manage.

Among the routine matters were some cases which were truly exciting. Of these far and away the most colorful in the first decade of Daniel's service was *Luther v. Borden*, arising out of Dorr's rebellion in Rhode Island in 1841. The matter was not finally disposed of by the Court until 1849, having been held on the docket for several years. Since the revolutionary party in Rhode Island was Democratic, there was some surprise when the entire Court, in a leading opinion by Chief Justice Taney, held against it.[4]

The case of the Rhode Island revolution illustrates the fact that Daniel's America had some markedly different moral values and some markedly different offenses than the twentieth century. Slavery is of course the greatest difference. But Daniel also participated in a piracy case, replete with pistols and daggers.[5] He joined in upholding the power of a naval officer to order the flogging of a marine in a native hut and in leg irons, and to order protracted jailing, all in a spirit of better navy discipline.[6] He participated in a decision involving a fraud by the man who had been chosen to pull out the winning ticket in a Virginia lottery undertaken to raise funds for road construction. The man who chose the lucky number had previously taken steps to be sure, by indirection, that he would himself be the winner.[7]

There were not enough cases relating to education or religion to make a pattern. An educational trust which presented substantial problems both in Daniel's century and in ours was that arising from the will of Stephen Girard. Girard left his immense estate, worth something over seven million dollars, to be administered by the City of Philadelphia for the establishment of an educational institution for "poor white male orphans." The program of the school was duly outlined in the will and was thoroughly wholesome, but was subject to a restriction that no clergyman should be permitted to hold a position in the college, indeed that none should even be allowed on the premises. Daniel Webster attacked the will, noting that heathens could come to the college but that good Christian ministers could not: "The clause, as it stands, is as derogatory to Christianity as if provision had been made for lectures against it." With passion he told the Court that if he could aid in setting aside this iniquitous trust, it would be the crowning achievement of his professional career. A unanimous Court, speaking through Justice Story, was unimpressed and upheld the trust.[8]

When the Methodist Church split apart on the issue of slavery and on the issue of division of church property, the Court presided at the divorce and by its development of the doctrine of class actions made it possible for the schism to take place in an orderly way.[9] An attempt was made to make a Federal constitutional issue of the validity of a New Orleans ordinance barring the exposure of corpses in churches, as was the practice in Roman Catholic funerals; but the Court held that whether the exposure of the corpse of Louis Le Roy was or was not legal must be decided by Louisiana law, since Federal rights did not apply against the states.[10] A religious case peculiar to the age involved the Harmony Society, which was founded in 1805 by German settlers. The society established a community in Indiana and another in Pennsylvania, both based on biblical models and each with a community of property. One of the faithful became discontent and wanted not only to leave Harmony, but also to take his share of the property. The Court was wholly unsympathetic to his desires.[11]

A surprisingly large number of family relations cases turned up on the Supreme Court docket. The *Gaines* case, involving a problem of common-law marriage and wills, gained the most notoriety. In *Jewell v. Jewell*[12] the Court divided equally on just what constituted a common-law marriage. Benjamin Jewell, a Jew from Savannah, Georgia, had an ambiguous relationship with Sophie Prevost, a French-speaking Roman Catholic girl from the West Indies. According to her account the couple had a civil marriage because they could not agree on a church, but there was no record of their marriage. They had eight children, and then separated, each going through a marriage ceremony thereafter with a second person. Jewell died intestate and thus certain property interests passed to his wife. The problem was whether Sophie or the second wife had the legal right to the property. If Jewell had been either ceremonially or at common law married to Sophie, then the second relationship was bigamous. The Court divided four to four on just what made a common-law marriage and what was mere concubinage.

In pre–Civil War America the women's rights movement was in the period of its boisterous beginning. While Daniel was on the Court very real progress was made by the stalwart if sometimes eccentric champions of the cause.[13] Nonetheless women were far from free agents. Once married, a wife lost control of her property unless it was adequately protected by an antenuptial agreement. Daniel wrote the opinion of the Court concerning such an agreement.[14] In 1816 Ann Wood De Lane, "a widow lady" with valuable real estate and slaves, married John Yancey. Before the marriage the parties entered into a written agreement under which Yancey was not to have the power to dispose of any part of the estate without Ann's concurrence, nor was any of her property to be subject to his debts. After the marriage they left South Carolina, where the agreement was made, and moved to Alabama. There, either before or after Ann's death, Yancey did sell a number of slaves to James Goree. An action was brought by the children of Ann against the executors of Goree, who had died. The defense was that Goree had obtained a Negro woman slave named Lindy and her child Becky in payment of a grocery account, and without any knowledge of the recorded marriage agreement. Daniel found that the children had been so extremely tardy in instituting their action that it was too late to be considered.

So far as the law was concerned, these were hard times for the ladies, and Daniel did nothing to make it any easier for them. No one would be likely to lend money on the security of a mortgage on real property if the wife's dower (one third) interest were not covered by the mortgage, and therefore wives commonly agreed to realty mortgages and subordinated their dower interests to the right of the mortgagee. In theory, the law was supposed to insure that no woman was forced to sign a waiver under threats or compulsion of any kind. But in one case the Court held that the substance of the waiver was all that mattered and that no particular form was required.[15] Another case involved a woman who had come to marriage with property worth about $88,000 and signed a $10,000 mortgage on part of it, quite obviously turning the money over to her husband. The Court held that if on the face of it the wife appeared to be making the loan for her own benefit, it was not up to the lender to inquire as to what was to become of the money and she was therefore obligated.[16]

In the cases just recited one has the impression that the ladies in question were taking advantage of the situation, claiming innocence and oppression when in fact they might well have been neither innocent nor oppressed. On the other hand when it was fairly clear that there was dirty business afoot and a maiden in distress, southern chivalry could be relied upon. Daniel carried the spear for the lady in distress in the case of Charlotte Taylor.[17] Shortly before she became 21, Charlotte's uncle died and left her a house with its furnishings and silver in Savannah, Georgia. While she was still living with her parents she conveyed the house to them. Later she sued to get it back on the ground of duress.

Daniel for a divided Court set the conveyance aside. He began by reciting all the cases and authorities he could find emphasizing the necessity of particular care and most scrupulous honesty in transactions of this kind. He stressed the "watchfulness, thus enjoined as a duty, this severe and peculiar scrutiny as applicable to contracts between parent and child" for the relationship is "aptly and naturally productive of powerful influence on the one hand, and of submission on the other." As against these principles he recited facts: A conveyance by the daughter of a valuable piece of property in return for nothing at all; the fact that the daughter was barely over the legal age and a young woman living at home: "She might be moulded to almost anything, in compliance with the earnest wishes (with her habitually yielded to as commands) of her parents." In such circumstances, filial affection could readily be "converted into means of wrong and oppression."

The Daniel who wrote the opinion is very obviously the father of two daughters. Quite without realizing that he did so, the Justice began to take judicial notice of the way in which young ladies in such a situation would react: "The natural effects of such appeals upon the feelings of an affectionate and sensitive girl, or even upon a spirit awaked to the impulses of pride alone, can easily be comprehended." He briefly etched the spiritual reaction of the young girl thus under pressure from her parents, acknowledging that these things could not be shown by any actual evidence in the record, but maintaining that they flowed from the very atmosphere of the case.

By now St. George had found the dragon, and he swung hard. There was a letter in evidence in which Charlotte purported to give her reasons for making the conveyance. Daniel tagged it as an obvious fraud and falsehood, written in a formal legal style which the girl could not herself conceive and obviously executed to whitewash a dubious transaction. Its recitals and those of the deed of conveyance he found "wholly irreconcilable with truth." And so the Court concluded that the deed was not fair or voluntary, that it was obtained by undue influence, and that it should be set aside.

In none of these cases did Daniel have occasion to say much on the subject of divorce. On his last day on the Court he dealt with the legal effect of a partial divorce, or a divorce from bed and board.[18] The parties were given a divorce of this sort in New York, and the wife was allowed alimony. Soon thereafter the husband moved to Wisconsin and failed to pay the alimony. The wife sued him there in the Federal court, and a basic issue was whether the two had become citizens of different states. The majority thought yes, but three Justices disagreed.

In dissent Daniel stated his conception of marriage, completely embracing the English notion that by marriage the husband and wife become one person. The wife has no separate legal existence but exists altogether under the wing of her husband. After a partial divorce, as Daniel saw it, the wife was no longer under the power of the husband but rather was freed from his control. Therefore she was entitled to take a separate residence. But this did not restore her separate citizenship. This being so, in the eyes of the law wherever the legal residence of the husband might be, there also was the legal residence of the wife, and hence there could not be diversity of citizenship of Federal jurisdiction. Daniel would thus leave all questions of divorce and alimony to the states.

The Court in this period heard Indian cases, too. In these years the country was still pushing the Indians west. In 1838 and 1839 the Cherokees were moved across the Mississippi under the superintendence of General Scott, who drew up a budget of $65,880 for the purpose, including provision for 80,000 rations at 16 cents each, and five dollars a day for a physician to travel with the tribe. Some fifty-one wagons and teams were involved. A claimant who had furnished four of the wagons filed an action which ultimately came to the Court.[19]

This Court was perhaps not always absolutely clear in its exposition of theory in regard to the tribes. In this case the Court observed that "The Cherokees are in many respects a foreign and independent nation." In another case also dealing with the Cherokees the Court held that "The native tribes" had "never been acknowledged or treated as independent nations by the European governments" and that the United States succeeded to the same point of view.[20] The Court did believe, however, that the United States had "exercised its power over this unfortunate race in the spirit of humanity and justice, and has endeavored by every means in its power to enlighten their minds, and increase their comforts, and to save them if possible from the consequences of their own vices." [21]

Daniel did not write any important majority opinions in Indian cases. He did however have a very prominent though unsuccessful role in the development of the law of conquest, serving as one of the principal dissenters in the Spanish land grant cases. The Mexican war brought a great deal of new business of this nature to the Court.[22] The Spanish crown had lavishly, corruptly, and — most difficult of all from the legal standpoint — haphazardly distributed the lands of California, New Mexico, and Arizona. After the expulsion of Spain the Mexican governments continued this practice. The treaty of Guadalupe Hidalgo at the end of the Mexican War committed the United States to recognize Spanish and Mexican land titles.

In passing upon these claims, the Court had behind it the substantial experience of adjudication of similar claims in the Louisiana territory based on French and Spanish grants. Indeed, one of the earliest cases on which Daniel sat involved title to land in Mobile, Alabama, which depended upon a Spanish grant from the governor of Florida.[23]

With the realization that a tremendous number of land titles remained to be settled after the war, in 1851 Congress established a commission on California Spanish and Mexican land claims, providing for appeals to the United States district judge in California and eventual appeal to the Supreme

Court.[24] The disposition of many of these cases stopped with United States District Judge Ogden Hoffman of the northern district of California.[25] The leading case to come to the Supreme Court was *Frémont v. United States*,[26] in which Daniel did not participate. The tract involved was ten square leagues of land granted in 1844 to a Mexican who in 1847 conveyed his interest to John C. Frémont. Taney noted with great care that it was one thing to have a grant made and another to have its conditions fulfilled; that any number of grants had been made by the Spanish government on which the grantees never met the conditions of the grant. He maintained that California should not be subject to the encumbrance of any such claims. However, the Court found that Frémont and his predecessor had done as much as could be done despite the fact that, as the dissent pointed out, the grant in effect was "a floating land warrant, seeking a location on any part of a large region of country containing 900 square miles." Though Daniel did not sit in this case, he later noted [27] that he would have dissented in this and in *United States v. Ritchie*,[28] decided the same day.

Daniel did not participate in these leading cases at the December 1854 term, but he had full opportunity to develop his point of view in a series of five decisions during the 1855 term.[29] Daniel believed that the course of decision upholding the Spanish grants was completely hostile to "the welfare of the people of California, by inciting and pampering a corrupt and grasping spirit of speculation and monopoly." The practical situation was that if the grants were upheld, these lands would belong to private owners, but if not, they would be held for the benefit of the public as a whole; insofar as he was concerned, if the public was to lose the lands, the private claimant had to have an unquestionably good title, the conditions of the title under Mexican or Spanish law had to be fulfilled.

As is so often the case, this meant that policy might well be determined by principles of the laws of evidence. Daniel wanted actual documentary proof that acts had been done which were required to establish title. He was unwilling to let the claims depend upon the oral testimony of what he regarded as a group of grasping and corrupt liars. He was brutally blunt about it: "It can hardly admit of a rational doubt in the mind of any man who considers the character of much of the population of the late Spanish dominions in America — sunk in ignorance, and marked by the traits which tyranny and degradation, political and moral, naturally and usually engender — that proofs of other statements might be obtained, as to any fact or circumstances which it might be deemed desirable or profitable to establish." He would not sacrifice the sovereign rights of the United States to those who had every incentive to perjure themselves. His credo, which he was to express alone, was clear and direct:

> Upon such a foundation, such a pretense, or rather such a defiance of authority, I will not, by an abuse of language, call it even a pretense of right, I cannot consent to impair or destroy the sovereign rights and the financial interests of the United States in the public domain. I can perceive no merit, no claim whatsoever, to favor, on the part of the grasping and unscrupulous speculator and monopolist; no propriety in retarding, for his advantage or profit, the settlement and population of new states, by excluding therefrom the honest citizen of small means, by his presence and industry the improvement and wealth, and social and moral health, and the advancement of the country are always sure to be promoted.[30]

Another kind of monopoly grant, industrial patents for invention, frequently led to litigation in Daniel's time. This was an era of great inventions, and many of them turn up in the Supreme Court reports, including the McCormick reaper, Morse's telegraph, and an improved sluice for panning gold. Daniel heard a case having to do with the waterproofing of cloth, a matter at the foundation of the Goodyear rubber fortune, and cases concerning a spike-making machine, a fireproof safe, and a method of laying railroad track across streets so as not to break carriage axles.[31]

Daniel approached the patent system as he did everything else, by starting from first principles. Once he had laid out his guide line, he stuck to it:

> It is undeniably true, that the limited and temporary monopoly granted to inventors was never designed for their exclusive profit or advantage; the benefit to the public or community at large was another and doubtless the primary object in granting and securing that monopoly. This was at once the equivalent given by the public for benefits bestowed by the genius and meditations and skill of individuals, and the incentive to further efforts for the same important objects.[32]

The fireproof safe was a rather simple affair, consisting of two metal cabinets, one inside the other, with the space between them filled with plaster of paris. The originality lay in the use of plaster of paris or gypsum for this purpose. The patent was issued in 1843, but four years earlier, in 1839, the inventor had sold his interest in the patent to a man named Wilder for $5000. The first question in the case was whether an interest in an invention could thus be assigned before it had been patented. The Court upheld the assignment system, which had long been in use throughout the country. The remaining principal question was whether this simple contrivance was an invention at all and hence subject to patent. The law provided for patents for new and useful improvements "not known or used by others before his discovery or invention," and it was proved that a similar previous device had been in use in New York City for some years before this "invention" was made. The Court held that if this was simply an isolated instance of which the patentee knew nothing, and certainly if the earlier product had been lost or abandoned, the inventor who in good faith proceeded to produce it over again was entitled to a patent.

Daniel dissented as to both points. He believed that until a patent had been issued, there was nothing to assign, that there was no right in an invention prior to the patent. He demonstrated his proposition with some very solid English materials, regarding it as "mischievous and alarming" that the Court should thus allow the creation of a new property interest of this sort.

On the second point, Daniel dissented rather more vigorously. It seemed to him absolutely preposterous to apply the conception of "lost art," which he thought applied to the discoveries of the Egyptians, the Greeks, or the Romans, to a plaster of paris safe lining which had been in use only seven years prior to the challenged invention. So far as he was concerned, when the first inventor had been willing to give his invention to the public, subsequent inventors should not be allowed to patent the same thing. The first inventor was considerably more "the benefactor of the public who makes a useful improvement which he generously shares with his fellow citizens" than was the person "who studies some device which he denies to all, and limits by every means in his power to a lucrative monopoly." To dramatize what he regarded as the ridiculous aspect of the situation, Daniel pointed out that the first inventor (who might still be using his invention) would now have to pay a tax to the second man for the use of what he had himself originally invented.

Daniel spoke for the Court in dealing with the problem of a combination patent,[33] a patent on an invention which puts together familiar objects to achieve a new result. In this particular case, rails and grooves had been combined to reduce bumpiness on car tracks. In holding that this lacked originality Daniel closely followed the earlier doctrine of Justice Story.

The best known patent case in which Daniel was involved was renowned more because Abraham Lincoln was the trial counsel than for any great significance in the case itself.[34] The issue was whether the divider on the Manny reaper conflicted with the patent for the McCormick divider. A majority held that there was no conflict, that the Manny divider was a distinct improvement on the McCormick.[35] Daniel dissented alone, and vigorously. He wanted no part of the expert testimony, regarding it as simply the reveries of paid partisans more skilled at obscuring than clarifying the truth. In his opinion the proper approach to the devices was to look at them, and he could see no significant difference.

In another patent case Daniel joined in one of the most pointed, as well as one of the briefest, denunciations of patent abuses on the books. The inventor had obtained a patent covering an improvement in the steam engine, plus a device for connecting it with the steering mechanism of a steamboat, plus an improvement in the steamboat paddle. The majority of five held that this was permissible, that three separate patents were not required, at least where the three new devices were connected in their operation.[36] Taney, Catron, Daniel, and Grier joined in dissenting. Justice Catron wrote that only one distinct invention can be patented at a time. He pointed to the potential abuse of attaching to a good claim many fictitious ones, so that a patentee would thus run no risk in getting a grant on items which were not new. He continued:

> By this mode of proceeding at the patent office, fictitious claims may cover and assume to monopolize the ordinary implements now in use on the farm and in the workshop, and even more than is now the case, harass the public with fictitious and ill-founded claims to make and sell exclusively things in daily and extensive use. Although the claim may be fictitious, still this does not protect the public from harassment, as usually men using cheap instruments can not afford to litigate in the

United States courts. It would be far better to allow the claim, just as it is, and pay the patentee his fraudulent demand, than incur the expense of a suit, which the patentee or his assignee may well afford to prosecute.

Criminal cases, cases relating to education and religion, to family relations, to Indian tribes, to land grants, to patents — this is the sort of business which constituted the workaday labor of the Court, its business below the level of the great constitutional questions and for the most part quite outside the news of the day. Below it there is an even larger substratum of matters too tedious to enumerate, too uninteresting to sample. These were the utterly routine cases on procedure, on commercial paper, on insurance policies — cases each of which depended so precisely on its own facts as to be of no interest to anyone but the litigants. And yet together their disposition was an invaluable service to the community — they were all disputes which in an ordered society must be disposed of somehow. In the beginning of each session there was a mighty pile of wood to be sawed, and by the end of it, Daniel had sawed his share only to return the next winter to find the pile higher than it had been before.

A word should be said as to Daniel's style and capacity. Daniel consistently reasoned from first principles. Nice analysis and close reasoning were not quite his forte. He was rather a bundle of principles and prejudices. If the principle was one in his constitutional hierarchy, then it controlled the case. Two other basic principles loomed large with him. One was a strong bias in favor of the jury system.[37] The second was his own strict morality. Over and over again cheats had a bad time before Daniel, and if he could find a way to set them at naught he did so.[38]

In terms of his general intellectual capacity, one can only make an overall judgment based on a survey of hundreds of cases. This survey suggests that Daniel was not the intellectual equal of Taney, Curtis, and Campbell, the three great Justices with whom he served, but was at least as good as all the rest. As a stylist Daniel was weak. His verbosity and his involved sentences frequently turn his prose into a twisting trail of parentheticals. His style was uneven — occasionally he rose to the heights of a Taney or a Curtis, and at his worst he was not as bad as Woodbury. His was, alas, an average legal prose.

Chapter XVII

THE CIRCUIT

IT DID NOT take the Whigs long to put Daniel out to pasture. They had been unable to prevent the confirmation of his appointment in the closing days of the Van Buren administration in 1841. Their bill abolishing the Virginia circuit, by combining Virginia and Maryland in one, and creating a new western circuit in its stead had not passed before Congress adjourned. But they had pledged publicly to deport the new Justice, and in 1842 the bill did pass. The new circuit, the Ninth, consisted of Arkansas and Mississippi.[1] The Court thereupon assigned this new circuit to Daniel. Daniel was thus able to sit for only one year as the circuit judge in his native Virginia before heading for the wilderness.

Given the transportation limitations of the time, geography was a major factor to be considered in the allocation of circuits. A gross imbalance in the number of miles to be traveled could make it impossible for a Justice to get about. Justice McKinley, who had previously been assigned to the circuit which included Arkansas, had solved his problem by the simple device of not going there.[2] This was not unreasonable; under the system as it existed before the 1842 amendment, Taney had to travel only 458 miles to cover his circuit, whereas McKinley would have traveled 10,000 miles to cover his. But the new arrangement was wholly disproportionate in relation to population, with the result that there was far more business in some circuits than in others. For example in 1857 the New York–Connecticut–Vermont circuit had almost four million white people while Daniel's circuit had fewer than a half million. His was by far the smallest circuit in this respect, with seven of the circuits running from three to eight times the population of his.[3]

Holding court on the Ninth Circuit was arduous, and Daniel was extremely bitter about it. In both 1843 and 1844 he made his circuit, the 1844 trip taking him three months and covering five thousand miles. In 1843 he wrote Van Buren from Jackson, Mississippi, to say,

> I am here two thousand miles from home (calculating by the travel record) on the pilgrimage by an exposure to which, it was the calculation of savage malignity that I had been driven from the Bench. Justice to my friends, and a determination to defeat the machinations of mine and of their enemies, have decided me to undergo the experiment, and I have done so at no small hazard through air of fever at Vicksburg and convulsive and autumnal fevers in this place and vicinity. The enormity of the usage I have observed is almost without an example, and I trust to the overruling protection of a good providence to disappoint its purposes, and to the justice and independence of my friends, and the friends of honor, magnanimity and common fairness to give me a redress.[4]

This sitting in Jackson consumed a month.

The Arkansas portion of the assignment was indeed rough. Arkansas had been admitted as a state in 1836. In terms of physical comforts and cultural standards it was a long way indeed from tidewater Virginia. During his stay there in April of 1844, Little Rock announced that it would begin the enforcement of its ordinance against hogs running in the streets. It was an enterprising community — a young lady about to be married shot her own wild turkey for the wedding feast.[5]

One of the worst aspects of these long trips was their loneliness. Daniel was a family man. If transportation of people was uncertain, that of the mail was worse. It was something to be noted and celebrated when a letter arrived at all. It might well take three weeks for a letter to go from Jackson to Richmond. In one three-week period Daniel wrote his wife five times but at the end of that period she had as yet received none of the letters.[6]

Daniel's loneliness was intensified by the limitations of his own personality. His was not a gregarious spirit and he did not mingle much with the people in the communities he served. In Jackson he stayed in the home of a genteel woman of reduced circumstances who played the piano well, and her music was almost all the entertainment he had.[7] He did, however, occasionally go to a semiofficial dinner given by the governor, whose wife, a Virginian, courteously sent him potable water from the capitol. Almost invariably he inspected the gardens of the communities and was duly delighted with the best roses.

Reaching Arkansas and Mississippi from Washington in the 1850's was considerably more difficult than reaching any other continent a century later. Daniel recorded some of his wanderings, and his correspondence with Elizabeth contains the best known accounts of the problems of western circuit travel.[8] In the 1840's he began his trips by going west on the Cumberland Road, but following a suggestion of one of his fellow Justices, he decided in 1851 to proceed instead to the Ohio River through the interior of Pennsylvania. He left Washington on a Saturday evening in 1851, taking the train to Baltimore through a heavy wind and rain storm. Sunday afternoon he left Baltimore by train and by early Tuesday morning he had reached Pittsburgh. For this thirty-six hour period he was unable to remove so much as his boots. The railroad proceeded from Baltimore through Harrisburg to Holidaysburg on the eastern side of the Allegheny Mountains, and this trip was fairly easy; but the trip over the mountains was slow and extremely difficult, the cars at times being at such a slant that one could not safely stand up. It took as long to cover the 36 miles over the mountains as it had taken to cover the preceding 220 miles. After crossing the Alleghenies, Daniel took a canal boat at Johnstown for the remaining 104 miles to Pittsburgh. This part of the journey took a little more than a day and a night and the average speed was around four miles an hour, giving him an impression of perfect stillness.

The physical condition of the boat and its passengers was at best unappetizing, and to a person as fastidious as Daniel it was downright loathsome. He found his fellow travelers the most vulgar and filthy in the world, the women being if possible even dirtier than the men. The washing facilities of the vessel consisted of two tin basins encrusted with filth, and one long towel for all the men aboard. Daniel's washing consisted of wiping his eyes and his mouth with his linen handkerchief, and for this 24-hour period he did not sleep at all. Pittsburgh, even in 1851, he found unlivable because of smoke, with an atmosphere like a closed room in which, after a rainstorm, all the soot has fallen out of the chimney.

From Pittsburgh Daniel took a two-day boat trip downriver to Cincinnati, and proceeded from there to Napoleon, a village at the mouth of the Arkansas River. This town was founded in 1820 and served as a shipping center for persons changing from the Mississippi River boats to the smaller vessels which went into Arkansas. It was abandoned in the 1870's A savagely irritable Daniel arrived at Napoleon on April 17, 1851, twelve days after he had left home. At Napoleon he was compelled to remain over night until he could get a vessel to Little Rock. He was furious with the steamboat captains who had brought him from Cincinnati because the boats ran on no fixed schedules, pulling in at any point at which they could hope to get a load, and staying there as long as necessary in order to get it. As a result he ran some three days behind schedule and had spent two days in Memphis, where he had not intended to stop at all.

Daniel found Napoleon the most miserable substitute for a village he had ever seen. It had a few little wooden buildings, some already collapsing and others with neither doors nor windows. The hotel was an abandoned steamboat which had been pulled up on the shore; his room was about four by six feet. So long as he stayed on the boat he was attacked only by mosquitoes; but if either to escape the mosquitoes or for variety he went outside, he was engulfed in swarms of buffalo gnats. That such a condition could exist shook his faith in his beloved South.

The next day he reached Little Rock, and after holding court there for a few days proceeded to Jackson. He had made the trip without any serious consequences to his health, although he had not had one decent meal for weeks.

When Daniel arrived in Jackson, his first thought was of mail from home, but at the end of his first month of travel not a single letter had reached him. He knew no one in Jackson. The hotel in which he was quartered was like an old barn. Parts of it had never been lathed or plastered; but his bed linen was clean and he was duly grateful. On his first Sunday in Jackson, out of sheer boredom, he went to the Episcopal Church twice and otherwise amused himself by reading *David Copperfield*, then newly published, as well as several other novels. For his further amusement he walked through the town, delighting in the profusion of roses, carnations, and honeysuckle.

Later his solitude would be alleviated. He was entertained at Jacksonville and later at Vicksburg, where his acquaintance was larger. In Vicksburg he could abandon hotels and stay with a friend with whom he was actually comfortable for the first time since he left Washington.

Getting to his destination was only half of Daniel's problem. There remained the task of coming home again. When he left Jackson he took a fine river steamer up the Mississippi. As it proceeded up the river, the boat was snagged in the night by a large tree which pushed through the guard which the ship carried to fend off such misfortunes. The impact created a violent shock, and the boat was halted for an entire night while the crew worked desperately to saw out the tree trunk and repair the damage.

The assault by the drifting tree was by no means the worst of the hazards of the return trip. Cholera broke out on the boat and at least five persons quickly died. With such a disease aboard, it was clearly unsafe to continue by boat, and Daniel abandoned the ship at Cincinnati. There was no direct route from Cincinnati to Richmond. He was compelled to take a train all the way across Ohio to Cleveland on the poorest, bumpiest railroad he had ever seen. At Cleveland he took another boat, this time across Lake Erie to Buffalo. From Buffalo he traveled south through Pennsylvania back to Virginia. The one pleasure of the trip was a visit to Justice Grier at his home in Pennsylvania, where he had a pleasant evening of family life and enjoyed a piano performance by the eldest daughter of the house.

On June 6, almost precisely two months after leaving the East, he was back in Richmond. He had covered some 7000 miles, including the extra 1000 caused by his leaving the riverboat. He had spent more time traveling than judging, and returned home not only exhausted from the constant strain of his movement but nervously tense from his everlasting rush from one means of transportation to another. He wearily settled down in Richmond to try to get caught up on his professional reading.[9]

The western circuit did not grow more comfortable with experience. In 1853 he made the same round again, this time going by the Baltimore and Ohio Railway to Wheeling and

moving downriver from there. Train travel was no comfort
— the train was about fifteen hours late on a scheduled nine-
teen-hour trip to Wheeling, and for all this time the passengers were without sleep, without opportunity to wash, and
without a chance to buy food. But this time Daniel took a
Wheeling boat, and the captain, remembering the *Wheeling
Bridge Case*, gave him the best quarters on the vessel. It took
ten days to get from Cincinnati to Little Rock. This time,
too, Arkansas was no pleasure, and Jackson was worse. He
found the town with more dogs than people and his quarters he could only compare to a hog sty. Perhaps as a result
of the canine population, he was assaulted day and night
by fleas.[10]

If at the end of these outward trips there had been litigation to decide worthy of the labor of coming, the pain might
have been easier to bear. But all this was expected of a Justice
of the Supreme Court of the United States in order that he
might decide some of the most miserably routine of cases.
There is no record of Daniel's judicial labors in Mississippi,
although there appears to have been a rather considerable
volume there.[11] However, there is a record of 18 cases which
he heard in Arkansas between 1844 and 1855.[12] They may be
divided thus: six involved Federal jurisdiction or matters of
procedure, five involved real property, five were criminal,
and two were in contract. None of the property problems was
sufficiently interesting to be worth stating. One of the contract cases was for breach of warranty in the sale of slaves
and the other was an action against an attorney for improperly
withholding funds. The procedural points were particularly
insignificant, dealing with the proper form of depositions,
length of continuances, and other highly specialized matters.
The jurisdictional questions were of a somewhat more general nature. Daniel held that in diversity cases both the gar-
nisher and the garnishee could not be of the same state, it

being immaterial that the judgment debtor was of another state;[13] he also held that a state court could not interfere with a matter which was pending in Federal Court, saying that "state courts can no more interfere in our business and proceedings than we can in theirs."[14]

The five criminal cases puzzled him a little. Four were murder charges involving murders committed in Indian country west of Arkansas. The underlying problem in each of them was the extent of Federal jurisdiction over such crimes. On one theory or another, all the defendants got off lightly. Two of the defendants were held to be outside Federal jurisdiction. In a third case the murderer received a two-year sentence but was pardoned by President Pierce.[15]

And yet, in this dreary frontier slum, Daniel was conducting that everlasting process by which the law spreads from culture to culture, from age to age. For example Sanders, a Cherokee, was indicted for wantonly murdering Billy, an idiot boy, in Cherokee country. Billy's father was white. His mother was said to be an Indian, and the defense was that the case was thus outside the jurisdiction of the Federal Court. Daniel instructed this frontier jury, citing Book I, Title 4, of *Justinian's Institutes*, to the effect that if Billy's mother was an Indian, so was Billy, and that if Billy was an Indian, Sanders must be found not guilty. The jury found the fact of parentage and released Sanders.[16]

On Daniel's first trip to Arkansas, he did have one genuinely interesting constitutional question. Statutes of limitations commonly provide that in computing the time after the lapse of which a person shall be barred from suing, there shall not be counted any period during which the defendant has been outside the state. In January of 1843 the Arkansas legislature repealed that provision, thus cutting off altogether actions which could otherwise have been brought upon the return of absent persons. Daniel's circuit court held that the statutory change violated the contract clause and was so radical a change as not merely to affect the remedy of a person, but also to abolish his legal right.[17]

Perhaps the most bizarre of all Daniel's circuit cases was *United States v. Rogers*. The defendant was a white man who had taken up residence years before in Indian country and had married a squaw. He was charged with the murder of an Indian. The defense was that the court was without jurisdiction — that for legal purposes Rogers was an Indian.

If the defendant were regarded as an Indian, the defense would be good. The Federal Court had no jurisdiction in a case of murder of an Indian by an Indian in Indian country. The United States attorney argued that a citizen could not thus expatriate himself, particularly to an Indian tribe. He contended that a decision to the contrary would encourage worthless Americans to take refuge on the frontier.

The Court took this question under advisement in April of 1845 with full appreciation that it was a genuinely serious question. While the judges were considering it, the local newspaper advised them that if the defendant's claim was good, then certainly there should be an act of Congress extending the jurisdiction of the Court. "The peace of the frontier and the enforcement of law and justice require this," the paper said.[18]

After thinking the matter over, Daniel and the district judge, Johnson, concluded that this was a matter which ought to go to the Supreme Court. Under the current practice a circuit and a district judge could agree to disagree, and by dividing could send questions on to the Supreme Court for answer; this the two did. Daniel left Little Rock, assuming that Rogers would be kept in jail until the questions could be answered by the Supreme Court and that, in his capacity as a Supreme Court Justice, he could participate in answering them in Washington.

This was April 28, 1845. On the night of May 13, Rogers and a runaway Negro slave attacked their jailer with Bowie knives when he raised the trap door to go down into the dungeon with their supper. The two men escaped, but two days later the body of Rogers was found floating in the river. He apparently tried to swim back to the Indian country, became exhausted, and drowned.[19]

Apparently no one told Daniel or the Supreme Court. At the next term these certified questions came up and an appearance was made for the United States by the Attorney General. No one appeared for Rogers, but even had he been alive this would not have been remarkable. The Court, in a unanimous opinion by Chief Justice Taney, proceeded to decide the case, holding that a white man could not thus expatriate himself and put himself beyond the reach of the law. The Court therefore directed that Rogers be tried and "that, if he is found guilty upon the indictment, he is liable to the punishment provided by the Act of Congress before referred to."[20] The Court obviously did not realize that Rogers has passed beyond the reach even of an Act of Congress.

Chapter XVIII

THE LAST DISSENT

AFTER THE *Dred Scott* decision, there remained to Daniel two terms of the Supreme Court and three years of life. It was a lonely time. The Justice had the responsibility for his two small children, and how he handled it is not clear. They were well, and their physical resemblance to their mother was a comfort to him; and yet the fact that there was no mother to care for them and that he could not possibly live long enough to bring them up was a constant source of depression.[1]

He was never able to re-establish his earlier relationship with Elizabeth. His second marriage had robbed her of her place as his hostess and she had gone to live permanently with her sister Anne in North Carolina.[2]

The Daniel of these last days was an old, thin man with long hair and metal rimmed spectacles. He was described by a courtroom observer hearing the *Dred Scott* argument as "old, and lean, and sharp in the visage, and simply wears the aspect of a tremulous and fidgety old gentleman in glasses." [3] His health was poor, his spirits low.

He saw little to cheer him on the political scene. He had known President Buchanan as a public figure for a long time, and had never expected much of him. Buchanan's performance he found far below even his dim hopes. He thought the cabinet uniformly poor with but one exception, the Attorney General, Jeremiah S. Black. Black was one of the foremost lawyers of his era and Daniel fully recognized him as such, but thought of him as a courtroom advocate rather than as a statesman.

It was especially annoying that the cabinet included Daniel's old enemy former Governor Floyd of Virginia, now Secretary of War. Floyd's principal assignment had been to send a force into Utah to conquer the Mormons, a task of which he had made a distinct botch; and it gave Daniel as much pleasure to criticize his old enemy in the 1850's as it had when Floyd was governor and he was lieutenant governor in the 1830's.

In all these things Daniel was essentially an outside observer. He did have a conversation with President Buchanan about the handling of the problems of Kansas. He strongly advocated to the President the same views he had taken in his *Dred Scott* opinion, that the question of slavery in Kansas was a matter to be determined altogether by the people of that territory without any interference of any kind from the Federal government.

Daniel saw Stephen A. Douglas moving up on the Democratic horizon, and did not like what he saw. He thought Douglas was a pure opportunist in relation to the Kansas question. He saw him as torn by the dilemma of whether to stick with the South or to desert to the abolitionists in an effort to obtain the presidency or at least to hold on to his Senate seat.

In this dark hour for the South, Daniel believed that the only alternatives were either complete submission to what he regarded as Yankee insolence and oppression or open resistance. He was for the latter course to the point of secession, but doubted that there was enough courage in the South to risk such a step. Of the senators of the time, he dismissed Douglas as a vulgar, low-minded adventurer but had great respect for Judah P. Benjamin of Louisiana, whom he regarded as the ablest lawyer to come before the Supreme Court.[4]

But if the old fires were banked by ill health, they were by no means out. Daniel's last two terms on the Supreme Court amount to a restatement of his entire life. At the 1857 and 1858 terms he carried his fair share of the work, and inflexibly held to the positions to which he had been committed for so long. Twelve times in these two terms he dissented alone on the ground either that the Federal courts were without jurisdiction over corporations or on the ground that the admiralty jurisdiction did not reach the inland waters. Most of these dissents were merely one line statements of position, but on each issue he restated his position fully once. On the corporate question he reviewed the entire amazing history whereby corporations had, by legal fiction, been given the virtual status of citizenship. There was some poignancy in the statement because Justice Campbell, who in earlier times had joined him in his position, in this case finally yielded to his brothers and adopted the majority view. Daniel, in a typical passage, declared that he could not thus go along. The entire philosophy of his life he compressed into one sentence: "I am bound to reassert all of which I have endeavored earnestly, however feebly, to maintain, and which I still believe." [5]

He reviewed the whole subject of the admiralty jurisdiction in a last fifteen-page comprehensive dissent. He decried to the end the deterioration of jury power by the expansion of admiralty jurisdiction and, as ever, "the ceaseless march of central encroachment" by which the Federal government expanded its powers. He feared that "under this new regime, the hand of Federal power may be tossed into everything, even into a vegetable or fruit basket; and there is no production of a farm, an orchard, or a garden, on the margin of these water courses, which is not liable to be arrested on its way to the next market town by the high admiralty power." He poured withering scorn on the importation of all the ancient admiralty wisdom into the common affairs of internal American commercial life. [6]

In these two years Daniel wrote his quota of majority opinions, some of which also involved restatements of basic points of view. He restated in some detail for the majority the reasons why the Bill of Rights did not apply to the states.[7] He stated both in majority and dissent his conviction that the purpose of the patent system was to protect the public as much as to protect the inventor.[8] And he wrote six majority opinions on fairly humdrum subjects, all of them competently turned out.[9] In what was by far the most important opinion of this two-year period, *Ableman v. Booth*,[10] Daniel was a member of the unanimous Court which spoke through Chief Justice Taney. In this great opinion the Chief Justice put down Wisconsin's almost open rebellion against the fugitive slave act and against the Federal courts and Federal power.

But the basic motif of the last two years was one of dissent, and familiar dissent at that. Daniel again restated his view that Federal judges should not tell Federal juries how to decide: "The power of the Court is limited absolutely to the legality or relevancy of the testimony. The weight or effect of the testimony, or the deductions to be drawn from it, were peculiarly and exclusively within the province of the jury." [11] And he joined in a dissent by Justice Clifford to a decision which upheld a claim of Spanish title to land in California based on considerably less than solid documentary proof.[12]

Daniel went out fighting. After a dissent on the last day of the 1858–59 term, he left the Court never to return. He moved back to Richmond, and died at his home there on May 31, 1860, after a period of poor health. By then the country was deeply interested in other things, and not much attention was paid to his passing. Very brief newspaper notices appeared, the New York *Times* noting principally that "he was strongly Democratic in politics and fully approved of the Dred Scott decision of his friend, Chief Justice Taney." [13] He was buried with Lucy at the Hollywood Cemetery in

Richmond under the simple inscription, "Here rests what was mortal of PETER V. DANIEL, who was born in Stafford County, VIRGINIA, on the 24th of April, 1784, and died in the City of Richmond on the 31st of May, 1860." In the same cemetery lie Presidents Monroe and Tyler, and Confederate General J. E. B. Stuart.

But the old man had one last dissent left in his system. When his will was read, it proved to be a typical Daniel document, lengthy, detailed, and precise.[14] He gave specific instructions for the disposition of every teacup, of the last silver ladle. His principal assets were in real estate, and he realized that for the care of his two infant children, it might be necessary to sell the real estate and convert the assets into something else. To meet the situation he authorized his executor to convert that property into "safe productive public stocks or bonds." But he added: "excluding the stocks or bonds of banks, railroads, or corporations or joint stock companies of any kind."

HERITAGE

Was Peter V. Daniel just a queer old man with queer old ideas, dedicated to principles which, whatever their validity once, are obsolete now?

In part, surely yes. The plain truth is that Daniel was largely obsolete before he died in the sense that he was a battler for causes which had been irretrievably lost even by 1860; and much of the rest of his philosophy was certainly dead by the twentieth century. Some of his viewpoints, though they once commanded the adherence of some of the best minds in America, are now as antiquated as the Franklin stove, or bundling — they may have had their merits in the eighteenth century, but not now.

In the category of the gone and forgotten is the slave system; the system of economics based on hard money rather than paper; the prebank and precorporation economy. Banks and corporations are so much a part of our economy that anyone who takes the position that they should not exist at all would seem today slightly daft. And yet Thomas Jefferson had this point of view. Similarly with the powers of the Federal government. There could be intense debate prior to say, 1830, on the proposition that the Federal government had no power to build roads or to lay a protective tariff, but for a hundred years these arguments have been so dead that their reintroduction today would be merely quaint. All these doors are closed, and if this were all of Daniel, he would only be, in a legal way, a sort of archaeological find, a bench mark by which we could compare eras, no more.

But this is not all of Daniel, and it is not all of agrarianism.

These are the aspects which make Daniel's views look queer and remote, but they should not obscure what is vital and important.

1) Daniel's views of the contract clause of the Federal Constitution are basically the foundation of today's views. This was in part a matter of fundamental economic outlook stemming from his conception of the power of the people to control large aggregations of capital. It would be a rare student of the Constitution in the twentieth century who would not believe that the views Daniel expressed both for the majority and in dissent would be the prevailing views in the same cases today. Without the tenacious adherence to his views by him and by like-minded justices, we might have a considerably different body of law on this subject than we do now.

2) There is a heavy contemporary opinion that Daniel's approach to the power of the states to regulate commerce was exactly and precisely right. In the view of many the Federal commerce power is not exclusive, and there is certainly substantial minority opinion in the United States today that the states do and should have the power to regulate and tax commerce which Daniel alone of his Court consistently and invariably wanted to give them. Daniel abhorred the Federal power to regulate, but he certainly did not shrink from the state power.

3) Daniel's views on the preservation of public lands strike a very responsive chord in our own century. This is an ideal from which we may fall farther and farther away, but the ideal maintains in the twentieth century the allure which it had for Daniel in the nineteenth.

4) Daniel's notions of limiting the admiralty jurisdiction and of keeping corporations out of Federal courts are, carried to his extreme, insignificant views today; but the underlying resistance to any expansion of the Federal jurisdiction

is retained by many. Congress, moving in the same direction in which Daniel had wished to go, recently cut down corporate jurisdiction.

5) Daniel's tenacious loyalty to the jury system and his intense desire to keep judges out of the business of juries has, after a long period of quiescence, become either a dominant or very nearly dominant view, and for very much the same philosophical reasons — esteem for the kind of folk wisdom which juries are supposed to represent.

6) Daniel's vigorous insistence on basic fairness in criminal law enforcement had its most eloquent expression when he was still on the Virginia Council and dealing with slaves. It is surely in accord with our finest contemporary sense of decency.

7) The antibank, anticorporate position of agrarianism has been wiped out, and in that sense Daniel — and Jefferson — are extinct. But the underlying purpose of the position, as Daniel often said, was resistance to monopoly and to bigness. The later push for antitrust laws and their militant enforcement represents the same spirit that motivated Daniel to resist the expansion of big business of his own era.

There is one thing more. It cannot be summed up in terms of a doctrine or a cause, and it is, happily, not peculiar to Daniel. The Justice leaves an example of a lifetime solidly devoted to hard work, and to unswerving pursuit of principle.

NOTES

CASES CITED

INDEX

A Note on the Location of Papers

The Grymes Papers, a collection of letters largely from Justice Daniel to his children, is in the possession of Mr. and Mrs. William R. Grymes, Orange, Virginia, but was on loan to the library of the University of Virginia, Charlottesville, when I studied it. Unless otherwise specified all cited correspondence among Daniel, his wife Lucy, and their three children, Elizabeth Randolph Daniel, Anne Daniel Moncure, and Peter V. Daniel, Jr., is in this collection. The letters from the Justice to his daughter Elizabeth, which constitute the bulk of the Grymes Papers, are cited throughout as PVD to ERD.

All letters from Daniel to Martin Van Buren, cited as PVD to VB, are in the Van Buren collection in the Library of Congress. Also at the Library of Congress are the papers of Jefferson, Polk, Jackson, Rives, Curtis, Story, and McLean; unless otherwise noted all references to their correspondence are to these collections.

The Joseph Carrington Cabell Collection and the Wilson Cary Nicholas Collection, referred to here as Cabell Papers and Nicholas Papers, are located at the University of Virginia, Charlottesville. The David Campbell Collection is located at Duke University, Durham, North Carolina, and is referred to as Campbell Papers.

All references to the papers of Chief Justice Roger B. Taney, Court Clerk William T. Carroll, or Reporter Benjamin Howard are to the collections at the Maryland Historical Society, Baltimore.

The minutes of the Council of State of Virginia and the records of the district and circuit courts for Virginia are in the Virginia State Library, Richmond. The minutes of the Council of State are cited throughout as C.S.R.

The orginal Journal of the Supreme Court of the United States is in the custody of the Clerk of that Court in Washington.

The Richmond *Enquirer*, cited as *Enquirer* throughout, for the period 1800–1860 is on file in the library of Congress and, in part, in the New York Public Library.

NOTES

I. The Early Years

1. See H. E. Hayden, *Virginia Genealogy* (Washington, 1931), *passim*, and esp. no. 52. C. B. Heinemann, "Daniel Families of the Southern States," typescript, 2 vols., in the Library of Congress Genealogy Room is comprehensive.

2. Henry Howe, *Historical Collections of Virginia* (Charleston, 1845), p. 484; and for other information on the county see the WPA Writers Project volume, *Virginia, A Guide to the Old Dominion* (New York, 1940).

3. Daniel itemized part of his library in his will, County Will Book 3, p. 261, Henrico County Courthouse.

4. For details on the Princeton of Daniel's time see Thomas J. Wertenbaker, *Princeton, 1796–1846* (Princeton, 1946), esp. chap. IV.

5. Princeton College Records. I am indebted to Mr. Ike Hayman for supplying these records.

6. *Vindication of Edmund Randolph* (Richmond, 2nd ed., 1855). As the introduction shows, Daniel thought of his grandfather as a "bright exemplar" for succeeding generations.

7. *Enquirer*, March 5, 1805.

8. *Enquirer*, July 12, 1805.

9. Mrs. V. Scott, *Houses of Old Richmond* (Richmond, 1941); Samuel Mordecai, *Virginia, Especially Richmond, in By-gone Days* (Richmond, 1860).

10. R. R. Howison, "Duelling in Virginia," *William and Mary Quarterly* (2d series), Oct. 1924, p. 217, places the date at "certainly" between 1810 and 1820, and probably 1812. The correct date is 1808.

11. See A. W. Patterson, *The Code Duello* (Richmond, 1927), p. 28.

12. John L. Wilson, *The Code of Honor* (Charleston, 1838), p. 19.

13. Patterson, *The Code Duello*.

14. Howison, "Duelling in Virginia."

15. Patterson, *The Code Duello*.

16. *Enquirer*, Nov. 15, 1808; Virginia *Argus*, Nov. 15, 1808, quoting the release as from the Washington, D.C., *Federalist*. The details of the duel in the text are taken from this statement, and are in part

independently confirmed by the Fredericksburg, Va., *Herald* of Nov. 9, 1808.

17. The nephew, John M. Daniel, dueled with E. W. Johnson in 1852 and apparently had another duel the year before; Lorenzo Sabine, *Notes on Duels and Duelling* (Boston, 1854), p. 138. For Daniel's comments, see undated letter to ERD from Washington in 1851, and letter to ERD dated Jan. 31, 1852.

18. These details are taken from a memoir prepared by PVD for his children after Lucy's death in 1846. Grymes Papers.

19. Marriage records, Henrico County Court House.

20. The pieces seen by the author were in the possession of William Randolph Grymes of Orange, Va.

21. PVD's memoir, Grymes Papers.

22. Aug. 7, 1811, Lucy Randolph Daniel Papers in Grymes collection.

23. PVD to William Brent, Jr., Nov. 18, 1836, Brent Papers, University of Virginia.

24. *Enquirer*, Aug. 23, 1811.

25. C.S.R., Jan. 9, 1812.

26. *Ibid.*, Jan. 11, 1812.

27. *Ibid.*, March 16, 1813, p. 107.

28. *Ibid.*, p. 108.

29. *Ibid.*, p. 109.

II. The War of 1812 and Council Duties

1. C.S.R., April 15, 1812.

2. *Enquirer*, June 2, 1812.

3. John B. McMaster, *History of the People of the United States* (New York, 1907), III, 445–447.

4. *Enquirer*, June 16, 1812.

5. *Ibid.*

6. *Enquirer*, July 6, 1812.

7. *Ibid.*, Sept. 1, 1812.

8. *Ibid.*, Sept. 5, 1812.

9. C.S.R., Dec. 30, 1812.

10. *Ibid.*, March 16, 1813.

11. *Ibid.*, March 24, 1813.

12. *Ibid.*, March 31, 1813, pp. 143–146.

13. *Ibid.*, Nov. 20, 1813.

14. *Ibid.*, Feb. 21, 1813, the Daniel dissent being at pp. 125–128.

15. In the discussion of the structure of Virginia politics that follows, I have had great assistance from Rex Beach, "Spencer Roane" (unpubl. thesis, University of Virginia, 1941). Particularly relevant

also are two works by Charles Henry Ambler, his *Thomas Ritchie* (Richmond, 1913), and his *Sectionalism in Virginia, 1776–1861* (Chicago, 1910); and, for later references, the very useful Henry H. Simms, *Rise of the Whigs in Virginia* (Richmond, 1929).

16. Beach, "Spencer Roane," p. 21.

17. See Ambler, *Thomas Ritchie.*

18. Of the many references on this subject, two particularly illuminating views similar to Daniel's are John Garraty, *Silas Wright* (New York, 1949), and Louis Hartz, *Economic Policy and Democratic Thought* (Cambridge, 1948).

19. For illuminating background see Henry H. Simms, *Life of John Taylor* (Richmond, 1932), and Eugene Mudge, *The Social Philosophy of John Taylor* (New York, 1939).

20. John Taylor, *Inquiry into the Principles and Policy of the Government of the United States* (Fredericksburg, 1814).

21. C.S.R., July 2, 1816.

22. PVD to Nicholas, Sept. 10, 1816, Nicholas Papers. These papers are quoted by permission of the University of Virginia Library.

23. Campbell to Nicholas, Sept. 23, 1816, Nicholas Papers.

24. C.S.R., Sept. 30, 1816.

25. *Ibid.*, Oct. 31, 1818. The first meeting at which Daniel presided in the absence of the governor was Nov. 2, 1818.

26. *Ibid.*, Sept. 12, 1823, pp. 216–220.

27. *Ibid.*, Sept. 6, 1823; Oct. 20, 1823.

28. Illustrative of the attitude toward Marshall is a jingle printed in the *Enquirer* when a statue of the Chief Justice by a sculptor named Rogers was erected after Marshall's death:

> "We are glad to see you, John Marshall, my boy
> So fresh from the chisel of Rogers.
> Go take your stand on the monument there
> Along with the other old codgers."

Undated clipping in ERD notes, Grymes Papers.

29. On Marshall's life in Richmond see Albert Beveridge, *Life of John Marshall* (Indianapolis, 1919); on the lawyer dinners particularly, see IV, 78–79.

30. 4 Wheat. 316 (1819).

31. Quoted in Beveridge, *Life of John Marshall*, IV, 339.

32. *Enquirer*, July 9, 1819.

33. C.S.R., Dec. 2, 1820.

34. *Ibid.*, Dec. 8, 1820.

35. *Cohens v. Virginia*, 6 Wheat. 264 (1821).

36. Beveridge, *Life of John Marshall*, IV, 360–362.

37. Thomas Jefferson to Randolph, July 30, 1821, Jefferson Papers, Library of Congress, vol. 220.

38. *Enquirer*, Dec. 15, 1821.

39. *Ibid.*, Dec. 20, 1821. As lieutenant governor, Daniel had the honor of being the first signer of the statement. The reply fills three newspaper columns in fine print.

40. *Ibid.*, Dec. 22, 1821.

41. The Council's reply of Dec. 20 had anticipated this point.

42. *Enquirer*, Dec. 3, 1822.

43. *Enquirer*, April 30, 1824.

44. *Ibid.*, May 28, 1824.

III. Family and Practice

1. *Enquirer*, Jan. 20, 1835. The phrase presumably means that to this observer, Daniel's courtesy was very formal.

2. Lucy Daniel to PVD, April 30, 1821, Grymes Papers.

3. The factual data in this and the next sentence are taken from the records of St. Paul's Church in Richmond.

4. Personal note of PVD, Cabell Papers. This collection quoted by permission of the University of Virginia Library.

5. Lucy Daniel to ERD, Oct. 6, 1840, Grymes Papers.

6. *Ibid.*

7. Lucy Daniel to PVD, July 2, 1821, Cabell Papers.

8. *Ibid.*

9. PVD to William Brent, Feb. 18, 1830, Cabell Papers.

10. PVD to William Brent, July 13, 1836, Cabell Papers.

11. As, from the Supreme Court, "Now let me see if in my humdrum life in this place I can rake up anything which may further contribute to your entertainment," and so into an anecdote about Henry Clay's lovesick ladies. PVD to Anne D. Moncure, Feb. 12, 1848, Grymes Papers.

12. Comment about Anne in letter to ERD, Jan. 3, 1850, Grymes Papers.

13. PVD to Anne D. Moncure, date indecipherable, probably 1851, Grymes Papers.

14. PVD to ERD, Feb. 25, 1843, Grymes Papers.

15. ERD papers.

16. ERD papers.

17. PVD to ERD, Aug. 3, 1851.

18. PVD to ERD, May 24, 1850.

19. The exact location was found by the author with the aid of the office of the Richmond City Engineer and the Henrico County Court House property records. The area is now completely urban; see Bessie Grabowsky, *The DuVal Family of Virginia* (Richmond, 1931), pp. 171–174.

20. Some of the accounts are in the Huntington Library Daniel collection.

21. Mary Wingfield Scott, *Old Richmond Neighborhoods* (Richmond, 1950), p. 150; Earle Lutz, *Richmond Album* (Richmond, 1937). The last work has an error in the Justice's initials.

22. PVD to William Brent, Nov. 13, 1836, Cabell Papers.

23. PVD to Thomas Jefferson, Dec. 22, 1809, Jefferson Papers, Library of Congress, asks whether Jefferson can recall a particular person relevant to the case. Jefferson dimly recollected the man and searched his papers but could find no real identification. Jefferson to PVD, Jan. 11, 1810.

24. PVD to James Madison, July 14, 1814, Madison Papers, Library of Congress.

25. PVD to William Brent, Dec. 13, 1824, Cabell Papers.

26. Daniel Papers, Huntington Library.

27. Records, Henrico County Court House.

28. *Farmers Bank v. Clarke*, 31 Va. 603 (1833).

29. *Seekright v. Moore*, 31 Va. 30 (1832).

30. "I have received of Mr. C. Lipscombe five dollars for a fee in the suit of Jones against Lipscombe in Hanover County Court." Receipt, July 29, 1821, by PVD in the Huntington Library files. This collection here and throughout quoted by permission.

31. In a letter to Van Buren after Daniel was on the district court, he claimed a pre-judicial income of $4000; with due allowance for puffing, the figure $3000 seems about right, and in any case his claim was for the height of his practice. PVD to VB, Nov. 13, 1836, Van Buren Papers, Library of Congress. A letter to his intimate friend Brent shows that if the governor's salary had been raised to $5000, it would have been enough to lure him off the district bench. PVD to William Brent, Nov. 13, 1836.

32. To his daughter he once made an expense estimate of $1000 for six months, but this was after Lucy's death. PVD to Anne Daniel Moncure, July 17, 1851, Grymes Papers.

33. Willard Hurst, *The Growth of American Law* (Boston, 1950), p. 311.

34. The data in this paragraph were drawn from the Richmond tax records, Virginia State Library, and from Daniel's will.

35. Herbert H. Rosenthal, "James Barbour, Virginia Politician" (unpubl. thesis, University of Virginia, 1942), pp. 47, 48.

36. In encouraging the purchase of a house slave he said, "A total dependency upon chance at the end of the year even for the simplest accommodations is so annoying to me that I know not how to endure it." PVD to ERD, Jan. 14, 1849.

37. PVD to ERD, Jan. 3, 1850.

38. PVD to ERD, Jan. 12, 1849.

39. PVD to ERD, Dec. 28, 1851.

40. PVD to William Brent, July 27, 1836, Cabell Papers.

41. PVD to ERD, May 9, 1850.

42. PVD to ERD, Feb. 6, 1849.

43. The details are reported in the *Enquirer*, Oct. 22, 1824.

44. *Enquirer*, Oct. 28, 1824.

45. *Ibid.*

46. The author observed the cloth in the possession of William Grymes of Orange, Va.

47. *Enquirer*, Oct. 26, 1824.

48. *Ibid.*

IV. Revolt, *Actual and Political*

1. PVD to the governor of Maryland, April 14, 1829, Executive Letter Book, Virginia State Library, refusing an extradition where the Maryland authorities had sent a *note* descriptive of the alleged offense, but not an *affidavit*, as required by law.

2. Executive Letter Book, Aug. 1, 1825, p. 102, Virginia State Library.

3. PVD to County Court of Goochland, April 14, 1829, Executive Letter Book, Virginia State Library.

4. C.S.R., July 31, 1829.

5. W. S. Drewry, *The Southampton Insurrection* (Washington, 1900), based upon contemporary newspaper accounts. The text description draws heavily from the *Confessions of Nat Turner, as Made to Thomas R. Gray* (Baltimore, 1831). While Gray undoubtedly contributed far more than Turner to the language used, there seems to be no reason to doubt the essential facts.

6. C.S.R., Aug. 23, 1831.

7. *Ibid.*, Sept. 8, 1831.

8. *Ibid.*, Sept. 16, 1831, p. 116.

9. Drewry, *The Southampton Insurrection.*

10. C.S.R., Sept. 28, 1831.

11. *Ibid.*, Sept. 29, 1832.

12. *Ibid.*, pp. 145–146.

13. C.S.R., Oct. 18, 1832, reprinted in John P. Frank, *Cases and Materials on Constitutional Law* (Chicago, 1952), p. 178.

14. *Ibid.* Depressingly enough, the United States Supreme Court reached the opposite result, over strong dissent, on this point in *Lyons v. Oklahoma*, 322 U.S. 596 (1944).

15. *Enquirer*, Dec. 12, 1826.

16. *Enquirer*, May 19, 1829. Marshall had at first declined to be

considered because of his health, but then accepted; *ibid.*, March 31, 1829.

17. *Ibid.*, March 17, 1829. That the idea met some resistance is shown by a demand from one group at the district convention that they be represented by "farmers" and not "office holders." *Ibid.*, April 28, 1829.

18. The best source on the convention, from which the text description is taken, is its own published record, *Proceedings and Debates of the Virginia State Convention of 1829–30* (Richmond, 1830).

19. The vote in the 1831–32 legislature on the resolution "it is expedient to adopt some legislative amendment for the abolition of slavery" was 58 for, 73 against. Ambler, *Sectionalism in Virginia, 1776–1861*, p. 199. The representatives from the western 60 percent of the state were solidly in favor of the proposal.

20. *Debates of the Virginia State Convention*, pp. 474, 479, 491.

21. *Ibid.*, p. 711.

22. *Ibid.*, p. 716.

23. *Ibid.*, p. 594.

24. *Enquirer*, Jan. 7, 1830. The Richmond *Whig*, quoted in the Alexandria *Gazette*, Jan. 11, 1830, noted the scratch of two "excellent citizens and good councillors." It continued, with reference to "the fungus to which they recently belonged," that it hoped this would be "the last time Virginia will ever witness so absurd a proceeding."

25. *Enquirer*, Jan. 12, 1830.

26. *Enquirer*, Feb. 12, 1831.

V. A Growing Role in National Politics

1. Martin Van Buren, *Autobiography*, ed. John C. Fitzpatrick, Annual Report, American Historical Association, 1918 (Washington, 1920), pp. 125, 126.

2. *Ibid.*, p. 127.

3. The Van Buren Papers in the Library of Congress are the principal repository of these materials.

4. *Enquirer*, Feb. 24, March 2, 1824.

5. *Enquirer*, Feb. 12, 1824.

6. *Enquirer*, Feb. 18, 1824.

7. *Enquirer*, Oct. 16, 1824.

8. The result was controlled by the vote of one indecisive congressman, Van Rensselaer of New York. For an amusing account of how this gentleman finally made up his mind, see Van Buren, *Autobiography*, pp. 149–153.

9. *Ibid.*, p. 149.

10. *Ibid.*, p. 162.

11. Margaret Coit, *John C. Calhoun* (Boston, 1950), p. 159.

12. *Enquirer*, July 6, 1827.

13. On August 21, 1827, the *Enquirer* claimed Virginia as, next to Tennessee, "the most certain state in the Union for General Jackson."

14. *Enquirer*, Oct. 26, 1827. One handicap for this group was its mental reservation about Adams himself; Clay was their real favorite.

15. *Ibid.*, July 31, 1827, reports that among those for Jackson in Stafford County were William Brent, Jr., Walter R. Daniel, R. C. L. Moncure, and John M. Daniel.

16. *Ibid.*, Oct. 26, 1827.

17. *Ibid.*, Nov. 2, 1827.

18. *Ibid.*, Jan. 10, 1828; Simms, *The Rise of the Whigs in Virginia*, p. 30.

19. Marshall stated that he was voting "from the strong sense I felt of the injustice of the charge of corruption against the President and the Secretary of State." *Enquirer*, April 4, 1828.

20. *Enquirer*, March 8, 1827, and Feb. 5, 1828.

21. *Enquirer*, Oct. 7, 1828.

22. See Claude Bowers, *Party Battles of the Jackson Period* (Cambridge, Mass., 1922), chap. 2.

23. One Junto publication recounted the attacks on Jackson: "The dart which was aimed at him would have pierced at the same time the bosom of his wife. He was painted as a seducer and an adulterer"; as a "murderer," "butcher," "assassin," "Negro trader," "as a man abandoned by his own temper to the most shocking profanity." The pamphlet then came to the point: "Is the patriot hero to be sacrificed at the feet of John Q. Adams and Henry Clay?" *Enquirer*, Oct. 25, 1828.

24. PVD to William Brent, Feb. 12, 1830, Cabell Papers.

25. *Ibid.*

26. PVD to William Brent, Aug. 10, 1836, Cabell Papers.

27. Coit, *John C. Calhoun*, p. 164.

28. Albert Beveridge, *The Life of John Marshall* (Cambridge, Mass., 1919), p. 318.

29. Those mentioned are some of Daniel's many pseudonyms.

30. The principal basis of identification is in references to the letters in private correspondence. The author has claimed a few for Daniel on the basis of content, style, and other circumstances but has been extremely cautious in this regard.

31. These epithets are taken from a number of sources and particularly PVD to William Brent, July 13, 1836, Cabell Papers.

32. PVD to William Rives, Dec. 29, 1837, Rives Papers, Library of Congress.

33. PVD to VB, Nov. 2, 1832.

34. PVD to VB, March 9, 1835.

35. PVD to VB, Sept. 25, 1835.

36. PVD to ERD, Feb. 25, 1843.

37. *Enquirer*, Feb. 20, 1835.

38. *Ibid.*

39. The Miller reference is in the second Crito letter, *Enquirer*, Feb. 11, 1832.

40. PVD to Thomas Ritchie, Feb. 17, 1832, Cralle Collection, Library of Congress.

41. Miller to PVD, Feb. 22, 1832, Cralle Collection.

42. PVD to Miller, Feb. 29, 1832, Cralle Collection.

43. *Enquirer*, Sept. 30, 1828.

44. *Enquirer*, Nov. 7, 1828.

VI. *The Campaign for Van Buren*

1. On Van Buren generally, see his *Autobiography*. There are no really good biographies.

2. Daniel occasionally complained of Van Buren's failure to answer letters; see, for example, PVD to VB, Feb. 22, 1835, Van Buren Papers.

3. A leading work on Calhoun is Charles M. Wiltse, *John C. Calhoun* (Indianapolis, 1944). I have also made much use of the one-volume Coit, *John C. Calhoun*.

4. For a full account see Chauncey M. Boucher, *Nullification in South Carolina* (Chicago, 1916).

5. Coit, *John C. Calhoun*, pp. 184–191.

6. For an account the accuracy of which is open to some doubt, see M. L. Eaton, *Autobiography of Peggy Eaton* (New York, 1932).

7. PVD to William Brent, Aug. 10, 1831, Cabell Papers.

8. "Ambition with him seems to be a perfect mania, a frenzy." PVD to VB, March 9, 1835, Van Buren Papers.

9. *Enquirer*, April 22, 1831.

10. *Ibid.*, Sept. 9, 1831.

11. Charles H. Ambler, *Life and Diary of John Floyd* (Richmond, 1918), p. 204.

12. *Ibid.*, p. 161.

13. *Enquirer*, July 12, 1831.

14. C.S.R., Feb.–Aug. 1831, *passim*.

15. *Enquirer*, July 12, 1831.

16. As reprinted in the *Enquirer*, July 12, 1831.

17. *Enquirer*, July 19 and 22, 1831.

18. Ambler, *Life and Diary of John Floyd*, pp. 152, 154.

19. *Telegraph*, July 22, 1831.

20. *Telegraph*, July 8, 1831.

21. The statement appears in the *Enquirer*, July 8, 1831. I claim it for Daniel on the grounds (a) that he was with Jackson at Old Point Comfort; (b) that he is the only person mentioned in the party for whom the *Enquirer* was a natural press outlet; (c) that the statement has a quality of comfortable arrogance which was a dominant quality of Daniel as, referring to a statement by Eaton, "I expressed my regret [to Jackson] that he should have put himself in the wrong"; (d) that the adjectives are Daniel's — as, the "reckless, profligacy of the falsehoods"; (e) that the style throughout is Daniel's; and (f) that it was so very like Daniel to wish to be the vehicle for such a statement.

22. The text details are taken from the *Enquirer*, Dec. 19, 1831.

23. *Ibid.*

24. *Ibid.*

25. PVD to VB, April 22, 1831.

26. Ambler, *Thomas Ritchie*, p. 145.

27. *Enquirer*, March 17, 23, and 27, 1832, records the debate.

28. *Enquirer*, March 17, 1832.

29. *Ibid.*

30. Since Barbour and Daniel were later to sit together on the circuit court bench, it is noteworthy that no hard feelings between the two were manifested. Barbour did write the *Enquirer* to correct one alleged error by Daniel. The error consisted of an implication that Barbour had not voted against the charter of the second Bank of the United States when in Congress in 1816, thus implying that Barbour had then supported the Bank. The fact was that Barbour had not voted either way on that question. *Enquirer*, April 10, 1832.

31. *Enquirer*, May 15, 1832.

32. The details of the convention, particularly those that relate to the Virginia delegation, are taken from the *Enquirer*, Feb. 5 and May 25 and 29, 1832.

33. Letter to the editor, *Enquirer*, Feb. 5, 1832.

34. *Enquirer*, May 25, 1832.

35. Coit, *John C. Calhoun*, chap. 15.

36. "General Jackson expressed a wish that I would do what I could with my friends in Congress to promote a satisfactory adjustment of the matter." Van Buren, *Autobiography*, p. 541.

37. For shadings of Virginia opinion, see Simms, *The Rise of the Whigs in Virginia*, pp. 65–69.

38. The leading biography is Carl B. Swisher, *Roger B. Taney* (New York, 1936).

39. PVD to Governor David Campbell, May 13, 1837, Campbell Papers, by permission of Duke University Library.

40. Taney to Thomas Ellicott, Feb. 20, 1832, Taney Papers. Md. Hist. Soc.

41. On political aspects of the beginnings of the bank fight, see Swisher, *Roger B. Taney*, pp. 180–184.

42. James Richardson, ed., *Messages and Papers of the Presidents* (Washington, 1898), II, 576.

43. PVD to William Brent, Feb. 29, 1840, Cabell Papers.

44. Letter from [*indecipherable*] at Albany to VB, July 29, 1832, enclosing PVD to VB of July 2, 1832. Van Buren Papers.

45. PVD to VB, Nov. 2, 1832.

46. *Enquirer*, Oct. 16, 1832.

47. *Enquirer*, Oct. 30, 1832.

48. *Ibid.*

49. Granted, Van Buren was nominated at Baltimore on the first ballot *without* the Virginia votes. But question whether he would have thus been swept in if it had not been known that he would get those votes on the next ballot.

50. PVD to VB, Nov. 2, 1832.

51. *Enquirer*, Dec. 8, 1832.

52. See Boucher, *Nullification in South Carolina*, for details.

53. *Enquirer*, Dec. 3, 1832.

54. "It is the extreme medicine of the Constitution." *Enquirer*, Dec. 20, 1832.

55. Legislative debates, reported in the *Enquirer*, Dec. 15, 1832, and Jan. 3, 1833. Calhoun stopped off to hear the debate in the Virginia legislature and to meet his supporters on his way home from Washington to lead the nullificationists. *Enquirer*, Jan. 3, 1833.

56. Legislative action, reported in the *Enquirer*, Jan. 19, 1833.

57. On the tariff of 1833 see Frank W. Taussig, *The Tariff History of the United States* (New York, 6th ed., 1914), chap. 3.

58. *Enquirer*, July 9, 1833.

59. C.S.R., May 4, 1833.

60. *Ibid.*, Jan. 2, 1834.

61. Claiborne W. Gooch, coeditor of the *Enquirer*, to VB, Sept. 27, 1830, State Department appointment records, National Archives.

62. *Enquirer*, Jan. 20, 1835, references on legislative debate.

63. *Enquirer*, March 7 and 9, 1833.

64. Quoted in *United States Telegraph*, Nov. 4, 1833.

65. *Ibid.*, Oct. 29, 1833.

66. *Ibid.*, Nov. 12, 1833.

67. Quoted in the Washington *National Intelligencer*, Nov. 1, 1833.

68. *Enquirer*, Oct. 29, 1833.

69. Quoted in *Enquirer*, Nov. 5, 1833.
70. *Ibid.*
71. *Enquirer*, Oct. 29, 1833.
72. Washington *National Intelligencer*, Nov. 1, 1833.
73. Stevenson to Taney, Nov. 5, 1833, Taney Papers. Md. Hist. Soc.
74. State Department appointment records, National Archives.
75. Stevenson to Taney, Nov. 5, 1833, Taney Papers. Md. Hist. Soc.
76. Taney to Stevenson, Nov. 15, 1833, Taney Papers. Md. Hist. Soc.
77. *Enquirer*, Nov. 8, 1833.
78. Martin Van Buren, *Political Parties in the United States* (New York, 1867), pp. 322, 323.
79. *Enquirer*, Dec. 31, 1833.
80. The debate is reported in the *Enquirer*, Jan. 9, 1834. A typical pro-Daniel view was a letter of Jan. 7 emphasizing Daniel's great experience, his "firmness, perseverence, and ability; who has devoted himself to the state and refused three offices under the government of the U.S.; who is an inflexible friend of the rights of the states, whilst he is vehemently opposed to the dangers of nullification."
81. Based on comparison of reports in the *Enquirer*, Jan. 23, Feb. 13, and Feb. 15, 1834.
82. Simms, *The Rise of the Whigs in Virginia*, p. 83.
83. *Ibid.*, pp. 83, 84.
84. *Enquirer*, July 11, 1834.

VII. Defeat and Victory

1. Simms, *The Rise of the Whigs in Virginia*, p. 81; *Enquirer*, Sept. 19, 1832.
2. *Enquirer*, Dec. 9, 1834.
3. *Ibid.*, Jan. 17, 1835.
4. *Ibid.*
5. *Ibid.*
6. *Ibid.*
7. *Enquirer*, Jan. 20, 1835.
8. *Ibid.*
9. *Enquirer*, Dec. 19, 1835.
10. *Enquirer*, Jan. 31, 1835.
11. *Enquirer*, Feb. 7, 1836.
12. *Ibid.*, Feb. 28, 1836.
13. PVD to VB, June 7, 1836.
14. Daniel charged that an attack was planned by a Joseph Selden in conspiracy with Daniel's arch-enemy Hampden Pleasants, the editor of the Richmond *Whig*; PVD to VB, Aug. 8, 1838, Van Buren Papers.
15. *Enquirer*, May 26, 1835. The guiding principle of the Virginia

delegates was expressed in a resolution in which they pledged to "resist any other rule" than a two-thirds rule. *Enquirer*, Feb. 2, 1835.

16. *Enquirer*, Feb. 2, 1835.

17. *Ibid.*

18. *Ibid.*

19. *Enquirer*, Dec. 19, 1836.

20. Richard Parker to Van Buren, 1835 (precise date illegible) Van Buren Papers.

21. C.S.R., April 25, 1836.

22. *Enquirer*, May 6 and 27, 1836.

VIII. *District Judge*

1. Parker to VB, 1835 (precise date illegible), Van Buren Papers.

2. Three petitions and letter to Jackson, March 21, 1836, in State Department section, National Archives. The three had a total of sixty-nine signatures.

3. Morgan to Jackson, March 22, 1836, enclosing Mrs. Morgan to Jackson, State Department section, National Archives. Charles Morgan's letter noted that "not until Sunday last was it publicly known here that the name of any gentleman would be presented to your consideration for the office of District Judge other than that of Mr. Daniel."

4. John Campbell to Jackson, forwarding note of John Rutherford of March 21, 1836, State Department section, National Archives.

5. Morgan to Jackson, March 22, 1836, State Department section, National Archives.

6. PVD to William Brent, July 13, 1836, Cabell Papers.

7. Paragraph from undated, unidentified Ms., signed "W.S." University of Virginia Papers.

8. PVD to William Brent, July 13, 1836, Cabell Papers.

9. PVD to governor, May 15, 1837, University of Virginia Papers.

10. On the relations between the two brothers see Rosenthal, "James Barbour, Virginia Politician." The two were in Congress together, where Philip was regarded as the closer reasoner. Rosenthal reports, on p. 58, that someone wrote the following couplet on the wall of the House of Representatives:

"Two Barbours to shave our Congress long did try;
One shaves with froth; the other shaves dry."

11. PVD to William Brent, Nov. 18, 1836, Cabell Papers.

12. The following summary is based on a comprehensive study of the records of the district court, the order book of the circuit court, and the fee book of the circuit court, for Daniel's years on the bench, and on a study of the actual circuit court records for the year 1838,

nothing more being available. The files and records were obtained through the combined efforts and courtesy of Judge Sterling H. Atcheson, Federal district court, eastern Virginia, in 1952, and Mr. Van Schrewen, head archivist, Virginia State Library.

13. *Clarke v. The Schooner Alfred*, district court records, Nov. term, 1838.

14. *United States v. James Henderson*, district court records, Nov. term, 1838.

15. *United States v. Koster*, district court records, May term, 1838.

16. District court records, order, Nov. term, 1838.

17. "The Post Office under Barry's management made a most dismal showing from every point of view." Wesley Rich, *History of the United States Post Office to 1829* (Cambridge, 1924).

18. District court records, Nov. term, 1840.

19. For sources see note 12, above.

20. PVD to Senator William Rives, Sept. 7, 1837, Rives Papers, Library of Congress.

21. PVD to Rives, Dec. 29, 1837, Rives Papers; and PVD to VB, May 23, 1838, Van Buren Papers.

22. PVD to VB, Jan. 23, 1838.

23. S. 218, 25th Cong., 2d Sess.

24. PVD to VB, May 23, 1838.

25. PVD to Rives, Dec. 29, 1837, Rives Papers.

26. PVD to VB, May 23, 1838.

27. PVD to Rives, Nov. 7, 1837, Rives Papers.

28. The discussion is reported in the Washington *National Intelligencer*, May 11, 1838.

IX. *The Supreme Court Appointment*

1. *Enquirer*, April 6, 1839.

2. *Enquirer*, March 23, 1837.

3. *Enquirer*, March 5, 21, and 23, 1839; Feb. 22, 27, and 29, and April 10, 1840.

4. *Enquirer*, April 10 and Sept. 22, 1840.

5. *Enquirer*, Aug. 21, 1840, quoting letter from Daniel of July 24, 1840.

6. *Enquirer*, Aug. 21, 1840.

7. *Ibid.*, Sept. 23, 1840.

8. *Ibid.*, Oct. 9, 1840.

9. For a detailed account of the last hours of Justice Barbour, see letter of Justice McLean to Mrs. Barbour, Feb. 26, 1841. McLean Papers, Library of Congress.

10. Dr. John Brockenbrough to VB, Feb. 27, 1841, Van Buren

Papers. The appointment of Tucker "would be more satisfactory to the Republicans than that of any other person in the state."

11. Letter of sixty-two members of the Assembly to VB, Feb. 27, 1841.

12. Richmond *Whig*, March 5, 1841.

13. *Enquirer*, March 2, 1841.

14. The debate is summarized from Cong. Globe, 26th Cong., 2d Sess., pp. 213–216.

15. The account of the discussion on the appointment itself is taken from the *Enquirer*, March 6, 9, and 11, 1841, which includes letters from its Washington observers.

16. The Richmond *Whig*, March 5, 1841, pledged that as soon as their party took office, they would pass a redistricting bill which would deport Daniel all the way to the Indian country.

17. VB to Jackson, March 12, 1841, Van Buren Papers, reprinted in John Spencer Bassett, ed., *Correspondence of Andrew Jackson* (Washington, 1926–1935), VI, 93; Jackson to VB, *ibid.*, p. 96. Jackson added: "Mr. Clay got so wroth at the appointment of that pure patriot Mr. Daniel to the Supreme Bench, knowing that he did believe there was no power granted to Congress to charter a national Bank, or any beyond the limit of the District, and then not a bank of paper issues."

18. PVD to VB, Sept. 11, 1837.

19. PVD to VB, May 23, 1838.

20. PVD to ERD, Feb. 1, 1851.

21. PVD to VB, Nov. 19, 1844.

22. PVD to VB, Oct. 28, 1838.

23. PVD to VB, Dec. 16, 1841.

24. "There seems to be so general a sickening at the effects of the banks that I hope the country is ripe for suppressing them by degrees, but entirely in the end." Jefferson to Thomas Randolph, Jefferson Papers, Library of Congress, box 216, no. 38533.

25. PVD to VB, July 6, 1843. It will be noticed that Daniel deletes "liberty" and "the pursuit of happiness" from the classical trinity of the objects of government without being aware that he has done so.

26. PVD to VB, July 6, 1843.

27. PVD to VB, Nov. 1, 1847.

28. PVD to ERD, May 15, 1847.

29. PVD to ERD, Feb. 26, 1848.

X. *Daniel Takes His Seat on the Court*

1. 16 Pet. 25, 10 L. Ed. 73 (1842).

2. 16 Pet. 1, 10 L. Ed. 65 (1842).

3. *Erie Railway v. Tompkins*, 304 U.S. 64, 58 Sup. Ct. 817, 82 L. Ed. 1188 (1938).

4. *Cocke v. Halsey*, 16 Pet. 71, 10 L. Ed. 891 (1842). Many of these details as to dates are taken from the minutes of the Supreme Court which are in the custody of the clerk at the Supreme Court Building.

5. The two most important were *United States v. Eliason*, 16 Pet. 291, 10 L. Ed. 968 (1842), involving a claim for compensation, a problem not much different from the type of claims issues which had once confronted the lieutenant governor of Virginia; *Roach v. Hulings*, 16 Pet. 319, 10 L. Ed. 979 (1842) on a problem of transfer of a contract.

6. Charles Warren, *The Supreme Court in United States History* (Boston, 1922), II, 139.

7. Such merit as there was in the criticism of Peters is summarized in Warren, *The Supreme Court*, II, 106. The act was not in a technical sense a removal because Congress had only just authorized an official appointment; Howard thus became the first appointee under the new act.

8. Peters to Story, March 1 and 5, 1843, Story Papers, Library of Congress.

This was not simply a quiet, intracourt affair — it became openly notorious. Peters, despite the fact that he had been dismissed, proceeded nonetheless to bring out an additional volume of reports for the year 1843. Peters announced that he intended to continue his unofficial publication annually, which he did not in fact do. He reviewed the whole controversy in a preface in which he asserted that the minority of the Court which had been present and which had voted for him were men of the highest capacity, and that the absent members, who had they been present would have made a majority, had told him that if they had been present they would have voted for him. Meanwhile, Reporter Howard in his own first volume carried "a card" telling the Bar that since he was now the reporter and would be at the Court from day to day in that connection, he was taking "this opportunity to tender his professional services in arguing causes before the Supreme Court" for lawyers too far away to present them themselves. The two volumes also contain in their prefaces a host of claims by Justice Catron of alleged mistakes by Peters, countered with a rebuttal by Peters which does in truth demolish Catron, leaving the clear impression that most of the errors were Catron's own fault. Indeed, in Catron's error list as published by Howard there were additional errors, leading to a biting comment in still another communiqué in the Peters book by the printer that perhaps Justice Catron "may find it necessary to print a list of corrections" to his corrections. This unedifying exchange occurs in the 1843 edition of 1 Howard and in the 1843 (and only) edition of 17 Peters. These volumes were examined in the Supreme Court Library and are not commonly available.

9. McLean to Story, Jan. 25, 1843, Story Papers. McLean told Story that "the Chief Justice, Thompson, and myself were for postponing the appointment until the close of the term, giving Peters the present term, and then in a kind manner give him an intimation which might induce him to resign."

10. McLean to Story, Sept. 30, 1843, Story Papers.

11. The routine is taken from a description by Senator Reverdy Johnson of Maryland, one of the foremost members of the Supreme Court Bar, as set forth in Alexander A. Lawrence, *James Moore Wayne* (Chapel Hill, N. C., 1943), p. 133. McLean's description is from an undated letter to a Methodist paper, probably the *Western Ohio Advocate*, in McLean Papers, Library of Congress, box 18.

12. PVD to ERD, Jan. 29, 1848.

13. PVD to ERD, May 24, 1850.

14. PVD to ERD, Feb. 25, 1843. As he told his daughter, "My slavish engagements forbid participating in anything in the way of amusement and rarely allow me more than six hours in bed in the 24." PVD to ERD, Dec. 23, 1845.

15. PVD to ERD, Feb. 25, 1843. Colonel Benton was then senator from Missouri.

16. PVD to ERD, Jan. 3, 1850.

17. PVD to ERD, Jan. 2, 1851.

18. PVD to ERD, Jan. 3, 1852.

19. PVD to ERD, Feb. 1 and 23, 1851.

20. 16 Pet. 539, 10 L. Ed. 1060 (1842).

21. The quotation is taken from Warren, *The Supreme Court*, II, 85, as is the immediately subsequent account of the popular reaction.

XI. *Daniel's Role, in General and on Exclusiveness*

1. The cases listed are *Thomas v. Lawson*, 21 How. 331, 16 L. Ed. 82 (1859); *Fenn v. Holme*, 21 How. 481, 16 L. Ed. 198 (1859); *Connor v. Bradley*, 1 How. 211, 11 L. Ed. 105 (1843); *Gilmer v. Poindexter*, 10 How. 257, 13 L. Ed. 411 (1850).

2. The case is *White v. Nicholls*, 3 How. 266, 11 L. Ed. 591 (1845) holding that even a privileged communication may be libelous if actual malice is proved in the making of it. This case came to the Supreme Court, as did much of its business at this time, from the District of Columbia, for the Supreme Court was not only the Court of last resort for the rest of the country on those matters which the Constitution had assigned to it, but was also in a very immediate sense the Supreme Court of the District of Columbia on all sorts of essentially private disputes.

3. *U.S. v. Arjona*, 120 U.S. 479, 487, 7 Sup. Ct. 628, 30 L. Ed. 728

(1887), holds that offenses against the law of nations are punishable exclusively by the federal government but that some conduct (in this case counterfeiting of foreign money) may also be an offense against state law. The first patent act was passed in 1793, and its exclusiveness is considered in *Allen v. Riley*, 203 U.S. 347, 27 Sup. Ct. 95, 51 L. Ed. 216 (1906).

4. *Fox v. Ohio*, 5 How. 410, 12 L. Ed. 213 (1847).

5. The problems of the first presentation are revealed in McLean's dissenting opinion.

6. A subsidiary argument against Daniel's position, with which he felt it necessary to deal, was that this would permit both Federal and state prosecution, and thus double jeopardy, for what was essentially all one offense. Daniel's response was that he thought the likelihood of double prosecution extremely remote, but that in any case this was immaterial since the double-jeopardy clause was, like the rest of the Bill of Rights, a restriction upon the Federal government only. Subsequently, Congress did pass an act prohibiting the passing of counterfeit as well as the production of it, giving Daniel the problem of extricating himself from the situation created in *Fox v. Ohio*. This he managed to do; see *U.S. v. Marigold*, 9 How. 560, 13 L. Ed. 257 (1850).

7. 4 Wheat. 122, 4 L. Ed. 529 (1819).

8. *Ogden v. Saunders*, 12 Wheat. 213, 6 L. Ed. 606 (1827).

9. *Cook v. Moffat*, 5 How. 295, 312–313, 12 L. Ed. 159 (1847).

10. *Willson v. Black-bird Creek Marsh Co.*, 2 Pet. 245, 7 L. Ed. 412 (1829). The citations for *Gibbons v. Ogden* is 9 Wheat. 1, 6 L. Ed. 23 (1824), and for *Brown v. Maryland* is 12 Wheat. 419, 6 L. Ed. 678 (1827).

11. 11 Pet. 102, 9 L. Ed. 648 (1837).

12. *Groves v. Slaughter*, 15 Pet. 449, 10 L. Ed. 800 (1841), in the course of which Daniel Webster argued "that the whole subject of commercial regulation was taken from the states and placed in the hands of Congress . . . nothing which is a regulation of commerce can be affected by state laws."

13. *Thurlow v. Massachusetts* and other cases, commonly grouped together as the *License Cases*, 5 How. 504, 12 L. Ed. 256 (1847).

14. 5 How. 579.

15. 5 How. 613.

16. *Smith v. Turner* and *Norris v. Boston*, commonly referred to as the *Passenger Cases*, 7 How. 283, 12 L. Ed. 702 (1849). For discussion of the presentation of these cases and related matters see Warren, *The Supreme Court*, II, 174f.

17. 11 Pet. 102, 9 L. Ed. 648 (1837).

18. PVD to ERD, Feb. 6, 1849.

19. PVD to ERD, March 3, 1849.

20. "His place will no doubt be filled by some Federalist and rank abolitionist, some dirty tool of Fillmore and Webster, some inveterate enemy of southern rights." PVD to ERD, Sept. 19, 1851.

21. President Harrison had served for only a month in 1841 and was succeeded by Vice President Tyler, who cannot be considered as a Whig.

22. Warren, *The Supreme Court*, II, 226–227.

23. 12 How. 299, 13 L. Ed. 996 (1852).

24. Curtis to Webster, Aug. 21, 1850, Curtis Papers. Though Daniel loathed Webster, the senator had immense personal standing not only with Curtis but with McLean. An illustration is a letter from Webster to McLean asking in substance how and when one of Webster's cases was to be decided, a letter which would have resulted in a contempt citation if it had been directed to Daniel. Webster to McLean, Dec. 27, 1848, McLean Papers, box 16.

25. The argument is quoted at 9 Wheat. 1, 14, as made in 1824.

26. Curtis to George Ticknor, Feb. 29, 1852, Curtis Papers.

27. Warren, *The Supreme Court*, II, 238, suggests that Woodbury was moving toward Curtis' position. This is based on a passage in the *Passenger Cases*, 7 How. 559. In context I do not so read it, though I find Woodbury frequently so muddled and obscure that it is hard to be sure.

28. 13 How. 518, 14 L. Ed. 249 (1852).

29. In the long run, Daniel's view prevailed. Congress amended the statute clearly authorizing the bridge, and the Court upheld, six to three, its power to do so. The only other issue in the case arose from the fact that between the first decision and the act of Congress a storm injured the bridge and Justice Grier, sitting on circuit, enjoined its rebuilding. The company proceeded to rebuild anyway and the issue was whether it should be held in contempt. A five to four majority held that "in all the circumstances" it would be as well to forget the whole unhappy business and not attempt to punish the company.

XII. Regulation of Business

1. 6 Cranch 87, 3 L. Ed. 162 (1810).

2. *Dartmouth College v. Woodward*, 4 Wheat. 518, 4 L. Ed. 629 (1819).

3. *Bronson v. Kinzie*, 1 How. 311, 11 L. Ed. 143 (1843); *McCracken v. Hayward*, 2 How. 608, 11 L. Ed. 608 (1844); *Gantley v. Ewing*, 3 How. 707, 11 L. Ed. 794 (1845).

4. 3 How. 133, 11 L. Ed. 529 (1845).

5. *Charles River Bridge Co. v. Warren Bridge Co.*, 11 Pet. 420, 9 L. Ed. 773 (1837).

6. *Planters Bank v. Sharp*, 6 How. 301, 12 L. Ed. 447 (1848). The majority opinion seems so totally wrong in relation to the *Charles River Bridge* precedent that it is difficult to see how the majority reached its result. Whatever other sterling qualities Woodbury may have had, a gift for clarity and tight reason was not one of them.

7. 10 How. 190, 13 L. Ed. 383 (1850), a decision invalidating an Arkansas statute that repealed a previous provision making state bank notes payable for state debts.

8. *Ohio Life Ins. Co. v. Debolt*, 16 How. 416, 14 L. Ed. 997 (1854).

9. *Marshall v. B. & O. RR.*, 16 How. 314, 14 L. Ed. 953 (1853). Justices Daniel, Catron, and Campbell dissented solely on jurisdictional grounds, believing that the Baltimore and Ohio Railroad Company was a corporation which could not be in Federal courts at all. Daniel noted that if he thought there were jurisdiction, "I should probably say that it is a case without merits either in the plaintiff or in the defendants, and that in such a case they should be dismissed by courts of justice to settle their dispute by some standard which is cognate to the transaction in which they have been engaged."

10. 16 How. 369, 14 L. Ed. 977 (1854); 18 How. 331, 15 L. Ed. 401 (1856).

11. 18 How. 371.

12. 6 How. 507, 12 L. Ed. 535 (1849). Daniel's other majority opinion on a contract-clause matter is *B. & S. RR. v. Nesbit*, 10 How. 395, 13 L. Ed. 469 (1851).

13. *Kohl v. United States*, 91 U.S. 367, 23 L. Ed. 449 (1875).

14. Woodbury had doubts of a somewhat different sort, and concurred in a statement longer than the opinion of the Court. In an opinion studded with useless but scholarly citation, he set forth his own limitations on eminent domain. Not all property could be taken — only that essential and urgent for public good. The power could not be used, he said, in error so great as to be almost sublime, to condemn land "for a marine hospital or state prison." For such objects, he maintained, one location would do as well as another. He was satisfied as to the amount.

15. *Home Building & Loan Association v. Blaisdell*, 290 U.S. 398, 54 Sup. Ct. 231, 78 L. Ed. 413 (1934).

XIII. The State and the Nation

1. *Searight v. Stokes*, 3 How. 151, 11 L. Ed. 537 (1845).

2. Daniel followed this view in *Neil, Moore & Co. v. Ohio*, 3 How. 720, 746, 11 L. Ed. 800 (1845), extending it to cover the Ohio portion of the road.

3. 3 How. 180–181. When President Polk vetoed an internal improvements measure, Daniel congratulated him and called this dissent to the President's attention, pleading that for the future he would always dissent emphatically on the issue. PVD to Polk, Aug. 5, 1846, Polk Papers, Library of Congress.

4. *Barber v. Barber*, 21 How. 582, 16 L. Ed. 226 (1859).

5. *McNutt v. Bland*, 2 How. 9, 11 L. Ed. 159 (1844); *Gwin v. Breedlove*, 2 How. 29, 39, 11 L. Ed. 167 (1844); *Hays v. Pacific Mail Co.*, 17 How. 596, 15 L. Ed. 254 (1855); *Clements v. Berry*, dissent, 11 How. 398, 13 L. Ed. 745 (1850); *Miners Bank v. Iowa*, majority, 12 How. 1, 13 L. Ed. 867 (1851); *Bennett v. Butterworth*, dissent, 8 How. 124, 12 L. Ed. 1013 (1850). In *Smith v. Hunter*, 7 How. 738, 12 L. Ed. 894 (1849), Daniel announced for a unanimous Court the even then familiar doctrine that state court decisions would not be reviewed by the United States Supreme Court if the decision might possibly be rested on a valid state law rather than on rights claimed under the Federal Constitution or statutes.

6. *Bank of U.S. v. Deveaux*, 5 Cranch 61, 3 L. Ed. 38 (1809).

7. 2 How. 497, 11 L. Ed. 353 (1844).

8. The minutes of the Supreme Court for the January term of 1844 show that the case was decided on March 15, 1844, at which time only five Justices were present: Story, McLean, Baldwin, Wayne, and Catron. The case had been continued over from the preceding term, the minutes for March 8, 1843, showing that six Justices participated, including Daniel. The reporter at this period did not make it a practice, as has been done in more recent times, to show which judges were not participating in a case, so that one must have recourse to the minutes for the purpose of discovering this. Daniel in fact missed all the cases of the last ten days of the March portion of this term, and Taney had been absent beginning in mid-January, although this is not indicated in the official reports.

9. *Marshall v. B. & O. RR.*, 16 How. 314, 337, 14 L. Ed. 953 (1853).

10. *Phila. Wilm. & Balt. RR. v. Quigley*, 21 How. 202, 16 L. Ed. 73 (1859).

11. 21 How. 219.

12. For Daniel's views see *Rundle v. Delaware & Raritan Canal Co.*, 14 How. 80, 95, 14 L. Ed. 335 (1853); *Northern Ind. RR. v. Michigan Central RR.*, 15 How. 233, 249, 14 L. Ed. 674 (1853); *Marshall v. B. & O. RR.*, 16 How. 314, 338, 14 L. Ed. 953 (1853); and *Phila., Wilm. & Balt. RR. v. Quigley*, 21 How. 202, 215, 16 L. Ed. 73 (1859). Campbell's cases were *Marshall v. B. & O. RR.* and *Dodge v. Woolsey*, 18 How. 331, 414, 15 L. Ed. 401 (1856), in which Daniel concurred.

13. *Marshall v. B. & O. RR.*, 16 How. 314, 347, 14 L. Ed. 953 (1853).

14. *Ibid.*, Campbell's dissent.

15. *Hawes v. City of Oakland*, 104 U.S. 450, 26 L. Ed. 827 (1881).

16. 10 Wheat. 428, 6 L. Ed. 358 (1825).

17. Louis C. Hunter, *Steamboats on the Western Rivers* (Cambridge, Mass., 1949), p. 474.

18. *Waring v. Clarke*, 5 How. 441, 12 L. Ed. 226 (1847); *New Jersey Steam Nav. Co. v. The Merchants Bank*, 6 How. 344, 12 L. Ed. 465 (1848).

19. *Genessee Chief v. Fitzhugh*, 12 How. 443, 13 L. Ed. 1058 (1851).

20. *The Steamboat New World v. King*, 16 How. 469, 14 L. Ed. 101 (1854).

21. *Brittan v. Barnaby*, 21 How. 527, 538, 16 L. Ed. 177 (March 7, 1859). *Chamberlain v. Ward*, 21 How. 548, 572, 16 L. Ed. 211 (March 11, 1859). March 11 was the last day of the 1858–59 term, and Daniel did not sit again after that date.

XIV. Personal Relations

1. Lucy to PVD, Feb. 20, 1847, with an unimportant postscript which has not been included.

2. Richmond *Enquirer*, Nov. 16, 1847; Richmond *Times*, Nov. 18, 1847.

3. The memoir, dated Dec. 8, 1847, is included in the Grymes Papers.

4. For shirt talk see PVD to ERD, Jan. 12, 1849.

5. Peter V. Daniel, Jr., survived to 1889.

6. PVD to ERD, Jan. 26, 1850. In 1848 Daniel incapacitated both feet in separate accidents, injuring one while paring corn and the other with scalding water, but within four days he walked four miles before breakfast and so celebrated his recovery. PVD to ERD, Feb. 19, 1848.

7. His courtesy was noted in the memorial exercises in the Supreme Court, Court Minutes, Dec. 1860, and was particularly remarked by Justice Wayne in a letter to Elizabeth after her father's death, Jan. 11, 1861.

8. 15 How. 233, 14 L. Ed. 674 (1853).

9. This resolve could not have lasted more than moments since the dissent which raised the issue is recorded; *Fontain v. Ravenal*, 17 How. 369, 396, 15 L. Ed. 80 (1855). The Howard-Daniel correspondence of January 22–24, 1855, is included in the Howard Papers in the Maryland Historical Society. As for Daniel's handwriting, it was uniformly good though not flawless. In these pretypewriter days handwriting was the eternal problem. The dismissal of Reporter Peters and his replacement by Reporter Howard had occurred in part because of errors by Peters in printing the opinions of Justice Catron,

but the printer had defended himself on the grounds of the "extreme difficulty of printing from crabbed or confused manuscripts." 17 Peters, preliminary unpaged, letter of printer dated August 11, 1843.

10. The experience was repeated more than once: "The Chief Justice is so careful of me, that he will not consent to my sitting in court, and in the variable weather he prevented my going out for exercise, so that I have been walking back and forth in my room as impatiently as a caged bear." PVD to ERD, May 9, 1850.

11. PVD to ERD, Aug. 22, 1851; PVD to Anne Daniel Moncure, Sept. 1, 1851.

12. PVD to ERD, Feb. 17, 1850.

13. Polk's principal prominence prior to the presidency had been as Speaker of the House of Representatives from 1835 to 1839 and Daniel appears to have had no business with him during that period at all.

14. PVD to Jackson, Dec. 29, 1844.

15. PVD to Polk, March 22, 1845, Polk Papers, Library of Congress. Daniel told Polk, "Perhaps you can scarcely conceive the excess of political intolerance which has long characterized, and still marks the conduct of the dominant party in this place. It has extended its merciless sweep, even down to the humble men who patrol the streets as watchmen in the night, and has embittered and almost destroyed social intercourse in all the ranks of life, separating the ties of kindred."

16. PVD to ERD, Feb. 19, 1848. A few years earlier a silly and completely false story had been circulated that Daniel, former President Tyler, and others had jumped out of a window to avoid a social meeting with Clay. In fact, Daniel had not been present on the occasion in question, and the others all had a pleasant visit with the Kentuckian. *Enquirer*, Oct. 24, 1845 ("A Silly Fable").

17. PVD to Anne D. Moncure, Feb. 12, 1848.

18. For a good concise account see Lawrence, *James Moore Wayne*, pp. 123–127. For a fuller account see Nolan B. Harmon, Jr., *The Famous Case of Myra Clark Gaines* (Baton Rouge, La., 1946).

19. *Gaines v. Relf*, 12 How. 472, 540, 13 L. Ed. 1071 (1852).

20. PVD to ERD, Aug. 3, 1851.

21. PVD to ERD, Aug. 3, 1851.

XV. Sectionalism and Slavery

1. PVD to VB, June 11, 1844. Daniel found a way to stick with Van Buren on annexation, but his fellow Virginia Democrats could not; in May 1844 the state Democratic central committee issued a statement expressing regret over the former President's stand and

began looking for a candidate who would put Texas first *Enquirer*, May 10, 1844.

2. PVD to VB, Oct. 17, 1844.

3. PVD to ERD, Sept. 9, 1847.

4. PVD to VB, Nov. 1, 1847. Daniel also stated: "I have ever regarded what has been called the Missouri Compromise as utterly without warrant from the Constitution."

5. VB to PVD, Nov. 13, 1847.

6. PVD to VB, Nov. 19, 1847.

7. PVD to ERD, Feb. 15, 1851.

8. *Ibid.*, narrating conversation the Justice had with a distinguished judge of New York State in which he took this point of view. Southern Whigs who cooperated with the northern branch of the party he regarded as no better than traitors.

9. PVD to ERD, Feb. 23, 1851, and March 7, 1851.

10. PVD to ERD, April 1, 1850.

11. *U.S. v. The Schooner Amistad*, 15 Pet. 518, 10 L. Ed. 826 (1841), involving the disposition of Negroes taken in Africa who revolted on the high seas. The case was argued on behalf of the Negroes by John Quincy Adams, which contributed to its considerable notoriety. The second case was *Groves v. Slaughter*, 15 Pet. 449, 10 L. Ed. 800 (1841), relating to the importation of slaves into Mississippi.

12. *Jones v. Van Zandt*, 5 How. 215, 12 L. Ed. 122 (1847).

13. 10 How. 82, 13 L. Ed. 337 (1851). This is not to say that no other cases concerning or relating to slavery in any way came before the Court in the meantime, but only that such cases did not rise to the level of interstate friction. For example, in *McClanahan v. Davis*, 8 How. 170, 12 L. Ed. 1033 (1850), there was a dispute among Virginia residents concerning the passage of title to slaves under a will, but the principle of decision would not have been materially different if property had been involved.

14. See Warren, *The Supreme Court*, II, 225–226, for reactions to the decisions. The chapter which encompasses these pages, chap. 25, "Slavery and State Defiance," is an outstanding portion of Warren's great work.

15. *Downs v. Kissam*, 10 How. 102, 13 L. Ed. 346 (1850).

16. 14 How. 13, 14 L. Ed. 306 (1852).

17. The only Justice with an enormous pile of crow to eat was Justice Wayne who had in *Prigg* written at great length to the effect that "No state can pass any law as a remedy upon the subject, whether Congress had or had not legislated upon it." In 1852 he also maintained a discreet silence.

18. See the brilliant account of the case in Warren, *The Supreme Court*, vol. II, chap. 26, on which the following summary is based.

The best almost contemporary account of the case is in *A Memoir of Benjamin Robbins Curtis* (Boston, 1879), a biography by Curtis' son with extensive quotations from the writings of the Justice. Vol. I, chap. 8, deals with the *Dred Scott* case.

19. It is only on this point — Curtis' stand — that I question Warren's account. He says (II, 293): "It was found that the two dissenting judges — McLean and Curtis — intended to write opinions discussing at length their sustaining and constitutionality of the Compromise Act." He cites nothing as authority for that proposition, but quotes a letter from Justice Grier to President-elect Buchanan, dated Feb. 23, 1857, which says, "It appeared that our brothers who dissented from the majority, especially Justice McLean, were determined to come out with long and labored dissent" on the compromise question. However, the *Memoirs of Benjamin Robbins Curtis*, pp. 234–235, shows that the original plan of the dissenters had been that McLean and Curtis were to dissent in an opinion by McLean. Since it would have been very like McLean to get into gratuitous discussion and very unlike Curtis, I assume that the primary responsibility for introducing extraneous material into the case was McLean's.

20. Wayne acknowledged that he was responsible for the shift on the part of the Court majority, and for this reason. See *Memoirs of Benjamin Robbins Curtis*, I, 235–236.

21. Quoted in Warren, *The Supreme Court*, II, 296.

22. Washington *National Intelligencer*, Jan. 5, 1857; Washington *Daily Union*, Jan. 6, 1857.

XVI. *Routine Court Business*

1. On the basis of a study of the work of the Court for each term from 1946 to 1954, an attempt was made to evaluate all cases from the standpoint of social importance. It was found that about 25 percent of the cases could be considered of substantial social importance and only 5 percent of great importance. See, for example, my "United States Supreme Court, 1949–50," *University of Chicago Law Review*, 18 (1950): 1, 41.

2. Felix Frankfurter and James M. Landis, *The Business of the Supreme Court* (New York, 1927), p. 52.

3. See letter of PVD to Attorney General John Mason, July 19, 1845, in Polk Papers, Library of Congress.

4. 7 How. 1, 12 L. Ed. 581 (1849). See also the related case of *ex parte Dorr*, 3 How. 103, 11 L. Ed. 514 (1845).

5. *The United States v. The Brig Malek Adhel*, 2 How. 210, 11 L. Ed. 239 (1844).

6. *Wilkes v. Dinsman*, 7 How. 89, 12 L. Ed. 618 (1849).

7. *Catts v. Phalen*, 2 How. 376, 11 L. Ed. 306 (1844).

8. *Vidal v. Girard's Executors*, 2 How. 127, 11 L. Ed. 205 (1844).

9. *Smith v. Swormstedt*, 16 How. 288, 14 L. Ed. 942 (1854).

10. *Permoli v. The Municipality No. 1*, 3 How. 590, 11 L. Ed. 739 (1845).

11. *Baker v. Nachtrieb*, 19 How. 126, 15 L. Ed. 528 (1856).

12. 1 How. 219, 11 L. Ed. 108 (1843).

13. For an excellent recent discussion of the movement see Eleanor Rice Hays, *Morning Star, A Biography of Lucy Stone* (New York, 1961).

14. *Delane v. Moore*, 14 How. 253, 14 L. Ed. 409 (1852). The text of a premarriage agreement had to be prepared with extreme care. For example, where a woman attempted to preserve property for her own children, it was held that this would not preserve the property for her grandchildren. *Adams v. Law*, 17 How. 417, 15 L. Ed. 149 (1855).

15. *Dundas v. Hitchcock*, 12 How. 256, 13 L. Ed. 978 (1852).

16. *Bein v. Heath*, 6 How. 228, 12 L. Ed. 416 (1848).

17. *Taylor v. Taylor*, 8 How. 183, 12 L. Ed. 1040 (1850). The influence of Sir Walter Scott and the South on Daniel was very strong. The Justice on occasion attended summer outings which included actual jousting and tournaments for a "Ladye Fair"; *Enquirer*, Sept. 11 and 18, 1846, Sept. 13, 1847.

18. *Barber v. Barber*, 21 How. 582, 16 L. Ed. 226 (1859) discussed above from the jurisdictional standpoint.

19. *Parks v. Ross*, 11 How. 362, 13 L. Ed. 730 (1850).

20. *United States v. Rogers*, 4 How. 567, 11 L. Ed. 1105 (1846).

21. *Ibid.*, 4 How. 572.

22. The war itself brought up a certain number of cases. Examples are *Cross v. Harrison*, 16 How. 164, 14 L. Ed. 889 (1854), concerning the effect of tariffs levied by American military governments in California before the treaty of peace; *Jecker, Torre & Co. v. Montgomery*, 18 How. 110, 15 L. Ed. 311 (1856), a Daniel opinion involving a vessel which had sailed out of New Orleans for the purpose of trading with the enemy and which was seized in Mexican waters; and the colorful and important case of *Mitchell v. Harmony*, 13 How. 115, 14 L. Ed. 75 (1851), involving the claim of a trader who was compelled by Colonel Doniphan to accompany the American forces with his wagons in the march on Chihuahua. In *Mitchell v. Harmony* Chief Justice Taney for the Court held the taking an illegal act for which the military officers were personally liable, a matter of great concern to them until they were relieved by an act of Congress. This was a precedent of great importance in World War II when the government was again faced with the problems of taking

of property, this time to avoid labor disputes. Daniel dissented in *Mitchell v. Harmony* on the ground that the trial judge, who had been Justice Nelson of the Supreme Court, had so commented on the evidence as to deprive the jury of a fair chance to decide the case.

23. *City of Mobile v. Emanuel*, 1 How. 95, 11 L. Ed. 60 (1843).

24. See acts of March 3, 1851, and Aug. 31, 1852.

25. Hoffman and the commission are worth a monograph of their own which has not yet, so far as this writer knows, been written.

26. 17 How. 542, 15 L. Ed. 241 (1855).

27. *Arguello v. United States*, 18 How. 539, 550, 15 L. Ed. 478 (1856).

28. 17 How. 525, 15 L. Ed. 236 (1855), which outlines the procedure for determination of these cases and then disposes of the particular claim.

29. *United States v. Reading*, 18 How. 1, 15 L. Ed. 291 (1856); *Arguello v. United States*, 18 How. 539, 15 L. Ed. 478 (1856); *United States v. Cervantes*, 18 How. 553, 15 L. Ed. 484 (1856); *United States v. Vaca*, 18 How. 556, 15 L. Ed. 485 (1856); and *United States v. Larkin*, 18 How. 557, 15 L. Ed. 485 (1856).

30. 18 How. 533.

31. Reaper: *McCormick v. Talcott*, 20 How. 402, 15 L. Ed. 930 (1858), following *McCormick v. Gray*, 13 How. 26, 14 L. Ed. 36 (1851); telegraph: *O'Reilly v. Morse*, 15 How. 62, 14 L. Ed. 601 (1853); sluice: *Teese v. Huntington*, 23 How. 2, 16 L. Ed. 479 (1860) (Daniel still on Court but no longer participating); rubber: *Hartshorn v. Day*, 19 How. 211, 15 L. Ed. 605 (1857); spikemaking: *Troy Iron & Nail Factory v. Corning*, 14 How. 193, 14 L. Ed. 383 (1852); safe: *Gayler v. Wilder*, 10 How. 477, 13 L. Ed. 504 (1851); railway track: *Landes v. Brant*, 10 How. 348, 13 L. Ed. 449 (1850). See also on a planing machine: *Wilson v. Rousseau*, 4 How. 646, 11 L. Ed. 1141 (1846).

32. *Kendall v. Winsor*, 21 How. 322, 338, 16 L. Ed. 165 (1859), opinion for the Court.

33. *Stimpson v. The Balt. & Susq. R. Co.*, 10 How. 329, 13 L. Ed. 441 (1850).

34. Though Lincoln had a minor and, it is usually believed, humiliating role in this case, he did earn a good useful fee from it; for a brief discussion see my *Lincoln as a Lawyer* (Urbana, Ill., 1961), p. 177.

35. *McCormick v. Talcott*, 20 How. 402, 15 L. Ed. 930 (1858).

36. *Hogg v. Emerson*, argued twice and reported at 6 How. 437, 12 L. Ed. 505 (1848), and (the relevant instance) at 11 How. 587, 608, 13 L. Ed. 824 (1851).

37. For an excellent statement of this point of view see *Mitchell*

v. Harmony, 13 How. 115, 138, 142, 14 L. Ed. 75 (1851), in which he attacked the practice of judges commenting on the evidence in such fashion as virtually to direct verdict: "It was the jury who were to find the facts for the judge, and not the judge who was to find the facts for the jury; and if the verdict is either formally, or in effect, the verdict of the judge, it is neither according to truth nor common-sense, the verdict of the jury; and these tryers of fact had better be dispensed with, as an useless, and indeed an expensive and cumbersome formula in courts of law, than be preserved as false indicia of what they in reality do not show."

38. See for example *Byers v. Surget*, 19 How. 303, 15 L. Ed. 670 (1856), in which a tricky fellow by use of a judgment for $39.10 got control of some $40,000 to $70,000 worth of property.

XVII. The Circuit

1. Act of Aug. 16, 1842, 5 Stat. 507; for illustration of the public pledge to send Daniel west see the Richmond *Whig & Public Advertiser*, March 5, 1841.

2. "I have never yet been at Little Rock, the place of holding the Court in Arkansas; but from the best information I can obtain, it could not be conveniently approached in the spring of the year except by water, and by that route the distance would be greatly increased." Report by McKinley to Congress in 1838 as quoted in Frankfurter and Landis, *The Business of the Supreme Court*, pp. 49–50.

3. Warren, *The Supreme Court*, II, 289.

4. PVD to VB, Nov. 4, 1843.

5. *Arkansas State Gazette* (Little Rock), April 1, 1844.

6. PVD to ERD, May 15, 1847.

7. *Ibid.*

8. These letters are included in the Grymes Papers. Three of them have been reprinted by William D. Hoyt, Jr., in *Archaeological Historical Quarterly*, 1 (1942): 158, and *Ohio State Archaeological Historical Quarterly* 51 (1942): 62.

9. The trip is reconstructed from letters of PVD to ERD, April 8, 17, and 28, and June 6 and 13, 1851.

10. PVD to ERD, April 7, April 17, and May 8, 1853.

11. PVD to ERD, May 15, 1847, refers to "more than 200 cases."

12. Hempstead's Reports as reprinted in the Federal Cases.

13. *Tunstall v. Worthington*, Fed. Cas. 14, 239 (1853).

14. *Greenwood v. Rector*, Fed. Cas. 5792 (1855).

15. *United States v. Dawson*, Fed. Cas. 14, 933 (1853).

16. *United States v. Sanders*, Fed. Cas. 16, 220 (1847).

17. This was duly reported in the *Arkansas State Gazette* (Little Rock) on April 24, 1844, as an "important decision." For Abraham Lincoln's dealing with a similar problem of retroactive alteration of the statute of limitations in his one argument before the United States Supreme Court, see my *Lincoln as a Lawyer*, pp. 79–83.

18. *Arkansas State Gazette* (Little Rock), April 22, 1845.

19. *Ibid.*, May 19, 1845.

20. *United States v. Rogers*, 4 How. 567, 573, 11 L. Ed. 1105 (1846).

XVIII. The Last Dissent

1. PVD to John M. Daniel, April 13, 1858, in the Huntington Library Daniel collection.

2. What became of ERD is something of a mystery. Her pre-Civil War notebooks had been filled with beautiful thoughts. A typical example is a poem beginning, "The scent of the flower is a wonderful thing!" A later notebook, discovered among the Grymes Papers not on deposit at the University of Virginia but reserved by the family, contained as gruesome a collection of horror news stories, and particularly brutal murders, as one would ever be likely to see. If one were a novelist, it would be easy to improvise a psychological tale centering on the effects of her father's second marriage; but there are certainly not enough facts at hand to permit the historian to come to any conclusion at all.

3. Quoted in Warren, *The Supreme Court*, II, 318.

4. PVD to John M. Daniel, April 13, 1858, in the Huntington Library Daniel collection. Benjamin later became Attorney General in the Confederate cabinet and, after the war, a leading English barrister.

5. *Phila. Wilm. & Balt. RR. v. Quigley*, 21 How. 202, 215, 219, 16 L. Ed. 73 (1859).

6. *Jackson v. Steamboat Magnolia*, 20 How. 296, 307, 320, 321, 15 L. Ed. 909 (1858).

7. *Withers v. Buckley*, 20 How. 84, 15 L. Ed. 816 (1858).

8. *Kendall v. Winsor*, 21 How. 322, 16 L. Ed. 165 (1859); and dissent in *McCormick v. Talcott*, 20 How. 402, 408, 15 L. Ed. 930 (1858).

9. *Leitensdorfer v. Webb*, 20 How. 176, 15 L. Ed. 891 (1858), on transfer of cases in the territory of New Mexico after the war; *Irvine v. Marshall*, 20 How. 558, 15 L. Ed. 994 (1858), a five to four opinion relating to territorial lands; *Leggett v. Humphries*, 21 How. 66, 16 L. Ed. 50 (1859), on the obligations of sureties; *Thomas v. Lawson*, 21 How. 331, 16 L. Ed. 82 (1859), on the effect of an Arkansas tax deed; *Brown v. Huger*, 21 How. 305, 16 L. Ed. 125 (1859), an

extended majority opinion on the method of measuring land boundaries along rivers; *Fenn v. Holme*, 21 How. 481, 16 L. Ed. 198 (1859), on distinctions between legal and equitable title.

10. *Ableman v. Booth*, 21 How. 506, 16 L. Ed. 169 (1859).

11. *Pennsylvania v. Ravenel*, 21 How. 103, 110–111, 16 L. Ed. 33 (1858).

12. *United States v. Sutter*, 21 How. 170, 183–184, 16 L. Ed. 119 (1859).

13. New York *Times*, Friday, June 1, 1860, p. 4.

14. The will is recorded in the records of the Chancery Court of the City of Richmond; see County Wills Book 3, p. 261.

CASES CITED

Ableman v. Booth, 21 How. 506, 16 L. Ed. 169 (1859) 288, 324

Adams v. Law, 17 How. 417, 15 L. Ed. 149 (1855) 320

Allen v. Riley, 203 U.S. 347, 27 Sup. Ct. 95, 51 L. Ed. 216 (1906) 312

Arguello v. United States, 18 How. 539, 15 L. Ed. 478 (1856) .. 321

B. & S. RR. v. Nesbit, 10 How. 395, 13 L. Ed. 469 (1851) 314

Baker v. Nachtrieb, 19 How. 126, 15 L. Ed. 528 (1856) 320

Bank of U.S. v. Deveaux, 5 Cranch 61, 3 L. Ed. 38
(1890) 218, 220, 225, 315

Barber v. Barber, 21 How. 582, 16 L. Ed. 226 (1859) 315, 320

Bein v. Heath, 6 How. 228, 12 L. Ed. 416 (1848) 320

Bennett v. Butterworth, 8 How. 124, 12 L. Ed. 1013 (1850) 315

Brittan v. Barnaby, 21 How. 527, 16 L. Ed. 177 (1859) 316

Bronson v. Kinzie, 1 How. 311, 11 L. Ed. 143 (1843) 313

Brown v. Huger, 21 How. 305, 16 L. Ed. 125 (1859) 323

Brown v. Maryland, 12 Wheat. 419, 6 L. Ed. 678 (1827) .. 189, 312

Byers v. Surget, 19 How. 303, 15 L. Ed. 670 (1856) 322

Catts v. Phalen, 2 How. 376, 11 L. Ed. 306 (1844) 320

Chamberlain v. Ward, 21 How. 548, 16 L. Ed. 211 (1859) 316

Charles River Bridge Co. v. Warren Bridge Co., 11 Pet. 420, 9
L. Ed. 773 (1837) 202, 204, 212, 314

City of Mobile v. Emanuel, 1 How. 95, 11 L. Ed. 60 (1843) .. 321

Clarke v. The Schooner Alfred, district court records, Nov.
term, 1838 308

Clements v. Berry, 11 How. 398, 13 L. Ed. 745 (1850) 315

Cocke v. Halsey, 16 Pet. 71, 10 L. Ed. 891 (1842) 310

Cohens v. Virginia, 6 Wheat. 264 (1821) 41–42, 86, 297

Connor v. Bradley, 1 How. 211, 11 L. Ed. 105 (1843) 311

Cook v. Moffat, 5 How. 295, 12 L. Ed. 159 (1847) 312

Cooley v. The Wardens, 12 How. 299, 13 L. Ed. 996 (1852) 195, 313

Cross v. Harrison, 16 How. 164, 14 L. Ed. 889 (1854) 320

Dartmouth College v. Woodward, 4 Wheat. 518, 4 L. Ed. 629
(1819) 201, 313

Delane v. Moore, 14 How. 253, 14 L. Ed. 409 (1852) 320

Dodge v. Woolsey, 18 How. 331, 15 L. Ed. 401 (1856) 206, 221, 315
Ex parte Dorr, 3 How. 103, 11 L. Ed. 514 (1845)   319
Downs v. Kissam, 10 How. 102, 13 L. Ed. 346 (1850)   318
Dundas v. Hitchcock, 12 How. 256, 13 L. Ed. 978 (1852)   320

Erie Railway v. Tompkins, 304 U.S. 64, 58 Sup. Ct. 817, 82 L. Ed.
    1188 (1938)   310

Farmers Bank v. Clarke, 31 Va. 603 (1833)   299
Fenn v. Holme, 21 How. 481, 16 L. Ed. 198 (1859) 311, 324
Fletcher v. Peck, 6 Cranch 87, 3 L. Ed. 162 (1810) 200, 313
Fontain v. Ravenal, 17 How. 369, 15 L. Ed. 80 (1855)   316
Fox v. Ohio, 5 How. 410, 12 L. Ed. 213 (1847)   312
Frémont v. United States, 17 How. 542, 15 L. Ed. 241
    (1855) 268, 321

Gaines v. Relf, 12 How. 472, 13 L. Ed. 1071 (1852) . . 239, 262, 317
Gantley v. Ewing, 3 How. 707, 11 L. Ed. 794 (1845)   313
Gayler v. Wilder, 10 How. 477, 13 L. Ed. 504 (1851)   321
Genessee Chief v. Fitzhugh, 12 How. 443, 13 L. Ed. 1058 (1851)   316
Gibbons v. Ogden, 9 Wheat. 1, 6 L. Ed. 23 (1824) 189, 197, 312
Gilmer v. Poindexter, 10 How. 257, 13 L. Ed. 411 (1850)   311
Gordon v. The Tax Court, 3 How. 133, 11 L. Ed. 529 (1845) 201, 313
Greenwood v. Rector, Fed. Cas. 5792 (1855)   322
Groves v. Slaughter, 15 Pet. 449, 10 L. Ed. 800 (1841) 312, 318
Gwin v. Breedlove, 2 How. 29, 11 L. Ed. 167 (1844)   315

Hartshorn v. Day, 19 How. 211, 15 L. Ed. 605 (1857)   321
Hawes v. City of Oakland, 104 U.S. 450, 26 L. Ed. 827 (1881) . .   316
Hays v. Pacific Mail Co., 17 How. 596, 15 L. Ed. 254 (1855) . .   315
Hogg v. Emerson, 6 How. 437, 12 L. Ed. 505 (1848) and 11
    How. 857, 13 L. Ed. 824 (1851)   321
Home Building & Loan Association v. Blaisdell, 290 U.S. 398,
    54 Sup. Ct. 231, 78 L. Ed. 413 (1934)   314

Irvine v. Marshall, 20 How. 558, 15 L. Ed. 994 (1858)   323

Jackson v. Steamboat Magnolia, 20 How. 296, 15 L. Ed. 909
    (1858)   323
Jecker, Torre & Co. v. Montgomery, 18 How. 110, 15 L. Ed. 311
    (1856)   320
Jewell v. Jewell, 1 How. 219, 11 L. Ed. 108 (1843) 262, 320
Jones v. Van Zandt, 5 How. 215, 12 L. Ed. 122 (1847)   318

Kendall v. Winsor, 21 How. 322, 16 L. Ed. 165 (1859) 321, 323

Kohl v. United States, 91 U.S. 367, 23 L. Ed. 449 (1875) 314

Landes v. Brant, 10 How. 348, 13 L. Ed. 449 (1850) 321
Leggett v. Humphries, 21 How. 66, 16 L. Ed. 50 (1859) 323
Leitensdorfer v. Webb, 20 How. 176, 15 L. Ed. 891 (1858) 323
License Cases, 5 How. 504, 12 L. Ed. 256 (1847) 190, 192, 193
Louisville Railway v. Letson, 2 How. 497, 11 L. Ed. 353
    (1844) 218, 219, 220, 315
Luther v. Borden, 7 How. 1, 12 L. Ed. 581 (1849) 260, 319
Lyons v. Oklahoma, 322 U.S. 596 (1944) 300

McClanahan v. Davis, 8 How. 170, 12 L. Ed. 1033 (1850) 318
McCormick v. Gray, 13 How. 26, 14 L. Ed. 36 (1851) 321
McCormick v. Talcott, 20 How. 402, 15 L. Ed. 930 (1858) . 321, 323
McCracken v. Hayward, 2 How. 608, 11 L. Ed. 608 (1844) 313
McCullough v. Maryland, 4 Wheat. 316 (1819) 40, 297, 313
McNutt v. Bland, 2 How. 9, 11 L. Ed. 159 (1844) 315
Marshall v. B. & O. RR., 16 How. 314, 14 L. Ed. 953 (1853) . 314, 315
Miners Bank v. Iowa, 12 How. 1, 13 L. Ed. 867 (1851) 315
Mitchell v. Harmony, 13 How. 115, 14 L. Ed. 75 (1851) 320, 321, 322
Moore v. Illinois, 14 How. 13, 14 L. Ed. 306 (1852) 249, 318

Neil, Moore & Co. v. Ohio, 3 How. 720, 11 L. Ed. 800 (1845) .. 314
New Jersey Steam Nav. Co. v. The Merchants Bank, 6 How.
    344, 12 L. Ed. 465 (1848) 316
New York v. Miln, 11 Pet. 102, 9 L. Ed. 648 (1837) ... 190, 193, 312
Northern Ind. RR. v. Michigan Central RR., 15 How. 233, 14
    L. Ed. 674 (1853) 232, 233, 315

Ogden v. Saunders, 12 Wheat. 213, 6 L. Ed. 606 (1827) 312
Ohio Life Ins. Co. v. Debolt, 16 How. 416, 14 L. Ed. 997 (1854) 314
O'Reilly v. Morse, 15 How. 62, 14 L. Ed. 601 (1853) 321

Parks v. Ross, 11 How. 362, 13 L. Ed. 730 (1850) 320
Passenger Cases, 7 How. 559 (1849) 192, 193, 195, 313
Pennsylvania v. Ravenel, 21 How. 103, 16 L. Ed. 33 (1858) 324
Pennsylvania v. Wheeling Bridge, 13 How. 518, 14 L. Ed. 249
    (1852) 198, 281, 313
Permoli v. The Municipality No. 1, 3 How. 590, 11 L. Ed. 739
    (1845) 320
Phila. Wilm. & Balt. RR. v. Quigley, 21 How. 202, 16 L. Ed.
    73 (1859) 315, 323
Piqua Branch Bank v. Knoop, 16 How. 369, 14 L. Ed. 977
    (1854) 206, 314

Planters Bank v. Sharp, 6 How. 301, 12 L. Ed. 447
(1848) 204, 212, 314
Prigg v. Pennsylvania, 16 Pet. 539, 10 L. Ed. 1060
(1842) 177, 247, 249, 311

Roach v. Hulings, 16 Pet. 319, 10 L. Ed. 979 (1842) 310
Rundle v. Delaware & Raritan Canal Co., 14 How. 80, 14 L. Ed.
335 (1853) 315

Scott v. Sanford, 19 How. 393, 15 L. Ed. 691
(1857) 172, 248, 250, 257, 285, 286
Searight v. Stokes, 3 How. 151, 11 L. Ed. 537 (1845) 314
Seekright v. Moore, 31 Va. 30 (1832) 299
Smith v. Hunter, 7 How. 738, 12 L. Ed. 894 (1849) 315
Smith v. Swormstedt, 16 How. 288, 14 L. Ed. 942 (1854) 320
Steamboat New World v. King, 16 How. 469, 14 L. Ed. 101
(1854) 316
Stimpson v. The Balt. & Susq. R. Co., 10 How. 329, 13 L. Ed.
441 (1850) 321
Strader v. Graham, 10 How. 82, 13 L. Ed. 337
(1851) 247–248, 251–253, 318
Sturges v. Crowninshield, 4 Wheat. 122, 4 L. Ed. 529 (1819) . 187, 312
Swift v. Tyson, 16 Pet. 1, 10 L. Ed. 65 (1842) 168, 309

Taylor v. Taylor, 8 How. 183, 12 L. Ed. 1040 (1850) 320
Teese v. Huntington, 23 How. 2, 16 L. Ed. 479 (1860) 321
Thomas v. Lawson, 21 How. 331, 16 L. Ed. 82 (1859) 311, 323
Thomas Jefferson, 10 Wheat. 428, 6 L. Ed. 358
(1825) 222–224, 225, 316
Thurlow v. Massachusetts, 5 How. 504, 12 L. Ed. 256 (1847) .. 312
Troy Iron & Nail Factory v. Corning, 14 How. 193, 14 L. Ed.
383 (1852) 321
Tunstall v. Worthington, Fed. Cas. 14 (1853) 322

United States v. Arjona, 120 U.S. 479, 7 Sup. Ct. 628, 30 L. Ed.
728 (1887) 311, 312
United States v. The Brig Malek Adhel, 2 How. 210, 11 L. Ed.
239 (1844) 319
United States v. Cervantes, 18 How. 553, 15 L. Ed. 484 (1856) .. 321
United States v. Dawson, Fed. Cas. 14 (1853) 322
United States v. Eliason, 16 Pet. 291, 10 L. Ed. 968 (1842) 310
United States v. James Henderson, district court records, Nov.
term, 1838 308

United States v. Koster, district court records, May term,
1838 .... 144, 308
United States v. Larkin, 18 How. 557, 15 L. Ed. 485 (1856) ... 321
United States v. Marigold, 9 How. 560, 13 L. Ed. 257 (1850) .. 312
United States v. Reading, 18 How. 1, 15 L. Ed. 291 (1856) 321
United States v. Ritchie, 17 How. 525, 15 L. Ed. 236 (1855) . 268, 321
United States v. Rogers, 4 How. 567, 11 L. Ed. 1105
(1846) 284, 320, 323
United States v. Sanders, Fed. Cas. 16 (1847) 322
United States v. The Schooner Amistad, 15 Pet. 518, 10 L. Ed.
826 (1841) 318
United States v. Sutter, 21 How. 170, 16 L. Ed. 119 (1859) 324
United States v. Vaca, 18 How. 556, 15 L. Ed. 485 (1856) 321

Vidal v. Girard's Executors, 2 How. 127, 11 L. Ed. 205 (1844) .. 320

Waring v. Clarke, 5 How. 441, 12 L. Ed. 226 (1847) 316
Watkins v. Holman, 16 Pet. 25, 10 L. Ed. 73 (1842) 168, 309
White v. Nicholls, 3 How. 266, 11 L. Ed. 591 (1845) 311
Wilkes v. Dinsman, 7 How. 89, 12 L. Ed. 618 (1849) 320
Willson v. Black-bird Creek Marsh Co., 2 Pet. 245, 7 L. Ed.
412 (1829) 312
Wilson v. Rousseau, 4 How. 646, 11 L. Ed. 1141 (1846) 321
Withers v. Buckley, 20 How. 84, 15 L. Ed. 816 (1858) 323
Woodruff v. Trapnall, 10 How. 190, 13 L. Ed. 383 (1850) . 204, 314

INDEX

Abolitionism, 163–164, 209, 243, 246

Adams, John Q., 79–82, 165–166, 179, 246; election (1828), 83–91

Administrative law, 183

Admiralty cases, 146, 182, 183, 221–226, 287, 291–292

Agrarianism, 34, 161–167, 209, 290–292

Albany Regency, 78, 79, 80, 163–164

Alien and Sedition Acts, 4, 153

Ames, Samuel, 238

Archer, William, 108, 113, 128

Attorney generalship, 119–125

Baldwin, Henry, 170, 171, 190, 237

Baltimore *Republican*, 99

Bank of the United States, 33, 34, 37, 40–41, 93, 119–126, 135, 153; and election of *1832*, 110–113

Banks and banking, 35–36, 56, 110–113, 162, 202–204, 289, 290–292. *See also* Bank of the United States

Bankruptcy, 185, 187–189

Barbour, Governor James, 31, 59, 143; and War of *1812*, 21–31, *passim*

Barbour, Philip, 42, 59, 137–138, 142–143, 147, 156, 190, 193, 237; role in election of *1832*, 103–116, *passim;* death, 154

Barry, W. T., 145

Benjamin, Judah P., 286

Benton, Thomas H., 157, 159–160, 176

Betsey, a slave, 59–60

Biddle, Nicholas, 112

Bills and notes, 182–183, 184

Black, Jeremiah S., 285

Brandeis, Louis D., 169

Brent, William, Jr., 97

Brockenbrough, Dr. John, 33, 58, 106, 125, 155

Buchanan, James, 157, 253–254, 285–286

Business, regulation of, 200–212

Butler, B. S., 123

Calhoun, John C., 33, 76, 83, 86, 92, 97, 118, 127, 243, 244; election of *1824*, 80–82; described, 93; events of *1828–30*, 93–95; tariff and politics, 94–95; Eaton affair, 95–96; role in election of *1832*, 104–116; death, 247

Calhoun, Mrs. John C. (Floride), 96

Campbell, John (Virginia Council member), 37

Campbell, John A., 173, 206–207, 216, 219–221, 236–237; and *Dred Scott* case, 251–257

Carroll, William, 175, 233

Catron, John, 169, 171, 172, 174, 175, 191, 193, 197, 206, 219, 231, 235–237, 272; as Daniel's living companion, 232; and *Dred Scott* case, 251–257

Chase, Samuel P., 6, 247

Choate, Rufus, 238

Circuit Court, 142–143, 146–147, 173, 260; bill to rearrange circuits (1841), 155–158; Daniel's circuit experience, 275–284; travel, 277–281

Clay, Henry, 80–82, 97, 105, 112, 118, 127, 129, 151, 158, 161, 198; argument, 238–239

Clifford, Nathan, 237, 288

Collamer, Jacob, 208

Columbia *Telescope*, 120–121

Commerce power as limitation on states, 184–196, 291

Compromise of *1850*, 250

Congress, powers of, 184–196

Constitutional law opinions, 182, 183

Constitutional theories of Daniel, as strict construction, 18–19, 30–31, 45–46, 153; on banking, 112–113; on tariff, 164–165; on internal improvements, 213–215; on importance of original intent, 224

Contract clause, 200–212, 282–283, 291

Contracts, 183, 184, 281

Corporations, 161–162, 164; contract clause and, 200–212, *passim*; federal jurisdiction, 217–221, 287, 289, 290–292

Council of State, 15, 63–76, 118–119, 292; business, 17; role in War of *1812*, 21–31, *passim*; post-1812 problems, 34; resistance to Marshall, 42–43; friction with Thomas Randolph, 43–47; attack on, 48–49; revised in Convention of *1830*, 73–75; end of Daniel's service on, 139

Counterfeiting, 185–187

Crawford, William H., 79–81

Criminal procedure and justice, 64–71, 281–282, 283–284, 292

Crow's Nest, 2, 55

Curtis, Benjamin R., 172, 173, 182, 231, 237, 242; appointment and commerce decision, 195–198; and *Dred Scott* case, 251–257; controversy with Taney, 257

Daniel, Anne, *see* Moncure, Anne Daniel

Daniel, Elizabeth, 59, 174, 176, 235, 240–241, 323; family interests, 1, 52, 53–54; reading taste, 54; health, 54–55; relationship with Daniel, 227, 229–231

Daniel, Elizabeth Harris, 241–242, 285; death, 257–258

Daniel, Lucy Randolph, 7, 56, 60, 62, 102, 134, 141, 147, 166, 174, 176, 238, 240, 241, 288; Daniel meets, 6; courtship, 11–12; marriage, 12; personality, 12, 13; religion, 13, 50–51; relationship with Daniel, 49–52; death, 227–229; trip North, 244–245

Daniel, Mary, 242, 285, 289

Daniel, Peter V., Jr., 5, 49, 50, 52–53, 60, 228–230

Daniel, Travers, 242, 285, 289

Daniel, William, 1

Davis, David, 237

Democratic (formerly Republican) party, 33, 40–42, 77–91, 97, 134–135, 163–164, 236; Virginia Central Committee, 77–78, 83, 85; and election of *1832*, 104–116; defeat and victory, 127–139; second national convention and two-thirds rule, 135–136; and election of *1836*, 137–138; and election of *1840*, 151–154; and Daniel's appointment to Supreme Court, 155–161

District Judge: Daniel's appointment, 138–142; circuit duties, 142–143, 146–147; district duties, 143–146, 147; salary, 147–149

Divorce, 265–266

Douglas, Stephen, 286

Duel, 7–10, 158–159

Eaton, John, 95–96, 100–101

Eaton, Peggy O'Neill, 92, 95–96, 100–101

Education, 261

Elections: of *1824*, 78–82; of *1828*, 83–91; of *1832*, 103–116; of *1836*, 134–138; of *1840*, 151–154

Eminent domain, 207–212

Equity, 181–184

Exclusiveness of congressional powers, 184–196, 249–250, 291

Federal jurisdiction, 182, 183, 215–226; and corporations, 202, 217–221; in *Dred Scott* case, 251–257,

266, 281–282, 283–284, 287, 291–292. *See also* Admiralty cases.

Federalist, The, 185

Federalist Party, 14, 22, 39, 83, 150, 151, 161, 173, 197

Field, Stephen, 237

Fillmore, Millard, 176, 195, 243

Floyd, John, 66–67, 76, 96, 101, 102, 106, 115, 117–118, 128, 133, 286; described and quoted, 98; controversy with Daniel, 98–100; renewed controversy with Daniel, 118–120

Force Bill, 117–118

Frémont, John C., 163, 268

Giles, William Branch, 3

Gooch, Claiborne W., 79

Governorship of Virginia, 34, 44, 47, 48, 98

Green, Duff, 96, 99–100

Grier, Robert C., 182, 191, 197, 205, 231, 272, 280; as Daniel's living companion, 232, 235–237, 249; and *Dred Scott* case, 251–257

Hamilton, Alexander, 185

Harris, Dr. Thomas, 241

Harris, Thomas, Jr., 242

Harrisburg *Reporter*, 121

Harrison, William Henry, 137, 152–153, 155, 157

Hayman, Ike, 295

Hayne, Robert Y., 94

Henry, a slave, 64

Hoffman, Ogden, 268

Howard, Benjamin C., 171–172, 232–234

Hughes, Charles Evans, 212

Income of Daniel, 14, 56–57, 177; and attorney generalship, 120–125; as district judge, 147–149

Indians, 266–267, 282–284

Internal improvements, 85, 135, 153, 213–215

Jackson, Andrew, 63, 76, 77, 82, 93, 97, 100–101, 127, 130–139,

passim, 153, 170, 238, 244; election of *1824*, 78–81; election of *1828*, 83–91; Eaton affair, 92, 95–96; re-election and campaign of *1832*, 103–116; nullification controversy, 116–118; chooses Daniel for Attorney General, 119–125; appointment of Daniel as district judge, 140–142; reaction to Daniel appointment to Supreme Court, 160–161

Jackson, Rachel, 84, 96

James, a slave, 60

Jefferson, Thomas, 2, 4, 5, 24, 32, 33, 40, 56, 58, 79, 83, 151, 246, 290, 292; on Supreme Court, 41; on governorship of Virginia, 44

Johnson, Reverdy, 311

Johnson, Richard M., 108, 135–136

Johnson, William, 188

Joshua, a slave, 69–70

Juries, 273, 292

Kansas-Nebraska Act, 250–251

Kearney, Philip, 163

Kent, James, 209, 225

Lafayette, Marquis de, 60–62

Law practice of Daniel, 56–58

Lee, Charles, 3

Leigh, Benjamin W., 47–48, 74, 75, 118, 121, 125, 128, 133, 151

Letters to editor, 78, 85–91, 138

Lieutenant governorship of Virginia, 16, 38, 44, 48, 74, 98

Lincoln, Abraham, 170, 247, 250

McDuffie, George, 94–95

McFarland, W. H., 133

McKinley, John, 169, 171, 191, 196, 237, 275

McLean, John, 170, 171–172, 173, 187, 190, 191, 197, 198, 206, 231, 234, 235–237, 249–250; on court work methods, 174; in *West River Bridge* case, 210–212; and *Dred Scott* case, 250–257

Madison, James, 2, 3, 4, 24, 27, 28, 32, 33, 56, 73, 75, 79, 140, 151, 246

Marshall, A. J., 204–205
Marshall, John, 4, 39–43, 62, 83, 86, 98, 118, 150, 170, 171, 187, 225; resentment at Roane attacks, 43; convention of *1830*, 72, 73, 75; death, 138; commerce power, 189–191, 197, 200, 202, 204, 217–218
Mason, John Y., 155
Massillon, Jean Baptiste, 51
Mexican War, cases arising from, 320–321
Militia, 26–27, 29, 44–46
Miller, Samuel F., 237
Miller, Stephen D., 89–90
Missouri Compromise (Compromise of 1820), 250–257
Moncure, Anne Daniel, 49, 50, 52–53, 230
Monroe, James, 27, 28, 33, 73, 78, 79, 93, 98, 170, 246, 289
Morgan, Charles S., 141
Morgan, Mrs. Charles, 141

Nelson, Samuel, 191, 193, 197, 237; and *Dred Scott* case, 251–257
Nicholas, Philip N., 58, 72, 74, 75, 78, 79, 83, 106, 113, 125
Nicholas, Wilson Cary, 31, 33, 35, 36
Norfolk *Herald*, 121
Nullification, 110, 116–118, 243

Old Party, 32
Opinions: of Daniel, 181–184; of Court, 181–184; style of Daniel's, 273–274
Original Package Doctrine, 191–192

Parker, Richard, 137, 140–141
Patents, 182, 183, 185, 269–273, 288
Pendleton, Edmund, 4
Pendleton, John S., 128–133
Peters, Richard, 171–172
Phelps, Samuel, 208–210
Phil, a slave, 59
Pierce, Franklin, 250
Pittsburgh *Advertiser*, 120
Pleasants, Hampden, 306

Pleasants, Thomas H., 88–89
Polk, James K., 238, 244
Post Office, 185
Prentis, Samuel, 149
Preston, John, 38, 46, 48, 74
Princeton, 2, 3
Procedure, 181–184, 281
Prunty, John, 17

Railroads, 198–199
Randolph, Edmund, 4, 5, 6, 29, 31, 32, 141; family silver, 58
Randolph, John, 75
Randolph, Peyton, 23
Randolph, Thomas, 43–48, 72, 74, 83
Real property law, 181–184, 291; Spanish land cases, 267–269, 281
Religion, 51, 261–262
Richmond, City of, 39, 40, 83, 106, 142; description, 5, 14–15, 32; and War of *1812*, 21–31, *passim*; role in Constitutional Convention of *1830*, 72–76; Van Buren in, 79; hostilities in, over Bank of United States, 125–126; and election of *1840*, 153
Richmond *Enquirer*, 11, 14–15, 23, 24, 33, 41, 55–56, 78, 83, 97, 120–121, 122–123, 129, 130, 131, 134, 137, 153–154; Daniel's letters in, 86–91; on Eaton, 101; on Daniel, 102
Richmond *Junto*, 31–34, 36, 40, 44, 55, 72, 78–81, 82, 91, 117, 125–126, 156; role in election of *1832*, 103–116; defeat and victory (1834–35), 127–139
Richmond *Whig*, 100, 120, 150, 155, 277
Ritchie, Thomas, 14–15, 33, 40, 55, 78, 83, 88, 90–91, 96, 122, 125, 130–131, 134, 231; on Van Buren, 97–98; role in election of *1832*, 103–116, *passim*; defeat as public printer, 128; restoration of, 136–137; deterioration of relations with Daniel, 140–141
Ritchie, Thomas, Jr., 88–89

Rives, William C., 118, 128, 133, 135–136, 148–149, 150, 151, 155, 157

Roane, Spencer, 32, 40, 43, 79, 86

Roane, William, 156–158

Scott, Walter, 2, 54

Scott, Winfield, 118, 266

Seddon, John, 7–10

Selbe, Mrs., 69–70

Seldon, Joseph, 306

Seward, William, 247

Sherrard, Representative, 128–129

Slaves and slavery, 57, 58–60, 63–76, passim, 243–258, 261, 281, 287; fugitives, 177–180, 186

Slavery in territories, 165, 243–246, 250–257

Smith, Oliver, 156, 160

Smith, Robert, 32

Smith, William, 136

Smythe, Alexander, 42

Social life of Daniel, 60–61, 175–176, 194

Southard, Samuel, 158–159

Spanish land cases, 267–269, 288

Spoils system, 97, 171–172

Spring Farm, 6, 12, 50, 55, 175

Stafford County, 1, 2, 7, 73, 82, 128–130, 161, 167, 227, 289

Stephens, Alexander, 252

Stevenson, Andrew, 78, 103, 113, 122–123, 125, 135

Stogdall, James, 30, 31

Story, Joseph, 169, 170, 171–172, 186, 187, 190, 231, 237, 249, 271; fugitive slave opinion, 177–180, passim; admiralty, 222–226; in Girard Will case, 261

Sumner, Charles, 171

Supreme Court: appointment of Daniel, 150–167; Daniel takes seat, 168–180; composition (1841), 169–170, 171–172; division over Reporter Peters, 171–172; work methods, 173–174; living quarters, 174–175; work load, 176–177, 259–260; work of, in Daniel's time, 181–184; Taney-Wayne alterca-tion, 194; routine business, 259–274

Swayne, Noah, 237

Taft, William Howard, 181

Taney, Roger B., 49, 111–112, 119, 122–124, 142, 157, 170, 171, 172, 173, 175, 176, 182, 188, 190–191, 196, 197, 198, 214, 216, 218, 240, 260, 268, 272, 275, 284, 288; appoint-ment to Court, 138; relationship with Daniel, 174, 232, 234–237; altercation with Wayne, 193–194; contract clause, 202, 203, 204; admiralty, 223–226, 231; in slav-ery cases, 248–257; controversy with Curtis, 257; on death of Elizabeth Harris Daniel, 258

Tariff, 85, 93, 94–95, 105, 135, 153, 164–165, 183, 184; revision of, 109–110; nullification, 116–118

Taylor, John, of Caroline, 34, 35, 41, 151, 161

Taylor, Zachary, 176, 243

Tazewell, Littleton, 83, 125, 127

Texas, annexation of, 244

Third degree, 71

Thompson, Smith, 170, 171, 237

Timberlake, John B., 95

Toasts, 5, 41, 63, 118, 150, 152

Travis, Henry, 65

Tucker, Henry St. George, 155

Turner, Nat, revolt, 65–69

Two-thirds rule, 135–136

Tyler, John, 75, 83, 118, 151, 288, 289

United States Telegraph, 99–100

Van Buren, Martin, 33, 63, 76, 77, 82, 84, 126, 127, 130, 134, 135, 137, 140, 148–149, 164, 170, 231, 236, 256, 275, 276; career, 78; relation to Virginia, 78–80; effect of elec-tion of 1824 on, 81; described, 92–93; relations with Calhoun, Jackson, and Eaton, 93–96, 97; campaign for vice presidency (1832), 103–116; appraisal, 114;

Daniel and attorney generalship, 119–125; election as President, 137–138; Daniel's appointment, 150–167, *passim*; election of *1840*, 151–154; end of relations with Daniel, 243–246

Virginia and Kentucky Resolutions, 4, 117, 153, 161

Virginia Constitutional Convention of *1830*, 72–76

War of *1812*, 17–18, 21–31, 93

Washington, Bushrod, 83

Washington, George, 4, 5, 61, 246

Washington *Intelligencer*, 122

Watkins, J. S., 135

Wayne, James M., 157, 169, 171, 172, 173, 174, 187, 190, 197, 201, 206, 211, 216, 231, 235–237, 240; reproached by Taney, 193–194; on jurisdiction as to corporations, 218–220; as Daniel's living companion, 232; and *Dred Scott* case, 251–257

Webster, Daniel, 51, 88, 165, 175–176, 190, 238; Curtis and commerce, 195–197; on contract clause, 201, 208–209, 211; in *Girard Will* case, 261

Whig Party, 51, 82, 87, 97–98, 100, 104, 120, 142, 145, 150, 164, 165, 232, 238; Virginia disputes, 127–139; opposition to Daniel for Supreme Court, 155–161; and revision of Daniel's circuit, 275

Whipple, John, 238

White, Hugh, 137

Will of Daniel, 289

Wills, 183

Wilmot Proviso, 245

Wilson, Allan, 132–133, 137

Wilson, D. A., 137

Women's rights, 263–265

Woodbury, Levi, 191, 193, 195, 203, 237, 247

Wright, Charles Alan, 237

Wright, Silas, 160, 244–245